# BECOMI

Laura Jane Williams has written about love, lust and her feelings everywhere from the *Guardian* to *Buzzfeed* to *RED*, the *Telegraph*, *Stylist*, and more, and in the autumn of 2016 was appointed *Grazia* magazine's single girl dating columnist. BECOMING is her first book.

# BECOMING

## A Memoir

### Laura Jane Williams

HODDER

First published in Great Britain in 2016 by
Hodder & Stoughton
An Hachette UK company

First published in paperback in 2017

3

Copyright © Laura Jane Williams 2016

A CIP catalogue record for this title is available from the British Library

ISBN 978 1 473 63560 9

Typeset in Avenir by Hewer Text UK Ltd, Edinburgh
Printed and bound by Clays Ltd, St Ives plc

Hodder & Stoughton policy is to use papers that are natural, renewable
and recyclable products and made from wood grown in sustainable
forests. The logging and manufacturing processes are expected to
conform to the environmental regulations of the country of origin.

Hodder & Stoughton Ltd
Carmelite House
50 Victoria Embankment
London EC4Y 0DZ

www.hodder.co.uk

*for who I was,*
*and who she became,*
*and for him, because he set me free before I knew how*

# AUTHOR'S NOTE

This is my truth. Of course, I'm a biased little shit. Biased because I am human, and that condition – humanness – renders all of us defective narrators, writer or otherwise. Because, well: we all have feelings. And emotions. And secrets, and lies, and inconvenient truths. All of it colours the story we tell ourselves about who we are and what made us that way. We rewrite our histories in shades of grey each time we learn something new about who we want to be, so that we might find the courage to keep on, one foot in front of the other, brave in spite of – and because of – that which terrifies us: break-ups. Change. Ourselves.

I've done my best. To demand any more would be forgivable, of course, but totally pointless. I've told a story about my past as honestly as I experienced it. But – if any other 'character' told you their version, it would undoubtedly be different. Their story would be coloured by different emotions, different feelings, different humanness. Their humanness. So please, allow me that. Allow me to be human, too. Allow me to be prejudiced. Unreliable. Subjective.

(Please also forgive all the name changes. My lawyer made me.)

This is *my* version of *my* truth. Because that's just the thing: this is *my* becoming. I might be confused about who said what, precisely, but I've never misjudged just how sad I was, and what a long way it felt to find a place where I wasn't any longer. This is the storified version of events – the most exciting way to tell it. I left out the bits that'd bore you. This isn't a court's transcript – these are the highlights. Lowlights. The bits that stick out in my mind. The bits I wrote down to make sense of.

The journey is my own. The journey is probably yours, as well, because what I wish I'd known is that we're all becoming more ourselves. I offer this story, this narrative, as my way of saying, *me too. I got hurt, too. I want to be better, too.* We're in this together, and for that I'm incredibly thankful. None of us is fucking up like we think we are.

# ONE

I sat in the sweltering shade of the veranda and watched him work with meticulous devotion. He yelled at me often, the grey-haired gardener, for tiptoeing on the planted beds, as I smelled the choreographed mass of flowers that spilled out in every corner of the courtyard. They were magnificent – reds and blues and pinks and purples, pushing out from the borders and on to the pebbles of our tiny walled piazza. One of the monks – the one I only ever referred to as *padre* – would tell me their names in Italian, the spaces between his words letting me know that I was doing no harm. I'd repeat what he said, incorrectly, misstepping over roots and conjugations both, and he'd shake his head in frustrated, amused contempt at my incapacity for his lessons. It was a dance we did daily – our way of being seen by the other. In the twelve weeks I spent within that gated convent I learned a whole new language – but it wasn't Italian. In that time, I learned the words I needed to like myself.

I tapped at my computer, trying to find the right sentences for the last paragraph to a chapter I'd just drafted. Valentino cast a shadow over my 'desk' – the spot near *padre's* office where I wrote every day until it got dark. He splayed out his hand over my computer screen, and his thick, workman's fingers struck my memory like a power cut. He had hands exactly like the man who had fucked me so hard that the next morning, as I cried getting out of the shower,

1

my housemate gently but firmly asked, 'Laura. Did he . . . did you consent to this?'

I'd had sores up the length of my back, from carpet burn. There were marks on my bum cheeks, and a smattering of bruises on the top of my arm. My neck was stiff and it hurt when I peed. The pressure of the water as I washed made me seize my breath in sharp shock, and I thought I could sleep for a hundred years. I'd wanted it like that, though. I'd wanted him to pin me down, to be rough. I'd wanted him to use me. Use my body.

'Working, working, working!' Valentino shrilled, waving in front of my face. 'You're too much serious for such nice girl.'

I never did figure out why a convent would be home to men. In my limited, caveman-like Italian I had ascertained that it used to be where the nuns lived, and when the ladies moved out it became a home for monks with limited mobility in older age: a sort of monk retirement home. *Chiostro di Sant'Agostino* was set back from the road that runs through the touristy, seaside town of Loano, just down the coast from the French Riviera. Hidden by trees, if you looked hard enough there was a small, engraved sign that said, simply, *Convento*.

*Padre* whizzed by, nodding at Valentino and me efficiently. He was an obese man, with brown religious robes homing rounded rolls. The weight of him meant he was bound to an electric wheelchair to navigate the grounds, and he'd sit just out of my eyesight for most of the day, round the corner, in his office, sucking on cigarette after cigarette with a mouth that accommodated four, yellowed, teeth. Monks do normal, human things like smoke. I didn't know. I didn't know they smoked and danced and ate ice cream. *Padre* loved his ice cream. We'd eat plain pasta and grilled vegetables at almost every meal, but at 9 p.m. there'd always be *gelato*.

Daily, I'd sit there for hours, Valentino teasing me in passing and *padre* going about his business of telling everyone else what to do. I'd 'do my studying', as Vale called it: writing and reading and looking at the lavender beside the statue of the Virgin Mary holding her rosary beads, repenting for that which only she knew. I was forgiving myself, too.

*

On the walk back to my house that first night, he'd pushed me up against the wall of a nameless street with my hands up against my head, and gyrated along the front of me. His dick was out – the largest, unruliest exhaust-pipe of a thing I'd ever encountered – my skirt hitched up around my waist, and he would've fucked me right there and then had I not said, breathlessly and just convincingly enough, 'Get me inside. Get me inside the house.'

It was like he was mad I'd made him wait. By the time my door was open his hands were on my neck, in my hair, on my waist, his mouth wet and heavy in my ear. He'd tossed me inside with a shove as soon as the door sounded its unlock.

He didn't give a shit what I wanted. Who I was. What this meant. This man, this stranger, he'd forced a tension up through my arms that stretched all the way down to between my legs, and as he grappled at my crotch, at my stomach, at my chest, he felt his way around my body as if memorising where he was going to use me next. He attacked me with his big, chunky paws, plotting a map of my curves.

He pulled away.

'Take off your clothes,' he'd said.

I took off my clothes.

'Good,' he'd said.

I awaited further instruction.

He stood, looking at me in my nakedness, and I let him see me. I wasn't embarrassed. My nipples prickled at his sight. I felt sexy. It was powerful to be wanted. To be looked at like he'd swallow me whole. Devour me. He was issuing the commands but it was me who'd gotten us this far, me who'd been confident and in control enough to engineer his desire this way. But it wasn't so much that we *had* sex, as much as he *did sex to me*. I was his willing participant, but I could've been anybody. I was a vessel.

*

I sought solace by proxy. In my time by *padre's* office there would be knocks at the convent's door, and another old or disabled monk would let in one more soul seeking their right selves. I was in good company. It was mainly Romanians or southern Italians down on their luck, and I spoke with them all. I was navigating my way out of the bad relationship I'd developed with, and against, myself, communicating in a tongue not mine to understand the stories of my own human-ness. Mistakes. Remorse. Clemency. They'd bring grimy-looking cakes and wilting flowers, and I'd tell them, *'Che bello,'* smiling and wide-eyed and desperate to step out of my own imagination, my mental jail, for the length of a stilted conversation about the death of their husband, the mouths they had to feed, how they didn't want to drink this way anymore if only God could help them. Folks far worse off than me. There was perspective in that.

*

I'd met Big Dick in a club. It was a friend's birthday and I'd found myself excited about a night out. I'd been running a lot, and felt fit. Toned, with that healthy glow regular, sweaty exercise gives you. When my body is strong, I feel strong mentally. It's my quickest way to

Superwoman. I remember posing for a photograph before we headed on out, and thinking, *Uh-huh. I feel GREAT.* Endorphins ran high.

'Oh god,' Calum said, when I commented out loud that maybe my legs weren't so bad after all. 'She's there. In the zone. I see it in her eyes.'

'The man-eating zone?' said his boyfriend, Liam, pouring double – maybe triple – shots of peach schnapps.

'Be nice to me!' I'd said, eyeing my reflection in the window with views across Derby city centre.

Behind me Liam and Calum exchanged a look. Calum said, 'It's us who have to stomach your stories the morning after the night before.'

I scowled over my shoulder, adjusting my boobs in their balconette bra. 'Spoken like a man who knows exactly who he's waking up to every morning.' Patting down my chest, I turned to them. 'Do my tits look shaggable in this top?'

Calum raised his glass in salute. 'Asked like a woman who has no idea who she's going to bed with.'

I seldom did in those years.

*

In the convent, I worked with visiting teenagers from all over the country as part of a special project that capitalised on their unique talents in science and art and dance. I taught English for less than three hours a day in exchange for room and board, and was given absolute free rein with them. We'd practise English by doing 'love parades' in the local town, handing out sweet notes and free hugs. We'd write letters to our past selves, reassuring our younger versions that everything would be okay. We penned letters to our future selves, to be mailed out in exactly one year's time, to remind us of what we were and how we'd hoped. 'Sometimes, we feel like we did something we shouldn't have done,' I'd tell my class of seventeen-year-olds. 'And we think we will be sorry for that until the day we die. But if you remember every time you make a mistake, you won't have room for the happy memories. So. Let's put it in a letter and then keep the bad memories there. Then we can write new, good ones, with the room left over. Doesn't that sound nice?'

*

It had been about midnight – two hours past my regular bedtime – that I stood at the bar, teetering in platform heels and tugging at my peplum skirt. I rubbed my lips together, massaging in remnants of red lipstick, and caught sight of myself in the mirror behind the bar. As I did, my reflection found the stare of eyes not my own. He was short and balding, a little chubby: cheeky looking. I refused to look away first. He smirked. I pursed my lips. He looked away and I ordered gratefully – I'd been on the dance floor for eight songs in a row, and hair was matted to the back of my neck in sweat.

'That's a lot of vodka,' a voice said, and turning, I saw it was the guy from the mirror.

'Just water,' I said, raising my glass and downing it. I put the empty down on the bar. 'I don't need booze to have a good time.'

'I'll bet,' he said.

I cocked an eyebrow.

A man stood next to him. Tall. Dark hair. Symmetrical face. Full lips. Rough around the edges. He tipped his head in greeting.

I don't remember how it happened, but the smaller, cheekier one, his attention went somewhere else for a minute. To the barman, I think. And . . . and, I don't know. I guess because the smaller, cheekier one was obviously interested, and willing, and wanting to engage in some kind of exchange, my attention went to the enigmatic, slightly out-of-reach one, the one who'd I'd have to actively pursue. The challenge. The ego-boost.

'Laura,' I said, with a tried-and-tested look that my friend Fern has come to refer to as 'Mona Lisa-ing': penetrative eye contact that follows you across the room.

I have no idea what name he replied with.

Afterwards, he'd asked to stay over. 'I have a girlfriend,' he said. 'If I go home at this hour she'll ask questions. It's easier if I go home in the morning and say I kipped at my mate's house.'

I was used to following his lead already.

'Okay.' My voice was small, now, stripped of the power of sex. 'Urm. I don't have a spare toothbrush for you or anything.'

He pulled me under his arm and held me into him. He smelt like men's deodorant and my cum. His hand drifted to the small of my back and after lying in silence for a while, he started tickling me, lightly.

'You haven't asked me anything about myself,' he said.

My brow furrowed in the darkness. 'Is there . . . is there something you want to tell me?'

'I'm an artist.'

'You are?'

'Yes. Acrylic, mostly. Big canvasses. They sell for a lot of money.'

I don't know why I was surprised. Maybe I expected an 'artist' to be more sensitive, less outgoing. But then, when I thought about it, he hadn't been outgoing. At the bar he'd been shy and reserved. I pursued him, and then he fucked hard and fast and impersonally.

'Why did you come home with me?' I asked.

He grabbed at my bum, plucking greedy handfuls. 'Because of this,' he laughed. Then, changing the subject, he added, 'I like my hands. That's my favourite part of myself.' He moved around me to extend both arms so I could see them in the moonlight peeking through the blinds. He had long, heavy-set fingers, and a wide span. I reached up to match my palm to one of his own and we suspended gravity and judgement for a half a moment – held hands, mid-air – our first and only sign of tenderness.

A week later, he texted. I didn't get it until I'd woken up the next morning, and it smacked of 'Do you wanna fuck?'

I texted back, 'A "How are you?" text after midnight? You could only have been after one thing . . .'

He messaged back right away. 'Am I that transparent?'

'You don't even know my name. Yes.'

'Your name is Laura. Wait – what's *my* name?'

I honestly could not remember.

'You're taking too long to text back. This deserves a punishment.'

I'd been saved from myself.

'Punishment? Oh, goodness. What will you have me do . . .?'

'First thing's first. Saturday night? You free?'

'Yessir.'

'Eight p.m. Saturday, wear something very short. So short that I can see your cunt.'

'Yessir.'

*

The convent had bare, empty rooms. Tiled floors and blank walls and a shared bathroom with a tub so stained that it made one thing surprisingly clear: if a monk needs to pee, he doesn't get out of the bath to do it.

The cook in the kitchen would always save a banana for me but pretend like he'd forgotten to, keeping behind the small token on the shelf above where he made the bread, until I rapped gently on the door at break time: 10.25, every morning.

My mattress was thin and hard, and I shared my living quarters with an American girl called Megan – a one-time model from the Magnum ice cream adverts who'd used the payout from a cycling accident to come practise her Italian *in situ*.

I moved slowly, in the convent, worrying that any false physicality would somehow ruin me. Undo the work I'd so desperately committed to doing. I thought if I lifted an arm too fast or widened my step too much I'd rip a seam of myself, burst open and spill out and never be able to stem the flow. I had so much fear.

I remember the hot, oppressive heat of the summer, as a wave the temperature of the devil, Lucifer, swept through the country, and how, three days before I finally left, the sky cracked and the clouds made way for rain and I stood on the balcony and let myself get wet because, somehow, it was that for which I had been waiting. For my sky to crack. For my pressure to ease. That was the day the man I thought I'd marry, a man I'd been with six years, married my friend instead. In many ways, that's what all this was about. Him. Her. Me.

*

Big Dick called me as he arrived and hung up before I answered. It was code for him being outside. I let him in to my university halls of residence wordlessly and he followed me upstairs, past the communal kitchen and into my single room. The first thing he said was in appraisal of my dress and heels and hair: 'Fuck. Good girl.'

He sat down on the bed and watched me linger, nervously, I suppose, at the door. I turned the lock, waiting for him to say something else. I was damp between my legs and my nipples rubbed against the lace of my bra. I took short, shallow breaths. Couldn't meet his eye.

'Pull your dress up,' he said. I pulled my dress up, to my waist.

'Go over there,' he said, 'And put your hands on the counter, by the sink.' Slowly, I did that. Moved towards the tiny tiled corner of the room, where I brushed my teeth every morning. 'Open your legs.' His voice came from behind me now. 'Wider.'

I was bent at a 90-degree angle, my forehead almost touching the worktop beside the taps. My chest rose and fell. I couldn't see him. The fabric of my thong brushed against one bum cheek as his hand caressed the other. He parted me, and spat on to my arsehole. He made me bleed.

# TWO

**Three years before convent life . . .**

I knew as soon as he got off the train. His eyes were sunken, the circles underneath them even bigger than the ones he danced in order to avoid embracing my hello. He had a cold sore on the left corner of his bottom lip – a condition he was prone to if he didn't sleep enough – and his gaze pooled with salty tears.

'*We need to talk*,' he said, voice breaking.

It was funny, but at the supermarket that morning, as I loaded up my trolley with smoked fish and Thai curry paste, croissants and jam and *Mâcon Villages* and coffee, a smorgasbord of his favourite things as a way to demonstrate I cared, that I missed him so very much now that we lived apart, I'd thought to myself, *This is an awful lot of money to spend if he's coming down here to break up with me.* I'd brushed it aside, amused at the darkness of my own mind, because we'd been together years – six as a couple, almost four more as friends who were always going to be more. He was based in Stockton, and I in Derby, because we'd both committed to heading to separate universities as 'mature students'. We weren't eighteen-year-old freshmen: we were almost twenty-three. Twenty-three is still childlike, if not childish, but I was old enough to know I'd marry him, despite a temporary distance. I was part of his family, and he mine. We weren't breaking up. We were inside each other.

Afterwards, in amongst a cloud of menthol cigarette smoke and midday beers, self-loathing ripe for analysis, I realised: I knew before I knew.

(I'm learning that often, we do.)

(Intuition can be a wildly problematic truth.)

The meander to my house was a silent one, save for the jangle of the buckle on the boots he had bought me two Christmases ago. Bile rose in my throat and, as my key turned in the door, I felt soundless tears spill down my face, rolling in tracks to fall on my shaking hand as it turned left in the lock. He reached out to steady it and I pulled away. A bodily recoil to mirror the emotional. He closed the door behind us and I said, without turning around, 'This is it?'

'I'm . . .' he said, unable to finish the sentence. But wasn't that just it? 'I'm' and not 'we're'? That *was* the sentence.

And then he started to cry.

David was the house that made me. We met at school when we were fourteen years old, and were known as belonging to each other long before either of us knew it ourselves. It was magnetic. Biological. Our friends, teachers, even our parents – they could all see it. By fifteen and a half we were on again, and off again, drawn to each other but unsure, in that particular teenage way, on exactly what to do about it. At seventeen we were boyfriend and girlfriend, bunking off sixth form to have sex in my car somewhere in the North Yorkshire hills. By eighteen we travelled the world: summers at his family château in France – a place I'd helped 'do up' when they bought it for a steal and in ruins – backpacking trips to India and Cambodia, Laos and Greece. At nineteen we moved in together, at twenty we decided we were far too young for such craziness, and two or so years later both pledged to build our brains at university, finally, and to both families' relief – 200 miles apart but still together.

Over the New Year, four months after setting up home in different parts of the country, we'd struggled to be alone. It was as if we'd forgotten how. We'd loved to cook together, to build things, make things, as a team, but a screaming row over the béchamel one evening left us with our backs to each other in bed that night, knowing that it wasn't about the fucking *sauce*. I'd been weepy. Clingy and in need of space at the same time. He lost his temper with me a lot, demonstrated his frustration through nit-picking at how I folded the bathroom towels and buttered my baguette. We didn't have sex, and we'd *always* had sex. Our bodies were our first tongue – we used them as a gateway to speech. It had taken four more months for one of us to build courage enough to say what it all meant, but it had been blindingly obvious for longer than I was prepared to admit: we didn't fit. Not any more.

'I'll make tea,' I said. 'I think we both need tea.'

We had tried. We had fallen in love very young and very hard, and knew nothing but each other. The man he was, was a man I had shaped, as a young woman he had moulded me. It was real, true love because how could it not be? How could it not be the kind of love you don't think of as *first love*? For us both, this was it. The Love. Until it wasn't.

I held on to his waist, knowing this would be the final time I'd get to and so committing to memory a list of things to remember. The way he smelt, the design of his pelvis against the soft of my upper tummy. I let make-up seep on to his T-shirt, a hand-me-down to him from my brother. I wondered if he'd still wear the things that came from me. I let him rest his chin on the top of my head, felt him stroke the length of my hair and cradle the arch at the back of my neck. There were vague suggestions that we would always be in each other's lives, that we were friends, above all else, with a decade's worth of falling and fighting, stolen chaste kisses and clumsy first times, all of that growing and learning and experimenting *and and and* . . .

'And thank you for the memories,' I said, as he left, less than an hour after he'd arrived, the tea I'd made untouched and cold in china mugs we'd bought together.

He turned and smiled at me – a heartbreaking, sad side-smile with only half of his mouth, robbing me of my relationship. As I closed the front door I collapsed to the ground, where I tried not to throw up, retching and heaving through solid and uninterrupted hours of primal sobs.

*He's gone*, I thought to myself. *He's gone.*

I called his mother. The phone rang out. I don't know what she could've said to me anyway.

# THREE

'Pete and Eduardo have offered to get you stoned,' Calum told me. 'And I think you should do it.'

Calum is my best friend. From our very first day at university together we spoke the same language in the same way, moving to the beat of the same invisible drum. Outrageous humour and a chiselled, beautiful face, falling in friendship lust with him was inevitable. We have an easy, light relationship, characterised by silly voices and impressions of our mothers, juxtaposed with a fierce determination to become published writers. Meeting him I was overwhelmed with a feeling of, *Oh! There you are!* He's the Darby to my Joan. The Nutella to my spoon. Everything.

We were on our way home from a writing class at the University of Derby, our fellow workshoppers Pete and Eduardo a short way behind. We were mates-by-circumstance, I guess, since we spent so much time in class together, or reading one another's work at home. Through each other's stories we knew sideways secrets and hidden desires, even if we didn't know last names or whether to sugar their tea. Writing is intimate that way. Pete and Eduardo were my favourite guys in a group of misfits as clichéd as a creative writing class should be, because they were both brilliant despite outwardly not seeming to give a shit in that green, earnest way so many 'creatives' have. Crap at punctuation but poets, the pair of them.

'I'm sorry – what did you say?'

'I told them about the break-up, and how this is the first time you've left the house in thirteen days, and they said what you need is a big old spliff so that you chill out for a minute.'

'You said that?'

Calum raised an eyebrow. 'Yes. You need some kindness, Laura, and not least from yourself. I understand that you're devastated, and rightly so. Obviously. I know. But you do this thing when you're sad; you shut down. Hide away. It's not healthy.' I went to interrupt, but he cut me off. I listened, resentful, arms folded. 'You've always been soft on Pete, even when you were with David. So as your best friend I'm taking it upon myself to break this ice maiden façade you insist on maintaining with him – *ah! Shut up! You're a bitch to him because you're worried he fancies you and you had that weird kiss thing and you fancy him a bit, too* – YOU *ARE* A BITCH TO HIM! Stop interrupting me! Anyway, where was I? Ah. Yes. As your best friend, I'm taking it upon myself to see to it you have somebody who cares to help you get through this wretched time in a way that I, as a homosexual, cannot. And today, I reckon that's Pete. I approve of Pete. He's a good one.'

I was incensed. 'But you don't get to tell people my business, Calum. You're telling them things I told you in confidence.' Tears pricked at my eyes. Again.

'Come on, duck, one look at you and it's obvious you're at the bottom of a hole. Fucking *crater*. I'm proud of you for getting it all out of your system, but let's figure out a way to make your eyes look a *little* less bloodshot, shall we? The show must, eventually, go on.'

My best friend's brutal kindness was a kick to the stomach. Rationally, he was right: I had to interact with the world at some point. Wars, famine, assault – folks endure human atrocity on a much grander scale than getting dumped. Emotionally, though, it was the privileged middle-class princess in me who couldn't think of anything worse than acting like everything was okay when I couldn't imagine a day when I might laugh again. Smile, even. It was inconceivable to me that there would ever be a night alone to be welcomed, only survived. I didn't know how to be without David. How to *be* alone. It had taken every ounce of my resolve to even make the end-of-term class; Calum had to practically dress me and frogmarch me there himself. Every minute of my day felt like an hour, and every hour was misery. I was empty. My heart was so heavy I carried it in my shoes – when I eventually wore them. I didn't know what to do with myself.

Calum stopped walking, causing me to do the same, and turned around to the boys behind us.

'That's right, isn't it, Pete?' Calum called. 'You're gonna take Laura home and get her stoned?'

Pete is cocky; he's got a cheeky-chappy swagger and a Brummie accent that mix to invoke Brand, Hemingway and Dylan. His army-green duffle coat and dark stubble make him look like an anarchist playboy. Even in the dark of an early evening he looked like he'd been on the lash for three days, and could do three more straight before knocking out 600 pages of an instant classic that he'd never give interviews for.

Pete caught us up and grinned. 'Well, yeah. If you've broken up with your fella and that, you should come and have some fun.'

Eduardo slowed beside him. He's South American with beautiful, brunette, incredibly shiny hair and mahogany skin, and when Ed reads his work aloud in our sessions his voice is as beautiful as his words. He trips on the '*th*'s and rolls on the '*r*'s, and makes little kissing motions with his lips at the end of most of his sentences – '*An*' '*dat is the rrreason she ne-ver loved a-gen (kiss)*', which get everyone

– even the boys – all hot and bothered, making it really tough to give constructive feedback.

'I'm not sure what Calum has tried to tell you,' I said. 'But don't believe any of it.' I struggled to make eye contact, and fixed to look at the toe of my boot as I scuffed it amongst a pile of dead, wet leaves on the pavement instead. My voice betrayed me.

'So you didn't start crying when Erica read out her piece about the cat and the tree, and that wasn't why you left the room for twenty-odd minutes?'

I gaped open-mouthed at Calum. He shrugged.

'Say no more,' Pete continued, slipping his arm around my shoulders. 'Don't be embarrassed by it, darlin'. The reason you can write like you do is because you feel things as deep as you do. I like that about you. In fact, you, my friend, are just the kind of girl I want to spend my evening with, if you'll do us the honour?'

His grip was electricity and I froze at the contact. I didn't want to be touched. Looked at. Seen. Pete sensed it, squeezed my upper arm hard, and dropped his clutch. He nodded at me, almost impercep- tibly. *I get it*, it said. *I'm listening.*

When I first met Pete, university was just starting. I was with David and content, and Pete was single and very actively looking. Because he is irritatingly handsome and full of happy-go-lucky banter – an observation made by my lesbian friend, so it must be true – he has a way with ladies and gents alike. I gave him shit for being such a charmer, and he couldn't sit on my face to shut me up because I wasn't offering. I think it threw him. When you're so charismatic, a wordsmith with the confidence to manipulate 100 per cent of those you meet, nobody tells you no. We'd always flirted, but it was flirting done on the understanding that nothing would ever develop – hurtling towards marriage as I thought I was. One night, not long after our first class together, Pete and I had sat in the corner of a club after bumping into each other in town, and for hours and hours we talked and talked – *battled and battled* – and he'd tried to kiss me as we bid each other goodnight. I realised what was happening almost too late, turning abruptly so that he caught my cheek, and the incident was never spoken about between us ever again – even though it cast a shadow over every interaction we subsequently had. We awkwardly went back to lunchtime fag breaks and meandering walks to the bus stop. After that, though, the no-holds-barred quips and insults continued to find basis in a sort of quasi- and restrained mutual attraction that would never be realised *especially* now that egos had been bruised. Not that shagging somebody else was on my mind, of course, even in new singledom. But I'd be lying if I said I hadn't harboured a small crush on him. I could begrudgingly see his appeal. I had always been faithful to David, head over heels in every way, but I'm human: I was aware other men – Pete – existed.

From the depths of my melancholy I currently wished that no men existed at all.

'What's in it for me?' I croaked, tentatively looking at them both from under my eyelashes, all Keira Knightley and contrived.

He kept it playful. Pete knew I was in a delicate state. I could tell by the way he stood – close enough to be sincere, far enough away not to crowd me. He didn't take his eyes off me. He silently willed me happy. 'You get to see the inner workings of the genius that is *Pete and Eduardo.*'

'I saw a TED talk that said the ancient Greeks believed that we couldn't *be* a genius, only *possess* genius when it chose to bless us with its presence to help our work along a little,' I detoured.

'That's exactly what I'm saying, beautiful.' He cracked a smile at my defrosting. 'Come be our daemon for the night.'

'He just called you a genius,' said Calum. I rolled my eyes.

Pete added, 'A genius who knows how to break hearts. Look at you! We're begging you for your time! Do you want me to get on my knees for you?' I scowled. Pete sank to the ground. 'Look. I wouldn't do this for just any woman, you know.' He pulled out a ready-rolled joint from a tin in his breast pocket. 'A gift, my stand-offish Athena.'

His earnestness made me giddy. Stood at the side of the road with them, I felt the small stirrings of something other than utter doom. Being with Pete was like cracking open a door to shed a sliver of sunlight on myself. It felt warm and comforting. Safe. An important baby step back into the world. I sighed. 'I've only ever been stoned once before, and I didn't like it,' I told them both. 'You'll look after me, won't you? You won't be dickheads?'

'Beautiful, with us in tow nothing can go wrong,' said Pete, sensing his victory and rising to a stand. 'It'll be good for you, doing something that isn't very *Laura*.'

'Stop trying to piss me off.' I willed myself to act as normal as possible, to be unbeaten by my own mentality.

'Stop letting him,' said Calum, signalling his intention to depart with a kiss on my cheek.

'Off you come, then, you naughty little girl,' said Pete. 'Ooooh, whatever would your mother say?'

I scowled. 'My mother'd love you, unfortunately.'

I'm a lot of things, but a drug-taker isn't one of them – even weed. I know that in theory smoking a joint isn't a big deal, but I hadn't done it since school. I was so desperate to impress a guy called Charles Newforest that I toked way too much, passed out, then woke up to vomit the spaghetti his mother had made us for tea over his bedroom carpet. Charles had cleaned up my sick for me, and never invited me back.

I didn't know why I was there, in Eduardo's bedsit. Pete was probably right – I was doing something that wasn't very *Laura*. Trying on a different part of my personality, maybe. Finding an excuse to spend some time with a man who made me feel hot as fuck, but wouldn't *actually* fuck me. In a tentative, reserved sort of way, I trusted Pete to be gentle with me. I didn't need to explain anything to him. He seemed to just . . . know. It was as if he wanted to help me, to bear witness to my struggle. I didn't know I needed that: somebody to say, *I see you hurting. I acknowledge you.* Somebody with enough distance to show awareness of my broken wing without swooping in to try to fix everything. Tenderness. Compassion.

The boys folded bits of paper and sprinkled tobacco everywhere – turns out the roll-up in Pete's top pocket was just a regular smoke. We sat in silence on Ed's floor as the spliff was handed back and forth, back and forth, and I tried to relax into the moment. I'd had a crippling time. After all these years, a decade growing up with David, I just did not have the mental tools to be suddenly without him. After he had left that day and I'd finally picked myself up off the hallway floor, I drank half a bottle or so of neat vodka (because that's what they did in films), and within forty-five minutes had thrown it all back up again. The crying and the booze was enough to exhaust me into a slumber that lasted until 3 p.m. the next day, when I woke up disorientated and confused. On suddenly remembering what the vodka was supposed to make me forget I retched again. There was nothing left in my stomach to vomit. I stumbled for the remainder of the bottle and stayed in bed for two more days before I finally called Calum to say, in a whisper, 'He doesn't love me anymore.'

'Oh, shit,' was his reply.

Suddenly, I sat bolt upright and turned to face Pete.

'What?' he said. I watched his mouth intently as he spoke. 'Laura? Hello? What?' I continued to stare.

It was really important to me – overwhelmingly so – to watch his mouth. Because it hit me: we weren't stoned. And even though my head felt funny and the room was woozy, I knew, with starling clarity, that I was being tricked by Pete and Eduardo. They were making me *think* we were smoking pot, but actually it was only tobacco and I was convinced I was high just because I wanted to be. And, probably, I was three puffs away from volunteering to do something really stupid, and they would tell everyone and laugh at me, and – they hated me, didn't they? Pete and Eduardo hated me, like everyone else, and – AND DEAR GOD. *Is this paranoia?* I asked myself. *Am I paranoid?* No. No way. What? Who said that? *This isn't a big deal,* I reasoned with myself. *Who's paranoid? Stop it. Stop it, stop it, stop it.*

'Don't kiss me,' Pete said. 'You look like you're going to kiss me. Don't do that. Don't ruin it.'

In my head I thought to myself, DON'T SAY ANYTHING! HE IS TRYING TO TRICK YOU! HE WANTS YOU TO ACT STONED SO THAT HE CAN LAUGH AT YOU! And so I didn't say anything. I continued to watch his mouth.

'Can you say something? Or do something? Anything?' he said. 'Look, I have a girlfriend now. I like you and everything, and I know what you must think, but . . .'

'Shut up,' I said. 'Just shut up.' And then I threw up on myself, of course.

*

The first time David and I kissed, we were barely just teenagers and in a church graveyard. I tripped over a stone, landing on my knees with a thud, and as I creased over double, laughing at my myself, he'd sort of launched on top of me, pinned me down and pressed his mouth to mine. I'd pushed him off, startled and embarrassed, got up, and carried on walking.

We had variation on variation of that several times over the course of the next few years. 'He's just my friend,' I'd squeal at weekend sleepovers and on school breaks. 'I don't fancy him or anything.' But neither of us ever did what our friends did, making out with different people at every party, getting and receiving handjobs that we'd dissect afterwards in groups. It was always a given that, no matter how an evening started, we'd always end up in the corner, together. When we finally kissed properly, both willing and more prepared, in Year 11, it was in a friend's garage that his parents had let him convert into a den. Matty Hill had a disco ball and two big speakers that played heavy beats you could feel through your feet from the other side of the room. We'd smoke stolen Lambert and Butlers and drink tinnies somebody's brother had got for us, and one night, on the sofa, when our lips brushed against each other, mouths parted and tongues danced. We only broke apart because of a sudden cheer, and when I opened my eyes we were confronted with twenty bystanders and somebody shouting, 'Finally!' as everybody else hoorayed.

I thought about that as I sat on a bench outside Eduardo's building, shivering but relishing the feeling of the stoned fog lifting from my mind. I'd done the best I could with my vomit-speckled trousers, and my shirt was now balled up in my bag. I was cold under Eduardo's borrowed jumper. Pete sat down beside me.

'You wanted me in there, didn't you?' he said, finally.

I looked straight ahead. 'Wanted you to get me some air, yes,' I said.

We watched the traffic.

'He'll regret this.'

I looked to my lap. 'Will he?'

Pete bumped his shoulder to mine. 'I'd snap you up in a heart-beat,' he said.

'I should go home,' I said.

A police car whizzed by with its siren spinning, blue lights making everything ugly.

'Why don't you talk to me properly?'

The traffic came to a standstill as the light glared angry red. A boy in a backwards baseball cap watched us through the window of his old Ford.

'I'm stoned,' I told him.

'Why are you always on your guard with me?'

'Nobody should enter battle unarmed.'

A young mother walked past with a toddler bundled up against the chill in a bright pink stroller. My hands were freezing. I held them together, blew into the gap, and let the warm air heat them as I brushed them against one another.

'Come here,' Pete said, as he took my hands and rubbed them for me. I let him – just for a tiny sliver of a second. I watched him work and in the softness of his eyes there was something I hadn't seen before.

Eventually I said, 'I have to go.'

He nodded. 'I know.' He loosened his grip gently and we stood to walk. I stuffed my hands into my pockets. 'You *were* going to kiss me,' he said, as my bus pulled up.

'You're delusional,' I replied.

# FOUR

It was four months after we'd broken up that my phone rang. I'd been about to go to bed and didn't much feel like talking to anybody. I saw that it was Elizabeth, an old school friend, and, knowing that Ibby is not somebody I could only afford five minutes for, I let it go to voice-mail, resolving that I'd call her back tomorrow. I washed my face and brushed my teeth, patting down lotions and potions as I dialled my answering machine to hear her voice before sleep.

'Hey Frou,' she said, using our nickname for each other in her sing-song plummy tones – the sort of poshness that can tell you your arse looks fat in the same breezy tone as the dog has died. 'I'm calling because . . . Well. It's the weirdest thing. I just thought you should know, and I love you and I'm here for you and I'm sorry but: he's here. At the bar. And you'll never guess who he has his arm around . . .'

I hit her number and she picked up immediately.

'He'll marry her,' I said down the phone. 'You mark my words. I know them both inside out. If they are in public, together, and don't care who sees, I'm telling you: they'll get married.'

I was right. They were engaged within the year.

*

Gwen had been in the crowd that night, one of the cheers as David and I kissed for the first time. She'd been there when we first had sex,

25

in the toilets of a Chinese restaurant, slipping a condom under the bathroom door and afterwards softly asking me if we'd used it. We'd taken flamenco classes together, ridden the bus to school side by side, I'd picked her up in my new Volkswagen Polo the day I passed my test and driven her around to show off my new wheels. As we'd grown up she'd listened wide-eyed over bottles of Veuve Clicquot we couldn't really afford but bought to demonstrate our young sophistication, to my stories of elephant rides and Delhi Belly, championing the travels David and I undertook without any judgement that we'd chosen aeroplanes and guidebooks over university and a degree. She studied away, south of London, and so we saw each other less and less often, as childhood friends often do. By the time she was working in a local hospital, newly qualified as a physiotherapist, it was me who lived away for my own studies. I'd thought we'd grown apart because that's just what happens sometimes, but now I wondered – casually, at first, and then with more conviction – if the reason we'd allowed nature to take its course was because she'd always had a soft spot for him. For my boyfriend.

\*

'You won,' I said down the phone, pacing my bedroom with my mobile in one hand and a glass of neat supermarket-brand vodka in the other. I'd seen the accruement of a glass and ice as an improvement on straight from the bottle, but I was slurring my words: consumption level was at the same consistent high. 'You won in a competition I didn't even know I was in. I'm not surprised you won't pick up the phone to me. You made me feel like shit for not being a better friend to you, for not being in touch more, but, fuck it, Gwen. I was there when it mattered. When I found out about your dad the first thing I did was call you, and when you broke up with Ian I shed fucking *tears* for you.' I jabbed at the air with my fist, forgetting I was holding my drink and feeling it splosh out on to the carpet. 'But this whole time you just wanted what I had, didn't you? When we had the huge fight, that night at Ziggy's, in York, you said something about his goddamn DICK SIZE for fucking fuck's fucking sake, and you acted like it was ME who was out of line! I didn't have a clue! You played the fucking injured fucking princess card with *everyone* that night, and I came off like the gobby cunt with no compassion.

'I can't believe you never even called me so that I could hear it from you first. I don't even want to know how long this has been happening for. I'm sure everyone must think this is the best thing since sliced fucking bread because of how you'll spin it. I'm honestly *physically nauseated* by you. Sick to my *stomach* at the thought of you plotting, lusting after my life, charming everyone into thinking it all just happened and you can't fight true love and, actually, you've wanted this for *years*, haven't you? You must really hate me, Gwen. Really fucking hate me. What a performance! You know, if you'd been honest about wanting to steal him from me right from the beginning I'd have more respect for you than I have right now. You liar. You filthy fucking *liar*. You whore. You piece of fucking shit on the bottom of my dirty fucking shoe.'

A thought occurred to me as I spat into the phone, hoarse at the stress of anger on a scale I'd only ever read about. Setting my empty glass down, I cradled the phone under my ear and undid the bottle for a refill.

'Shit the bed.' I slammed the bottle down in understanding. 'That's why you were so fucking weird that day at the hospital. When Mum fell over and we waited four hours to get seen and you walked on to the ward and went paler than pale could *fucking be* at the sight of us. And I thought that was worry! Concern for why we'd be in fucking hospital! But it's because he was there, wasn't it? With me. Together. You must've hated that, you spiteful little bitch. Seeing him with my family. Well. HE LOVED ME. He loved me, so much, so, so, much, and you . . . you . . . oh, shit.'

I gasped for air. 'You won, Gwen,' I said, finishing as I'd started. 'Enjoy your fucking prize.'

\*

I called Elizabeth nearly every day over the next few weeks, asking if she had any more news on them being together, and eventually she stopped answering my calls. David didn't pick up to me at all. Thorough online stalking confirmed that Gwen had visited him a few months ago with some other friends of ours, just before he'd dumped me. Gwen and I might've drifted – I'd drifted from a lot of old school friends, really – but David still kept in touch. He was good that way. Loyal. Willing to make the effort. I'd seen pictures of them in late winter sunshine, hiking through North England hills and hanging socks by real open fires. In nearly every photograph they'd been together and at the time I'd felt a pang of envy but I'd attributed that to jealousy because I wasn't cooking en masse and watching movies all snuggled up together in a house in the woods. I never thought that I was being made a fool of. I wondered how many other people knew. Mutual friends who'd silently had to pick sides. I'm proud of who I am but I'm well aware that Gwen is more palatable – she's smoother round the edges. Less opinionated. Rides horses, plays the piano, fluent in French. Speaks when spoken to. Looks like Audrey Hepburn, petite and packaged neatly. By comparison I'm a blonde, loud, hurricane of a mess, constantly asking why and demanding who and *talktalktalking*. I take up so much more space. Before embarking on university David had been a policeman and we'd always joked that

I'd make a terrible officer's wife. I can't make small talk and I challenge authority and, well, Gwen would be fucking perfect for that role, wouldn't she? Wife material in the absolute. Maybe it's right what they say; we're all either a Jackie or a Marilyn. Madonna or whore. Marriage material, or not. I knew which category I fell into.

*

'I'm just too much, aren't I?' I said to Calum, as I cooked our breakfast. 'This whole time I was just the warm-up act, the primer. Like a pig. Isn't that what pigs do? Isn't there a starter-for-ten pig who goes in to get the male all excited before they make him spunk in the one actually worthy of him?' I flipped a porcini and goat's cheese omelette out of the pan and on to his plate, passing it over. 'I'm the fucking primer pig.'

'You're not the primer pig, Laura,' said Calum, mouth full with his first bite. And then, 'Can I have some salt, please?'

'You shouldn't need salt.' I gave it to him anyway, and pushed my own food around half-heartedly. 'And, you're right, I'm not the primer pig. Pigs are too simple. If anything, I'm the primer . . . dolphin. Dolphins are clever.' Calum frowned.

'Dolphin?'

'I was ditched in favour of an easier life, wasn't I? He chose her instead of me because I am exhausting. You know, I was once in the garden with my dad, talking away, having a nice little conversation, *chat chat chat,* and after a while I noticed that he was sort of, slipping, like literally *slipping* down, into his chair. So I said to him, to Dad, "You look like a little flower wilting in the heat. Are you tired?" And do you know what he said?' I gave up playing with my food and slid it on to Calum's plate for him to eat instead. 'He said to me, "Laura, I'm not so much tired as exhausted. I find you . . ." and get this, my own father actually said this to me, "Laura," he said, "I find you debilitating." My dad! DEBILITATING!'

Calum was sympathetic. 'Dads are simple creatures – and you and yours have had, you know, *issues*. I mean – I know we all have. But. Don't pay that silly comment any mind.' I flung my head on to the table dramatically. 'Have you ever listened to the conversations in The Cottage? *That's* debilitating.'

The Cottage is the name of Derby's only gay club. I've passed many a drunken night in the gender-neutral bathroom, gratuitously gossiping in front of my own reflection instead of lusting after the sparkling abs and strong jawlines of men who only want to gawp at each other on the dance floor. (I've spent many a night peeing in front of my best friend in that bathroom too. Calum likes to impersonate me by crouching in the middle of the room to yell, DON'T LOOK ME IN THE EYE! DON'T LOOK ME IN THE EYE! Apparently my gay best friend and I are close, but not so close that I can maintain eye contact whilst wiping.) It was in The Cottage that I (interestingly, given the clientele) bumped into Pete, back when we almost kissed.

'Gay men *make* it complicated,' said Calum. 'It's like a hobby. Old women have crocheting and eating all the sausages, and teenage boys have masturbation with socks. Gay men have amateur theatre as a reference point for how to create melodramatic reality.'

'I'm not really sure what you're telling me now,' I said. 'What's your point?'

'That you're *fine*, sugartits. David did not dump you to marry that slaggy witch because you're incredible and droll and demanding and wild, and she's a quiet, unassuming and amiable pretty face. David dumped you because he is an arse. Plain and simple."

'I'm unloveable,' I said. 'It's okay. You can tell me so.'

Calum got up from the table and hugged me from behind. 'Laura Jane Williams,' he said. 'You are a whirlwind. A mass of contradictions and extremes. You exist in six different time zones simultaneously, on six different planets, and sometimes I have absolutely no idea where you've come from. But that's why you are remarkable, and I won't hear you say otherwise.'

I closed my eyes and let quiet tears escape. We stayed like that for a full minute.

'You need to stop reading these stupid magazines, for a start,' he finally said.

I lifted my head. 'Huh?'

'Well, gay men make it complicated, sure, but look at the bollocks you women have to contend with. Individually, you're all right. But collectively? Women don't half confuse themselves.' He picked up a monthly magazine off the sideboard and passed it to me. I opened it to a blurry photograph of a woman off morning telly in a bikini, on the beach, with big red arrows pointing to all her imperfections. 'You guys give each other so much advice you must have no idea how to behave.' He took the magazine back and flicked through it.

'Look – the pros and cons of first date sex. What's the big deal? Everyone knows it's not a real date without a handjob. And then, here – opinion columns on career over motherhood. Like you can't have both.'

'I'm unloveable, so maybe I'll just pick career,' I mumbled.

'Enough, you,' Calum said. 'And look, another one: "Why skinny celebs are our downfall" next to three pages on how to lose belly fat in ten days.'

I peered over his shoulder. 'Ooooh . . . A recipe for double choc-olate fudge cake . . .'

'How to be happy—'

'—without a man . . .'

'How to nab the perfect guy—'

'—because he exists . . .'

'Why we don't need men—'

'—buy Chinese love beads instead.'

'How to love yourself!'

'Stop reading these magazines?'

'Exactly! Look. Listen to your Uncle Calum. If David didn't want to marry you, sweet darling, then that doesn't mean you weren't the right one for him. It means he wasn't the right one for *you*.' I nodded. 'Are you still texting with Pete?'

'A bit,' I said. 'I told him about the engagement, and when we take our fag breaks he occasionally remembers to take the piss out of me whitey-ing at Ed's house.'

'Flirting? Are you gonna have his babies?'

'Don't be ridiculous,' I said. 'I'm never dating ever, ever again. And he has a girlfriend. And I hate men. Straight men, anyway. He's just being unexpectedly kind and sensitive, actually. It's nice. Most folks I know from back home have gone suspiciously quiet. But sod 'em. I've got you.'

'Good,' he said squirting ketchup on to the last of his omelette, 'Not about your shit non-friends from home who you didn't even like anyway. About Pete. I'm glad this is moving along.' His liberal dousing of sauce was ruining the perfect balance I had tried to achieve with the delicate flavour of the mushrooms and the Welsh cheese from the fancy deli in town. He didn't notice me scowling at him – or, if he did, he was ignoring me. 'Now. Heartbreak is all well and good but can we talk about me now? You've used up your self-obsessed allowance for the day. Concluding notes: woe is you.'

I snatched the ketchup out of his hands. 'Thank you,' I said. 'I'm glad that we agree. Woe is *absolutely* me.' I ran my dish under the tap and left it to soak in the sink – every neat freak's worst nightmare, but I excuse my own laziness above anyone else's. 'And, yes, over to you, you insensitive sod.' I laughed in spite of myself. 'Do you wanna melt some Dairy Milk and eat it with the last of the Rice Krispies? Now I'm going to be single forever I'm allowed to get as bloated as I like.'

'D'uh,' he replied.

'And Calum?'

'Yes?'

'If you ever ruin the breakfast I slavishly prepare for you with this shit again,' I said, brandishing the ketchup in front of his nose, 'I'll cut you.'

'Did you read an article on How to Ruin a Potentially Amazing Omelette by Not Using Enough Salt in one of your magazines?'

'It's a good job I adore you.'

'Melt the chocolate, love, and let's Google some naked boy band pics. That'll make us both feel better.'

*

The days had passed into weeks, into months unremarkably. I was on a sort of autopilot. I went through the motions: writing, working odd hours in a polyester T-shirt at a local toyshop, sleeping. A lot of sleeping. I drove myself crazy by Google stalking their every move, until I got sick of myself and hid them on every platform it was possible to spy from. I deleted his phone number, and hers. Hit 'unfollow' to most of our mutual friends, so that I wasn't accidentally confronted with images or updates that contained them. I miserably got fatter. Then he emailed something along the lines of:

ou are well. Life here continues to speed by – did you
Lena is pregnant? Can you believe it?! The first of our
have a baby. We're all growing up, aren't we? She looks
beautiful as she gets bigger and bigger. The father is a Brazilian
guy; I think they met through work.

My other news is that Gwen and I got engaged. I'm really
happy, Laura. We went backpacking around southern Africa, and
on a ranch in Botswana, at sunset, I asked her if she'd be my wife.
She said yes. We're hoping to marry the summer after I finally
graduate. Now I wish I'd gone to university sooner!

I wanted you to hear it from me. I don't think I'll email again – I
told Gwen I was going to send this, but it feels dishonest somehow. I don't want to do anything that might hurt her. So, this will
be goodbye from me.

Wishing you the best,

D x

I read it three times, blinking in disbelief. He didn't mention my voice-
mail to her, nor the scores of missed calls I'd left him. I hadn't spoken
to Lena since we left school, barely, even though I knew she was still
close to Gwen – why was he telling me about her? But most of all, the
bit that really bothered me, really got under my furious skin, was: *it
feels dishonest, somehow*. I hit delete on the email, and then added
him to my spam list. However I felt about what he'd said, about him
writing to me that way, I put it in a small box in my mind, closed the
lid, and buried it.

A fucking ranch in Botswana, at sunset? Fuck off.

# FIVE

Pete strolled through the door, and I felt him before I saw him. There were ten of us around the table, an impromptu 'social misfits' evening after a particularly brutal writing workshop – our second academic year was proving to be much more complex than the first. He'd texted me in the toilet break:

**I'll pay for your drink if you crack just one smile, beautiful.
p.s. your arse looks good in that dress.**

I'd laughed involuntarily, looking up across the room where he skilfully ignored me whilst knowing full well he'd provoked me just right. Since the night at Ed's something had shifted; it felt like he was keeping an eye on me. Making sure, with safe emotional detachment, that I was doing okay.

'I'll say it again: there are worse things you could do than have a fling with a man like Pete,' Calum had said as we'd left for the pub.

'That's a terrible idea.'

'No it's not. I think you both know what's going on here. You need somebody to remind you not to give up entirely on the idea of romance, one day, when you're better, and Pete is fond enough of you to be a little boost. I think that's a brilliant arrangement.'

'I had the love of my life stolen from me by my best friend, Calum.

I can hardly go and do that to another woman. He has a girlfriend, remember?'

Calum pulled open the door to the pub, letting me pass him to go through first. 'I remember it well enough, sweetheart. It's him who forgets . . . *when he's with you.*' He added, 'And time has passed, you know.' I scowled. 'It's been, what? Six months? Seven?' It was closer to ten or eleven, but I wasn't going to admit as much.

We crowded around a corner table, and I talked with John, a thirty-something skinny guy with a predilection for sci-fi fantasy and trouser braces. He was saying something to me about limiting the amount of autobiography in my work, and I was listening courteously when I should've been telling him to do one, the condescending oaf, except suddenly I didn't really hear him any more. Pete went straight to the bar. My eyes followed him and Calum watched me watching him. He was wearing a fresh T-shirt with his low-slung ripped jeans, and it looked like he'd been home to shave. When I noticed I'd been caught eyeing him I blushed, guiltily, and Calum shook his head in mock admonishment.

'I got you a pint,' Pete's hot, wet breath intoned in my ear. He smelled incredible. And then, louder, to John, he said, 'Budge over, son; make some room.'

Pete sat himself between us on the bench, his thigh pressing against mine. He watched me finish the tail-end of one beer in favour of the one he'd brought me, we cheers-ed, and over the table he raised his glass to Eduardo, who was busy being silent and brooding with Paris, a very talkative lass from Yorkshire who was scrolling through photos of her new puppy. He looked bored.

I let Pete tease me, and when we went outside for a smoke, he talked about Bukowski and anal sex, generally looking at me for longer than necessary and finding reasons to touch me. He undoubtedly flirted, like always, but tonight his tone had changed. Tonight he was overt, pushy almost. His jibes were more cutting, his gaze more penetrative. He was being less gentle with me.

'I'm not sure your arse does look good in that dress after all,' he said. 'I think I made a mistake.'

'Ouch,' I replied. 'That just hurt my feelings.'

'Maybe I'll ask to see Calum's bum instead. I hear your friends are much more obliging than you are anyway.'

His words were a slap.

'Pete?' I said. 'Fuck you.'

'I deserved that,' he said.

'He *knows* I'm still hurting,' I whispered to Calum at the bar. 'So why toy with me?'

'I thought you said he was being supportive and friendly?'

'He was. Do you think he's on something? Maybe he's on something.'

'On a Monday night at five past six?'

'So what, he's just going to be an asshole now?'

Calum's response was suitably helpful. 'You make boys act weird.'

I took a seat at the opposite end of the table from Pete, and looked at Paris's dog pictures. John joined us, and I asked leading questions of them both so that I didn't have to talk much, letting Paris go for a good twenty minutes at a time. Pete watched me, totally unabashed; I kept looking up to see him staring. Challenging me to be bothered by it. He was obnoxious in the extreme.

'Will you stop it?' I finally demanded. He'd asked to smell my perfume as he queued for a drink beside me, leaning in so that the tip of his tongue touched behind my ear, whispering, 'Mmmmm. I could eat you.'

He levelled at me, innocently. 'I thought you were always fully armed for battle?'

'The battle is making me weary.'

'I could do more to exhaust you.'

I was serious. 'Stop.'

'What?' he said. 'Stop this?' He laced his hand into mine, grabbing his drink off the bar with the other, and pulled me away. His concept of personal space vanished. 'I don't want to have to share you this evening,' he said, pushing me against the pillar of a small alcove that made our conversation private and putting his hand proprietorially beside my head so that he leaned in close.

'I'm sure your girlfriend would love to hear you tell me that,' I said, tersely.

Pete narrowed his eyes. 'Beautiful, I'm just playing.' He swigged from his glass. 'You're a bit sensitive tonight, aren't you? Is it that time of the month? Have you got the decorators in and so you have to knock me around with your words to feel a bit better?'

'Don't be a cock.'

'See? Sensitive.'

'I should go back to the bar. I owe Calum a round.'

He moved to block my escape. 'What's happening with John?' he said, side-stepping around me.

I had to think for a minute who John was. 'John, spits-when-he-talks John?'

'You haven't seemed to notice. Even Eduardo said there must be something going on there. You're hanging on to his every word. It's obvious you're going to fuck him.'

'Excuse me?'

'Are you taking turns with us all? Making us all feel a bit special so that you can build up that dented little ego after poor little Laura got dumped?'

I shook my head, confused. 'What? No.'

'Because he's welcome to you,' Pete said. 'I don't want you. Even if you could squeeze more than one fella into a night, and I bet you could.' He took a long pull of his drink, draining the glass. 'It's a bit pathetic, isn't it? The broken heart routine? Dragging on, some.'

He stung like acid. 'Good. I don't want you either,' I lied. I shook my head in disbelief. 'Like it's any of your fucking business what I do anyway.' Colour burned at my cheeks. I was utterly confused by him. 'And, if you don't care why are you being so mean?'

'You started it.' He let go of my hand. I hadn't realised he was still holding it. 'You never tell me how you really feel,' he said, voice changing. 'Every time we talk you hide from me. You don't give anything away. You're always . . . you're always gunning for an exit, or a fight.'

'No, Pete,' I said, turning on my heel. 'I'm trying to avoid a fight. By leaving.'

Calum bollocked me for taking too long to get his vodka orange, and I snapped back, 'Well fucking *excuse me* that the table service isn't up to scratch.' A few pints down and everyone was at that merrily pissed stage that three drinks and the shedding of professional inhibitions produces; the group chat had peeled off into little cliques, voices were louder and less restrained. I found myself in between Calum, who had his back to me to listen to Paris's puppy anecdotes politely, and a guy I didn't know very well but who seemed very passionate about describing a very particular nuance in the

US–Sudanese oil trading laws to Eduardo. I excused myself for another cigarette.

*People are so complicated,* I thought as I sucked on my fag. I watched the smoke dance out of my lips and into the dark night, resting on the brick wall of the pub and looking to the moon. In my quiet moments the same abusive monologue snaked its way into my psyche. *You're too much. Even tonight, with this crowd of out-and-out weirdoes, nobody really wants to talk to you for long. You're exhausting. A challenge. Too brash and loud. Learn to be smaller, Laura, for crying out loud. Learn to be more likeable. You're not likeable.*

'Penny for your thoughts,' said Pete from the doorway.

I sighed. 'I'm tired, Pete.'

He stood beside me and took the cigarette from between my fingers to light his own.

'You look like you've got the weight of the world on your shoulders, kid.' I said nothing. 'Is that why you're so prickly tonight? You're like a hedgehog balled up in the middle of rush hour.' We stared out into the dark together. Then he said, 'You don't like me much this evening, do you?'

'Now who's sensitive?' I said.

'You, I reckon. You've not said one nice thing to me lately.'

'That's what we *do*, Pete. Take the piss and wind each other up and then go home and fantasise about what would ever happen if we got naked with each other . . .'

He grinned. 'You fantasise about me?'

'Fuck off.'

'I have a girlfriend, Laura.'

'I have self-respect.'

'Ouch.'

'Look. Maybe I am mean to you, and push to see how far you'll push back. And you drive me crazy. Nuts! Totally fucking nuts. But this isn't ever supposed to happen, and if it was we would have kissed at the club, all that time ago, when you came on to me and I knew it wasn't right to kiss you back, and—'

'I didn't come on to you.'

'Yes, you did. On the steps. When I was leaving.'

'No.'

'You did.'

'I think you're imagining things.'

And he said it in such a way that I thought maybe I had imagined it, and then I thought that maybe I'd imagined any sexual chemistry at all, and then I had tears in my eyes because, well, because I liked Pete, and I hated Pete, and I'd been dumped, and if my ex didn't want me and he preferred my high school best friend to me then *of course* Pete didn't want me either. Nobody wanted me, and probably ever would. And then I was crying. I was trying really hard not to, but the tears came because . . . because I was empty and full, both at the same time, and it all seemed so terribly hard. I was drained, and didn't want to be strong, or brave, and to go another step alone, best face forward, terrified me. I was so goddamn *angry*. Full of hurt that I didn't have anywhere to put.

'Fuck. Come on, Laura. Don't do that,' Pete said, softly.

I sniffled, wiping at my nose with the back of my hand. 'No. I'm sorry. It's not you.'

'Maybe I did come on to you a little bit . . .'

I tried to push back the emerging tears with the heels of my hands. Pete moved to hug me, and my face was hot and heavy. We stood wordlessly until he shifted away to look at me, saying, 'I made you cry?'

I fumbled in my bag for a tissue, but couldn't find one. Putting it to the ground I crouched to scramble around a bit more, getting frustrated at my trouble. I started emptying out the contents on to the pavement: my purse and notebook, make-up bag and pens and loose change, and then I was whispering, 'It's not here. I don't have one. I thought I had. I always keep a tissue, for fuck's sake, I always have a tissue.'

I was frantic and Pete crouched down to hold my face, looking into my eyes, and said, 'Laura. I'll go and get you a tissue.'

He disappeared inside and I refilled my bag haphazardly. He returned bearing two drinks and a wad of loo roll to find me still on my knees, only this time clutching at a cigarette I'd fortuitously discovered in a secret side pocket.

'Baby, come on,' he said. 'Over here.'

Nobody had called me baby since David. Nobody else had called me baby, ever.

I followed him to a set of steps at the far end of the empty car park, hidden away from view of the door and in the shadows where I could be less embarrassed by my truths. We shared my cigarette and he pulled out a roll-up from his pocket that he lit off mine, and we shared that, too. It was wrapped in liquorice paper and the taste of it gave me a head rush. He put his arm around me and pulled me in so that my head could rest on his shoulder, and we sat like that for as long as it took us to finish the smoke and find my courage.

'If I tell you things and you repeat them back to me ever in my entire life I will kill you.'

'Deal.'

'What if I'm never loved again?'

I felt him smile in the darkness. 'You'll be loved,' he said.

'But not by my ex. Not by you.'

'Another time, another place, beautiful . . .'

'I know,' I said. 'I don't even know why I said that. This isn't about you. I promise you, it's not.' He tugged me back into his armpit and I wiped my face on his jumper. I closed my eyes to help with the pounding I could feel in my temple, and let myself cry. Proper, loaded sobs. We sat together in the shadows and I wailed. Clutching on to him and letting go of every sadness inside of me, I howled and shook and stopped being brave, and eventually, between breaths, as he patiently sounded it out with me, patiently let me hurt and cleanse and heal and process in the confines of the bottom step of a pub car park, I said, clearly, 'I'm really not crying for you, you know. I'm not. This is . . .'

'Beautiful,' he said. 'I'm a poet. I know what the tears are for.'

# SIX

I rang Calum's doorbell and huddled under his tiny porch from the early signs of spotting rain. The noise of his front door opening sounded, and then the footsteps of him skipping down the stairs of the communal hallway, heavy of step and light of heart – not unlike a baby bear waking up from a nap. He dramatically flung the door to the building open and then wobbled in surprise that I was stood quite so close to the entrance.

'Jesus!' he said, stumbling back a little. 'Personal space, Laura.'

I wasn't sure if I was about to ruin his day. 'The rain,' I said, motioning to the sky with my head. 'I didn't want to get wet.'

'It can be grey skies for a lifetime as long as the sunshine of my world is ringing my doorbell,' he sang. 'Did you text to say you were on your way over? I haven't checked my phone in a while. Do you know, the battery is getting worse and worse. I might just upgrade to a new one and pay the difference. What do you think? Or maybe I should just wait for the new model to get released . . . God, I'd be so mad if I got a new iPhone and then the improved version was released like, the next day.'

I hopped from one foot to the other. 'I have news.'

He didn't miss a beat. 'And you're telling me before Twitter?'

'I'm telling you before I've even called my mother.'

'You had sex with Pete, didn't you?'

44

'I'm not even having sex with myself, Calum. I might never cum again.'

'You're talking in riddles I don't understand, now.'

I sighed. 'I meant I'm not even really masturb—'

'I know what you *meant*, I just don't understand how that is *possible*.'

I swatted his segue away with my hand. Why was it always about sex? 'Listen,' I said. 'I'm going to America.'

Calum frowned, raised his eyebrows, and then clapped his hands together excitedly. 'Fantastic! Well, that's great, isn't it? I think a holiday is just what you need.' He hugged me lightly, pulling away quickly to hold me at arm's length. 'Why do you have a face like a slapped arse, then?' He patted my arm. 'Tell me everything from the beginning. You always do this – get dead dramatic. Let's go and put the kettle on. And why aren't you wanking? That's just not natural.'

I swallowed, inhaled, and said, almost in one breath, 'Next week I am going to Paris. To see my friend, Mary-Kate – the one who moved there ages ago.' I warmed to my theme. 'It's been booked for ages. I haven't been in forever, like, since before the break-up, and feel bad about not seeing her more often. It's so cheap on Ryanair; I reckon I paid about fifty quid return.' I pushed some loose hair out of my excited eyes. 'She's so lovely. I can't believe you guys haven't ever met! You'd enjoy her very much.' This wasn't what I came to tell him. Calum has a way of making me swerve off-topic – I realised I was digressing, and then forced myself to focus with a shake of my head. 'But that's not the important bit. You knew about Paris. The new bit of information is this: when I'm back, I'm moving for a bit. They've offered me a semester, with the chance to stay longer if I want. Which. Well. I might do. I don't know. But I'll be gone for the rest of the school year for sure.'

And then his *Good Morning!* smile dropped and his brows knitted in the middle and he pouted and said, 'No. Wait. What?'

He blinked several times in quick succession.

'I'm going to go and be somebody else for a while,' I said.

*

Crumbling into Pete's lap had been a turning point. I was boring. The constant crying. The lifelessness. I realised all I had in Derby was twelve hours a week of classes and a poorly paid job in a local toyshop. I'd find myself in the middle of dealing with a customer at work – searching in the stockroom for another colour variation on a bumper seat, say – and I'd just . . . stare. Lose minutes, chunks of time, to absolutely zoning out. I was eating pints of Ben & Jerry's ice cream a day. Calum had been good with me, letting me sit soundlessly on his sofa when I needed to, face set to screensaver mode in front of nothing in particular on the telly, as he played his life out around me. Or suddenly, I'd be full of energy and resolve, planning and plotting and dragging him to The Cottage where I'd buy his drinks for him and talk without taking a breath. Kudos to him, Calum rose to the discombobulating challenge of riding these moods out with me. He was a hero. I played in the clouds and then sank to the trenches, swinging back and forth with such elasticity that I was dizzy, and confused, and, above all else, successfully avoiding mentally processing the way David's email kept creeping into my imagination with visions of *her* boyfriend-stealing – *fiancée-stealing* – shit-eating grin, even almost a year after he'd left. I was stir-crazy. It felt as if people had started to talk at me rather than to me, speaking slower, as if I were a wild animal that could attack in a heartbeat. And, in truth, it did feel like at any given moment I could snap. I was drinking too much. Smoking too much. Abusing my body to numb my mind – the kind of over indulgence that meant I was occupied enough not to reconcile me to myself. I couldn't keep two thoughts together in my head. So I'd brought a plane ticket. I'd bought escape. Reinvention.

Calum's eyebrows unknitted, jumping to his hairline in surprise. 'You are *going* to America, or *moving* to America . . .?' He said the words slowly, deliberately. A bit squeakily.

'Both? Kinda?'

'When?'

'In about a month. I signed the paperwork this morning.'

He considered what I was saying for a second, eyes dotting back and forth like they were searching for something on the ground – possibly my common sense, or maybe just recognition that this wasn't some elaborate prank. Finally, he said, 'But you're not going forever? You're still enrolled at Derby?'

'I'm going for a few months to start with. The visa will allow me to be there for as long as I am enrolled at a university. It's basically an exchange programme. I'm not technically eligible on the course that we're on, but . . . well. I didn't take no for an answer.' I shifted my weight from one foot to the other. 'I don't know. I just need to get out of here. Like I said, be somebody else for a bit. Or more of myself. *Something.* I need *change.*'

He nodded as I spoke. 'Okay, okay . . .' He said it more to himself than to me. I wrapped my arms around my dampening shoulders, still stood on his porch and only half sheltering from the increasingly violent rain. I didn't want to interrupt his reverie to point out that my favourite suede boots were getting rain-marked. I'd had longer to get used to this sudden turn of events, after all. 'Are you going to be somebody else in New York?' he asked.

'Nope.' I said. 'Detroit!' I did a jazz-hands shimmy. I hoped a bit of animation might speed up the process of being invited in. *Yes, I'm leaving you for a bit. No, I don't know how we'll live without each other either. No, I won't forget to Skype on the daily. I love you.* I wanted Calum to understand that his strength had carried me this far, and now I needed reinvention to get me to the next part.

'Detroit?'

'Yes. Detroit.'

'Not New York?'

'No. De-*fucking*-troit. Eastern Michigan University, to be precise, about an hour outside the city.' He considered this. *Hmmm . . .* he intoned, and neither of us knew what to say, and so I said, 'Okay, so listen. I know this is kind of a big deal and everything, because who will you sit next to in the library now? But also it's only for a bit, a few months, probably, and you'll be fine, and my shoes are going to get ruined if we stay on the porch much longer. I'm cold. Are you going to invite me in?'

Calum stuck his head out of the door to look at the sky, assessing the situation. 'It depends if you are going to tell me anything else that will ruin my lunch.'

'That's all I've got today,' I said in a tiny voice.

'You'd best come in, then. I'll let you know it's not the end of my world in a minute.'

Whilst Calum brewed a shit cup of tea – always too weak, with too much milk, and often not hot enough because he gets impatient and doesn't let the kettle reach the boil – I explained. 'I've been offered the chance to go on a theatre tour of high schools in Detroit, doing some writing workshops at Eastern Michigan University, and, well, I'm going.' Calum nodded curtly to indicate he had understood. 'There is a programme out there I can do, and it's all happened dead fast. I was just sort of randomly Googling shit and it turns out it's all very straightforward, really, if you're good at filling out forms and demanding stuff. And so I said yes. When they agreed. Yesterday. Confirmation of everything came through on email this morning.'

'I don't see you for a week and this is what happens?' He delivered me the biscuits. 'Wow. Well, it all makes perfect sense, really. It does. You deserve to get away for a bit.' Slowly, as he pushed the teabag around the mug and searched for the semi-skimmed, Calum had acclimatised. 'I'm impressed that you've pulled together an actual plan. I mean – it's not like you are just quitting life and getting on a plane and hoping for the best. I'd be a bit more concerned if that were the case. And as long as it isn't permanent . . .'

'I don't even know what permanent means,' I said. 'I thought I had permanent. I don't really know what I want – I just know that I can't stay in bloody Derby. I just . . . I mean . . . I can't. I'm not better than this place, Cal, but I'm bigger than it, you know?'

'I know," he said, sadly. "Me, too. I know.'

I slurped at my tea and let the mug warm my hands.

'Why Detroit?' he asked.

'Just happened that way,' I shrugged. 'The opportunity presented itself, and I'm grabbing it with both hands.'

I was giddy at the thought of being somebody new. Being somebody other than 'the jilted one'. Becoming somebody else. I drained my mug and landed it on the table with a thud.

# SEVEN

'And so,' I explained over macaroons, a view of the Sacre Coeur peeking out over the Paris streets, 'I fly out in about three and a half weeks.'

My old school friend marvelled. 'Wow. Just like that?'

'It's no more impulsive than how you ended up out here.'

Mary-Kate, flawless skin and big, Bambi-like eyes, giggled. 'Well, no, I suppose not.'

'How did that go again? Oh yeah, *Sorry I haven't texted you back, it's just I got this new job in Paris and I leave tomorrow!* At least I'm giving you a little notice.'

She conceded, flicking ash blonde hair over a shoulder. 'Well, yes, it did happen a bit like that. But Paris is across the Channel, not halfway around the world!' She offered me the last macaroon. I took it, broke it in half, and handed a piece back to her. We said 'Cheers' and hit them against each other, before popping them in our mouths whole.

Mary-Kate implicitly understood the right things to say: she's considered and kind, generous with her judgements but merciless with her verdicts. She'd come over to Paris as an au pair, quickly demanding high levels of cash for her pristine and faultless childcare services that then meant she could afford to get a degree in the capital, too. A supremely handsome French-Chilean boyfriend and rent-controlled studio apartment later, she showed no signs of leaving Paris any time soon. Seeing slivers of her life, I couldn't argue with her choice. Having gone to school with and grown up alongside us all, Mary-Kate knew me and David and Gwen well enough to talk real sense to me in a way that I hadn't been subjected to from anybody else.

'Laura,' she'd said, the night I'd arrived. 'I love you, and I hate to see you like this. I do. I've watched all this unfold from a distance, but I know him, and I know her, too, and I'm so unreservedly sure that none of this was planned. Nobody ever wanted to hurt you. You know that, don't you?'

'I'm humiliated,' I'd told her. 'Out of everything, I'm . . . embarrassed. I wonder if it was obvious to everyone else that it was her who he really wanted.'

'Don't,' she'd said. 'Don't go down that rabbit hole.'

And so I didn't. I sidestepped it and swallowed down my curiosity, knowing that any more information about their dalliance, their courtship, would push me over an edge of jealousy that I'd struggle to get back from. Because that was it: I was envious in the extreme. David and I had been having problems – but that was an inopportune addition to the narrative I was giving myself as a faultless woman scorned. I wasn't ready to shoulder any burden of responsibility. Not yet. Mary-Kate saw that, and called bullshit.

Over the course of a week in Paris, she did me a lot of good. It was easier to feel stronger about the situation when I was in one of the world's most beautiful cities, eating sugar, getting some straight talking from somebody who had known me since I was wearing braces and frosted lipstick. She made me laugh, let me cry. I might've deleted a few people from my online life (as well as from my phonebook), but I was still able to access their public profiles, and Mary-Kate knew it.

She had me block the lot. She asked questions about Detroit, about my plans, and as we meandered the city she'd point out clothes in shop windows that she'd insist 'are just *perfect* for the Laura you're going to be in America'. It was cheering.

By my penultimate night she was quite insistent that no self-respecting French woman would let herself fall into the disrepair I was inflicting on myself – a sobering but very real truth, my bloated belly and puffy eyes confirmed. I looked in the mirror, at her firmness, and saw a shell of myself: hollowed cheekbones and grey skin. I looked like a woman on the edge. 'Let me give you a Parisienne night out, sweet girl,' she said. 'Remind you of how wonderful you are.' With Mary-Kate's help I painted on lip-gloss and curled my hair, and for solid seconds believed that I was going to be just fine. In fact, the more we talked about Detroit and all of the possibilities, the more I genuinely felt capable. And that's how I ended up basking in the attentions of a French scientist at a house party somewhere in the 11th arrondissement: Saturday night in Paris.

Tall, lanky, messy-haired and wearing the crispest of shirts, it was no wonder I noticed him: he was the spitting image of David. We were introduced, and he said, 'Ing-lish?' in a lazy French drawl exactly like all the clichéd Frenchmen who have ever been portrayed by horny female writers in the history of literature. There was a quick conversation about how Mary-Kate is actually English, too – her French is just so good that nobody can tell – and everyone agreed how wonderful she was, and then I decided I absolutely needed the startlingly handsome man's attention again and so I touched his arm with the tips of my fingers and said, '*Mais oui.* English.'

I was ambivalent on the inside, still feeling sorry for myself, but outwardly was apparently determined to charm. Mary-Kate had told me to. 'That is what a French woman would do,' she said. 'Flirt her way back to full health. Calum had that much right about that Pete guy. I can't wait to meet him, by the way. Calum.'

The advice was easier to follow amongst strangers. I smiled, offered my hand, turned my shoulder slightly so that it was clear I intended to have a conversation with him, and only him, and in return Raphael, as I learned he was called, tipped his head quizzically. He was amused, I think, at my brash behaviour, which came as something of a shock to me, too. An hour before we'd left for the party I'd let the tiniest single tear escape in Mary-Kate's studio apartment, unable to speak. 'No! No. I'm fine. Don't hug me,' I'd said. 'Let's just go.' And now, to look at me, all dressed up and 100 per cent committed to feeling all kinds of fabulous, nobody would ever have known.

The Frenchman shook my hand, holding on to it for a little longer than strictly necessary, and, as we maintained eye contact, he said, '*Enchanteé*,' making me melt into a puddle at his mercy.

In social situations my inner performer tends to rear her attention-seeking head, and with Raphael it was no different – even if it did take a little more effort on account of the weight on my heart. But, in spite of myself, it felt glorious to be holding a drink in a chic Parisian apartment, talking to a beautiful French man, asking him questions about himself and holding his gaze whilst undertaking a heavy demonstration in *brushing-hair-off-the-back-of-my-neck* that I supported with my very best *and-now-you're-thinking-about-kissing-my-neck* smile. I was an actress playing a lead part – Derby's own Elizabeth Taylor on tour. I giggled, I paused in a considered manner, I made what I assumed were intelligent observations about what he was telling me in the same breath that I took the piss out of his serious knitted brow and tendency to be very headmastery about the state of the European Union. I was, it seemed, *flirting*. And to success!

I gently corrected his pronunciation, after he asked me to tell him if he made a mistake with his 'Ing-lish'. I quickly noticed that doing so meant he had to watch my mouth to see how it moved in order to make a word sound correctly, and then I'd watch his mouth to see if he was, indeed, using it properly, and then we'd be saying things and staring at each other's lips and *shag me sideways* if that isn't the prelude to the hottest interaction between two fully-clothed virtual strangers ever undertaken. In those moments, I was worthy. Of what, I wasn't sure – but I didn't need to be. I was intoxicated by my own starring role.

Two hours and five cocktails later, Mary-Kate sought me out to pull on my arm and whisper, 'I know we decided that you're fine, but are you sure you're *this* fine?' She nodded her head in Raphael's general direction.

I was thinking about Raphael's mouth on mine, his hands on my waist; those rolling 'r's whispering rude, French things in my ear. She could see it. Everyone could see it: subtle I was not. It felt so terrifically good to know I could command a man's attention. *This man's attention.* To feel beautiful. As Raphael served me drink after drink we spoke for hour after hour, and I became more and more convinced that I was better off single anyway.

Oh, *booze*. Glorious, inhibition-smashing, reassuring *booze*.

Evening turned into midnight, turned into the small hours of the next day's morning. Mary-Kate appeared to interrupt us where I sat, suddenly inches away from Raphael's face, his elegant hand at the base of my spine. I have no idea what he'd been saying. By this point in the evening it was less about the words being spoken and more about how to stop speaking at all, really. Biology* (*the drink) had kicked in where my brain had ceased to function.

'We're going to miss the last metro,' said Mary-Kate.

'Stay here, then,' said Raphael.

And just like that the evening's events were confirmed.

We stared at each other. His eyes hinted secrets. 'We must go outside and make a smoke,' he said.

'Yes,' I said. 'We must.'

\*

I've thought of that moment in Paris many times over the years. I've told the story to friends and strangers, all women, in that way that we do when we pour wine and swap notes on what it is to be alive and female and young and unsure. I've said, time over, that when I flew out to Charles De Gaulle I was void. That the feeling of hurt and heartbreak had robbed me of something that I couldn't, at that time, put my finger on. I was functioning, but not living. Not one bit was I living. And I don't care what 'shoulds' there were – that I 'should' already be 'better' – I wasn't. But that night, in that apartment, with that drink in my hand and those fingertips dancing on my thigh, the horizon of a new adventure was just visible enough. Being somewhere where nobody knew I had failed was incentive enough to grant myself release. And, as it turns out, human beings are capable of thinking and feeling more than one emotion at a time.

\*

Raphael didn't pick up any cigarettes as we left the apartment and, as I made for the stairs in the dark hallway, he found my hand and tugged on it, pulling me back towards him. I did a sort of half-spin, stumbled, and he put his hands on my elbows to steady me. His mouth met mine.

He moved his right hand to cup the back of my head and used the other to pull me even closer. He kissed hard and deep, and I choked on my own breath a little in surprise. It took a moment to register what was happening, that this disarmingly handsome man wanted me *that much*, and then I was kissing back, and somehow we lay in the stairwell, and he was whispering what I can only imagine to be rude, dirty things to me and his hand was under my blouse, and then he was on my neck and ears and chest and I thought *this is what heaven feels like* because I forgot how to punctuate a sentence.

I knew that at any moment somebody could walk out of the apartment, though, and my brain wouldn't switch off. *You're making out with a French guy and he is so very hot,* I thought. *He kisses like he really means it,* I thought. *Goodness, he, errrr, he really knows what he is doing,* I concluded. Awkwardly, it occurred to me: Calum would be proud.

'*Aslkhfjbv,*' I mumbled. He said something in French. I tore apart from him, playfully resting a hand on his shoulder to say, 'People could see.'

'People *could* see,' he acknowledged, and I wriggled free to stand, presuming we'd go somewhere a little more private.

He'd sort of been lying at the side and on top of me, on the stairs, all at once, and from his quasi-horizontal position he moved to his knees and looked up to face me. I dropped my chin to stare back. He leaned closely to between my legs – looking at me, still, the whole time, deep and penetrating and so fucking *French*. He pressed his mouth to where my thighs met my pelvis and breathed, hot and sticky. My knees gave way a little and I closed my eyes. He tugged at the waistline of my leggings, and as he pulled them down suddenly I no longer minded that only a single door separated us from the party.

The focus and attention this man lavished on my vagina was like experiencing an artist at work. Inspiring. I could've applauded him.

That he was so invested in making me cum was incentive enough to let myself moan just a little too loudly, given the circumstances, and as quickly as I'd begged him in desperate whispers, I pushed him away again, sweaty and panting and glorious and satisfied.

'You taste sweet,' Raphael told me, gently re-dressing my bottom half and rising to a stand. 'I wanted to do that since you shook my hand.'

'Me, too,' I replied. I leaned over to meet his forehead with my own, breathy and sweaty. 'Fuck me,' I told him. He tensed. 'Please fuck me.'

As I understood sex, and all its tricky relations, oral was foreplay. A warm-up. I hadn't been with many other men besides David – I lost my virginity to a ginger guy a few years above me at school, in his parents' bed, and fooled around with the pot-wash at a waitressing gig I had, when David and I had temporarily broken up two years into our teenage romance. It hadn't lasted five minutes – the break-up, or the pot-wash. Men wanted to put their willy inside you, right? As a rule? And yet, as soon as I said to Raphael that this is what I wanted, everything changed. What had been a spontaneous, sexy encounter suddenly seemed dirty and uncouth. He stepped back from me.

'No,' he said. 'No. We don't do it like that here. I know British girls, they . . .' His sentence trailed off.

'They what?' I said.

'French girls don't do that.'

Self-respect dictates that at this point, I should've slapped the judgemental prick and flounced off, indignant but relieved at a narrow escape. It had been mutual seduction. We'd both wanted it. I had nothing to be embarrassed or ashamed about. But instead, I . . . begged. I fucking *begged*. 'Fuck me,' I repeated. 'I want you. I want to make you cum. *Fuck me*.' I sounded hysterical. Desperate.

I *was* hysterical and desperate.

I was also mortified.

Raphael couldn't have looked more repulsed by me if I'd asked to take a dump in his mouth. 'No, Laura. No, thank you.'

NO, THANK YOU? *Would you like a cup of tea?* No, thank you. *May I wash your clothes for you?* No, thank you. *Can I have sex with you?* NO, THANK YOU.

As if to prove to him, and myself, that he wasn't serious, that he couldn't possibly want to resist me and my body, I pulled at his belt. I rearranged my features so as not to betray my mortification, and focused on searching for his buckle. For a moment, a millisecond, he looked as though he would. His face suggested it would be easier to succumb than to continue refusing, and relief flooded me. He did want me, after all. I could make him want me. I'd get what I wanted. Needed. This man would be mine.

But catching his eye in the speckled moonlight of the hallway, one fact was clear: Raphael did not want me. An overhead light came on, blinding in its brightness and fact, and footsteps echoed in the hallway a few flights down.

'You should go back inside,' he said, and I snapped into some kind of sense. 'Your friend will wonder where you have been.'

Bile rose in my throat.

Before I could suggest otherwise, he'd spotted the middle-aged couple on the floor below, culprits of the light switch, and leant over the staircase to ask for a cigarette. He walked away from me to collect it. I let myself back into the party.

'You look awful. What happened?' Mary-Kate asked, as she spotted me reaching into the fridge for what looked like the last beer.

'He, errrr– we, we messed around,' I said.

'. . . Did you want to mess around?'

'Yes, yes – of course I did. He's lovely. Was lovely. I, errrr. You know. Do we have to stay tonight?'

Mary-Kate looked confused. 'Well, it's about two a.m. and the metro doesn't start again til six. We can't walk home, and a taxi will be impossible, too, I think. So. Yeah. We kind of have to.' She seemed a bit annoyed. 'I thought you wanted to stay?'

I pulled the bottle opener off the sideboard and clipped at my 1664. 'Oh god, yeah, that's cool. Totally cool,' I said. 'Just thought I'd ask.'

Raphael came through the front door then, saw Mary-Kate and me turn to look at him, and scurried into the living room. Mary-Kate stared at me. I drank my beer.

Two hours later we'd all collapsed in various states of drunken undress on several blow-up beds that had been thrown on to the living room floor. Mary-Kate was at the far end of the room, the little spoon to her boyfriend's big one, and I was in my knickers and a vest top breathing in the exhales of an athletic black man with an afro who somehow had ended up asleep next to me, despite me originally dozing off by the wall. I shifted and looked around for Raphael. Moonlight was peeking through curtains. The shadows of a dozen or so bodies were cast across the walls, and in the morning hour's silence, loneliness hit my stomach.

I wasn't sure what I had done wrong. I didn't really understand the situation. Raphael had seemed to want all the same things that I did, at least for that night, and then his hot blew cold in the time it took me to utter two short words.

I moved around, trying to get more comfortable, tears starting to leak from my eyes. Always tears. *Why her and not me? Why her and not me? Why her and not me?* My mind's favourite mantra played itself over and over again. I rolled over, and made eye contact with the guy with the afro. He was awake.

Putting his finger to his lips, he made a *sssssh* sound. I used my fingertips to slide away tears. He motioned for me to scoot over, and, sniffling unattractively, I did. He moved me on to my other side so that he could hug me from behind, and the compassion of it – of holding on to a stranger who needed to be held – made my whole body heave with silent sobs. We stayed like that, his grip on my body getting tighter. It felt safe in his arms. I found myself arching my back so that my barely clothed bum pushed into his crotch, tears continuing to fall. I felt him bulge. Wiping snot from my nose, I guided his hand to my crotch. I stopped crying.

# EIGHT

It was a case of identity: I didn't have to be the broken-hearted girl. I could, in fact, be whatever I wanted. I kept telling myself that it was powerful to be provocative and confident and sexual, and I came to believe it. I had two weeks until I flew to Detroit, and I wanted to practise my new self before I got there. This new self.

Raphael had wanted me until he hadn't, but instead of wallowing for months and weeks like I did when David rebuffed me, I'd replaced him quickly – literally, within the hour. The rejection didn't have to hurt, because without investing emotionally there was nothing to take personally. Men could, then, be interchangeable. That was staggering to me; enlightening in its bright convenience. I didn't have to get attached. My body could be a gateway to solace that my mind didn't have to indulge. I didn't tell Mary-Kate or Calum exactly why, but my change, my switch, was palpable. I wore it on my face. I was newly ravenous for male attention and delirious enough on hormones and control that I was going to get it.

I planned my next *liaison* via the Internet – an obvious choice now, but unchartered territory for a booty call in 2009. Tinder hadn't been invented yet; I didn't even have an iPhone. Casual sex with strangers was arranged either face-to-face, or via OK Cupid. I chose OK Cupid. I was riding a wave of cockiness, but not so much that I'd visit Derby's Wetherspoon's and dish out blowjobs after half a warm pint. There was, of course, a direct correlation between my drinking and my level of promiscuity. They fuelled each other, and I was fine with it.

'Isn't it a little shallow, Laura?' Liam asked me when I pulled up my dating profile in Calum's living room one rainy Tuesday evening. 'You're not normally so superficial. I'm surprised at you.'

After three days of a little post-Paris secrecy I'd admitted to Calum and his boyfriend that I was headed to the online realm, and they said they approved – but *obviously*, they countered, they'd need an insight into the process. I think they were laughing at me, but I couldn't be sure. Couples can be funny together – tag-teaming single folks to alleviate a curiosity that monogamy doesn't satiate. I know because I've been there, I've been the torturer, so I played along. They were pleased to see me happier, though, I knew that much. Calum had alluded to the open arms he had for the 'old Laura'. I can't blame him for having tired of my wallowing ways. Everyone was better off if I smiled.

'Okay, Judgey-Mc-Judgerson,' I replied. 'Let's keep this in perspective, shall we? I'm not looking for marriage'

'If she was she'd be on Jack Black lookalikes dot com,' Calum pointed out.

'I hear the jest in your voice, ass hat,' I said.

'Well, if you insist on having his picture as your computer's wallpaper I will continue to mock you and not feel one iota of guilt,' he said.

I feigned outrage. 'First thing,' I staccatoed, holding my finger to his face, 'He isn't even my background anymore. I changed it to a motivational quote about enthusiasm that I got from Oprah's website.' Liam guffawed. 'And, secondly, I *happen* to think I could do a lot worse than a man like Jack Black.' I sighed. 'It just makes me a bit sad in my belly that he is already married and adoring of his wife.'

Calum handed me my phone, which had just lit up. 'They all are at the beginning. You've got three missed calls.'

I punched in my access code and mentally noted that I needed to call my mother back. 'Jack Black would never cheat.'

'Everybody cheats.'

We let the words hang in the air for inspection.

\*

What's casually alarming is that you're *expected* to be self-destructive after a break-up. Nobody was about to criticise me for too many drinks or skipping class. Even my parents seemed to prefer a Sunday lunch story about a wild night out, to tears and an uncertainty they were powerless to fix. Stepping into that script of debauchery meant I easily bought into my own myth: I was keeping a blog where I'd frame my adventures as pithy, mildly outrageous vignettes of a girl totally unbothered by her life's circumstance. I got to literally pen a new story arc for my life. We all do it. We all live the story we tell ourselves. As I was living it, writing it, I chose to declare myself young and wild and free – and sexually unhibited. That was just so much more *fun* than any of the other stuff. Nobody suggested I was wrong.

'This guy lists *the gym* and *FHM* as his hobbies,' Calum giggled, scrolling the laptop over my shoulder. He flicked through the thumbnail photos with lightning quick speed.

'Small willy,' I said, feeling immediately terrible because small willies aren't bad, and it's the shittiest thing a person can say about a fella's sexual prowess. Intellectually, I know that a man's value is not proportional to length and girth. It's like dismissing a woman on her cup size. I revised my statement: 'Small willy with no sense of foreplay. Pounds like Jack Rabbit. Doesn't understand why you haven't cum.'

Calum rolled his eyes. 'Let the court's transcript of this conversation reflect your magnanimity towards all penises,' he said. And then, 'Ewwww, this one is a property lawyer and has only had one serious girlfriend.'

I looked closer at the screen. 'Take off his glasses . . . squint. Do you see it?'

'Maybe.'

We three tilted our heads in symmetry, trying to see it. Wanting to.

'And if he's only had one girlfriend,' I enthused, 'I'm sure he'll be very attentive.'

Liam nudged me in the ribs. 'Straight dating is weird. Who says "very attentive" when talking about a one-night stand?'

I swatted his limbs away. 'I do!' I said, indignantly. 'I'm . . . you know. Just getting used to all this. I'd like a gentleman, I think.' I looked to Calum for guidance. '. . . Wouldn't I?'

'You know we're in Derby, duck, don't you?' he said.

'Not for much longer,' Liam qualified.

We all saw Jay The DJ's profile at the same time. Sandy hair. Headphones around his neck. Tall. Looked mischievous – like he'd have a sense of humour.

'Ticks all the arbitrarily-chosen but necessary boxes,' Calum noted.

'He doesn't look insane or anti-feminist?'

'Looks like he'd call you a cab afterwards, and give the driver the cash to pay for it,' Calum reassured.

His accent reminded me of my cousin, and he used his hands to speak as much as he did his mouth. He laughed in all the right places, asked my opinion on things I was surprised to learn I had an opinion on, and listened – really listened. Jay The DJ made intelligent comments after I spoke, demonstrating that he'd understood what

I'd been trying to communicate, and I charmed him. I know I did because when I looked away he stole sideways glances that he was inept at hiding.

'I wasn't expecting this,' he said, as we supped our wine. 'I wasn't expecting to meet somebody like you.'

I designed a personality as I went along, enjoying both him, and the game of it all. The way it felt to practise a new personality, telling anecdotes and stories and using silly voices to add gravitas to my characters. Me, but more. When he kissed me goodnight, plans for date number two already established, I knew that by the very fact I *could* sleep with him, I would. I'd do it because, yeah, I fancied him – but because he was putty in my hands, I fancied *me* more. I felt more entitled, more worthy of the space, with a man at my side. Any man. This one.

'Did you whap out your pulling story, then?'

'What do you know about my pulling story?'

'I know you used it on Pete that night in The Cottage, when you were all over him without being all over him. You cock-tease.'

I was horrified at the accusation. 'I didn't!' I squealed, and then: 'Oh god, I did, didn't I? I flirted so hard with him that night. He's just so fucking *naughty.*' Calum laughed, but Liam was confused. 'A girl's gotta use what she's got,' I added, feigning nonchalance to navigate a new sudden reality about that evening. That kiss hadn't come from nowhere: I'd willed it to happen. That was happening a lot, lately: new information putting a slant on truths I'd previously held to be absolute. I was getting trickles of an idea that I had to accept more responsibility for my role in my own life.

Liam furrowed his brow. 'Pulling story?'

Calum put his hand over my mouth to indicate that *he* was telling this one. I let him, licking the palm of his hand with the tip of my tongue, playfully, grossing him out as punishment for shutting me up that way. 'Ewww, minging,' he said, wiping his hand on his jeans and then returning it to clap my mouth closed. 'So. You know how Laura wankily – albeit legitimately – starts sentences with, *It was exactly the same when I was on a houseboat in Kerala,* and, *Well, when I lived with some Burmese refugees in the Thai mountains for a week . . .?'* He adopted an airy, irritating voice to impersonate me. 'And most of the time we let her, even though it's disgustingly obnoxious, because we love her?' Liam nodded, eyeing me suspiciously. 'Well, she uses this to her advantage with people she needs to adore her, don't you, Laura? You little egomaniac?' He dropped his hand to signal that I may now speak.

'Yes, Calum.' I turned to Liam. 'Your boyfriend makes it sound ridiculous, and premeditated in a psychopathic way, but it's a tried and tested method for making people sort of, well, I dunno, like me, I guess. Is that pathetic to say? It's like, my way of being interesting at parties and dinners and stuff.' I rapidly felt very defensive. 'It's my party piece, if you like. It's dumb but it's a crowd-pleaser. I dunno.'

'Tell me, then,' Liam said impatiently.

'Well.' I settled into my chair. 'I feel stupid now.'

Liam had no time for my affected shyness. 'Shut up. Just tell me,' he said.

I took another breath. 'Okay,' I began. 'I get sort of misty-eyed as I tell the story, using the palms of my hands to create the visuals – swooping them from side to side like I'm in a music video and blinking a lot slower than I might otherwise do.'

'*It was in Sri Lanka,* I'll start. *In the jungle, there. A big national park. And it had been an awfully long day, I'll say. I remember I was absolutely wet through. My kaftan was positively sticking to me. I*

*suppose that is what you get for going on safari in monsoon season!'*
I shuffled closer to where Liam was sat. 'At this point I do a little knee touch or elbow graze. You know. I want my audience to feel included in what I'm saying.'

Liam nodded. 'That's what will get you laid, or whatever,' he commented. 'Even *I* feel more intimate with you, and I'm a homo. You touched my knee!'

'Works every time,' I said. 'Love a bit of physical contact. Anyway, then I say, *I remember literally wringing out my hair as I climbed out of the jeep, and then holding my breath as I realised that right out on the horizon, in the distance* . . . This is where the hand waving thing comes in, like this,' I gestured wildly. '*I could see mummy elephant, and daddy elephant, and baby elephant. It was truly beautiful. Majestic.* Normally I catch myself here to ask a question of the other, just to highlight how laid-back I am with the tales of my world travels.

'They always comment how wonderful that must've been, how magical, and then I reach my climax. I say, *And just when I thought it couldn't get any more perfect mummy elephant trumpeted; she sang right across the trees and the fields and the sky and the sound of her reverberated through my very soul. It was magical.'*

I stared at Liam expectantly. Nothing.

'O-kaaaaay,' he said slowly.

We stared at each other. He blinked.

'Is that it?'

'No, that's not it! There is the deal-clincher! After I told Jay my story I paused dramatically – he was such a courteous listener, it was kinda cute, actually – and I said, *I've never experienced a feeling like it. Not even during sex.'*

Calum applauded.

'Bring in sex and suddenly the conversation has taken a different turn . . .' Liam said slowly.

'Exactly,' I replied.

'I'll bet Jay The DJ was probably thinking, *Huh. I'll show her reverberating trumpets*,' Calum giggled.

'I'll bet he was, actually,' Liam agreed. 'I feel like I have just witnessed a really important, necessary stage event. I think even *I* want to sleep with you a bit. It makes you seem like an adventure. Like, being closer to you is being closer to the elephants or something. I'm quite awed.'

'Thanks,' I said. 'I feel less contrived now. Or . . . more contrived. One of the two.' I'd known it'd done the job on Jay when he'd gone quiet and looked at me in wonderment. *He'll do*, I'd thought to myself. *For a night, he'll do.*

Liam sighed. 'And now you're going to break his heart,' he intoned, and I hit him playfully.

'No,' said Calum. 'She's going to break his balls.'

# NINE

Same bar, same spot: Jay The DJ sat with a pint, swirling the dregs of it in the bottom of his glass. I was uncharacteristically nervous, and Jay's unease matched it. 'Wow,' he said, voice quivering just enough for me to notice. 'You look . . . you're perfect.'

I pulled up the stool next to him and, voice quivering just enough for him to notice, smiled and said, 'Down boy.'

My hands were shaking – I grabbed either side of the bar stool to hide it. I'd been hugely confident in Paris with Raphael – and two nights ago with Jay, when we met. But both of those had been natural. Unplanned. What was undoing me was the focus on getting out of the bar and into the bedroom. Of how to do it well. Of how to actually have sex this time.

'Wine?' Jay The DJ asked.

'Wine,' I replied.

It took a glass and a half for him to relax enough to stroke my leg, which, in a calculated move, I'd steered to push up against his thigh. I told him about my week, and then he told me about his new job – something to do with design. I might've stopped listening, to be honest, as my thoughts weren't really tuned into *conversation*. In my anxiousness I was struggling to be polite.

'And I suppose you haven't thought of me *once*,' I suggested, pouring the last of the bottle into our glasses – not bad work for under twenty minutes. He looked at me as the last drops hit my glass, and turned the bottle upside down in the cooler, a signal to the barman that we were ready for the next one.

He leaned in. 'I've thought of nothing but you, actually.' His look made the hairs on my arms bristle in shock. 'It's been driving me a bit crazy.' His face offered itself, open and kind. It occurred to me that Jay wasn't only in this to get laid – that he was genuinely interested in dating, in finding somebody to spend his time with. I'd lied by omission about Detroit, about leaving so soon. I lied by omission because I never mentioned that I only wanted him to get sex with somebody new over with.

I raised an eyebrow and matched his posture. 'And what exactly have you been thinking?' I reached out and put my hand on his shoulder, high up, so that it was at the base of his neck. He didn't say anything. 'Shall I tell you what I've been thinking?' He swallowed and nodded. 'I've been wondering what you taste like.'

Jay The DJ looked from my eyes to his lap, seemingly confused, shy, maybe, then back to me. 'Right then,' he said. 'Well.'

I laughed and told him I was kidding. Except – I wasn't. I wanted to know I could have this man, if I wanted to. To feel that thrill of command and charge. My motive was disgusting but I was honest with myself about it. We stared at each other for a minute – really, in matters like this the importance of a drawn-out silence cannot be overestimated, I marvelled – and then I looked away, back up at him from under my lashes, and he was blushing and it was electric and full of anticipation and we smiled.

'Let's grab that booth,' he said, finally, as we spotted a couple in the corner vacate. The barman followed us to the dimly lit crook with our next bottle, which Jay The DJ poured. We cheers-ed, put our drinks on the table, and instantly made out in a fit of furious desperation.

He ran both hands through my hair. I'd worn it up, and where he caressed me, held the back of my head, it came loose in messy knots, unfolding out of the grips it had been pinned in. I edged him closer to the corner of the booth. He kissed me hard and fast and feverishly, and I teased him by slipping my fingers under his shirt and tugging at his boxer elastic.

'God, I want you,' he said.

I kissed him some more. 'I want you, too,' I said. 'I want you very, very much.'

He pulled away. 'You're lovely.'

'Take me home,' I instructed, leaning back in.

We fumbled and kissed and necked. 'I can't,' he said, finding the gaps between kisses to respond. 'I'm at my parents',' he said, 'whilst I find my own place.'

We continued to maul at each other. I didn't want to take him back to mine. I didn't want him to see my life. I only wanted him for one thing. I only wanted to sleep with him.

'Hotel,' I said.

He stopped abruptly. 'Hotel? That's so fucking hot.'

Thirty-five minutes after first meeting at the bar, Jay The DJ was throwing me down on a Travelodge bed, hitching up my dress. I pulled at zippers and belts and buttons with frantic whispers, and then, just like that, I was naked with a man who was not my ex-boyfriend. It felt – notable, I think is the word.

Jay looked not at all as I expected he would. And not because I won't settle for anything less than my Richard Gere – I don't mean it like that at all. I mean – I mean that I was cripplingly aware that my only thought on loop was: *he isn't David*. I was naked with a man who looked at me with all the longing and lust a woman fantasises about, and I was thinking about my ex-boyfriend.

*I'm a god-awful person,* I told myself. *I need to get a fucking grip.*

In his nakedness, Jay The DJ seemed tiny. His legs were slight and a third of the width of my own. His head seemed too big for his skinny frame; a huge bush of blond pubic hair camouflaged his penis. From confident and strong at the bar, he seemed frail and unable in nakedness. It wasn't his body type that did it. A body is a body is a body. It was the way he held himself, the way he apologised for himself. As he embraced me, I almost felt like a mother holding her child to feed, not like a bold lover accepting another. He seemed to need looking after, to want to bear his nudity, and his soul. I was only prepared for one of those. I only wanted one of those. By the time he excused himself to go to the bathroom and I watched his miniscule bum disappear around the corner, I had to coach myself through what was about to happen. *I can leave,* I told myself. *That would be absolutely fine.* But leave to what? An empty bed and nobody to hold me?

That is what I reasoned. I was hungry for desire – even desire I had to manufacture.

He padded back carrying two plastic cups of water. Handing me one, he said, 'Don't know about you, but I'm parched.' I gulped it down to avoid responding; I worried in a moment of pure emotional honesty I might tell him what I was really thinking. I knew if I did, he'd listen and be kind because he was a thoroughly decent bloke, and that made it worse. *Get over yourself,* I scolded, internally. *This isn't the big deal you think it is. It's just sex. He's no monster.* I pulled him close and we kissed again. I wanted this to be *nice.* He was a good kisser, alternating between full, passionate tongues and light, feathery, playful lip brushes. And then his hands ran over my body, he pushed me back on to the bed again, rolled on a condom, and lay on top of me.

I was motionless as he entered me. I was turned on, after all that groping and kissing, but also slightly puzzled. This was it? Straight to the main attraction, with no hint of a teaser? He was the opposite of Raphael. He slid in and out slowly, and when I looked up I saw that his eyes were closed.

'Oh, yes.' He quietly trembled.

He kept saying it, that one word: yes.

I tried a few moans in response. I arched my back a little to try and feel him more, to join his rhythm. I pushed back against him, moved my arms above my head. He thrust. I did very little.

'Yeeesss,' he said.

*No,* I thought.

He felt so different to what I was used to: all wrong angles and positions, and he was entirely into the moment and I was . . . not. He wasn't taking me with him. I moaned a bit more, realised this was all a bit ridiculous, and pushed him off so as to straddle him. I lowered my head to kiss his neck, his cheek, his forehead. To *engage* him.

'You're good,' he whispered. And then: '*Yeeeessss!*'

He stopped thrusting.

Wiped sweat from his brow.

Opened his eyes.

He'd cum.

'That was AMAZING!' he hooted, withdrawing his arms from under me, clumsily, to tie a knot in the liquid-filled condom that he flung to the floor. We lay in a tangled embrace, the kind that should be romantic and tender in a post-coital flush, but inwardly had me cringing because I'd just had sex with a man who was now giving me the heebie-jeebies with his laboured caressing of my skin. It felt forced and wrong and like a lie.

'I'm so happy I met you,' he said, sleepily, into my hair.

By the time he climbed on top of me again I was counting backwards from sixty in my head, rationalising that it took about that long last time. When I got to zero he was still resting with his elbows either side of me, rocking his hips back and forth, and I resolved to count again. I could hear the bin men outside.

*God, I miss him. I miss David. I miss him so, so much.*

'Yes!' I abruptly cried, needing both him to hurry up and my internal monologue to hush. 'Oh yes! YES!'

Jay opened his eyes as if in surprise that I was there.

'Yes?'

'Yes.'

There was much concurring before mutual agreement meant that he breathed his final *yes*, and I breathed a sigh of relief as I wondered what the etiquette was when somebody had paid for a hotel room to have sex with you, but because the sex was excruciatingly poor one didn't want to spend the night. Couldn't spend the night.

Turns out, there is no etiquette – none that I could faithfully execute. You have to, in my case, have soul-crushingly mismatched sex four times, until six thirty in the morning comes, bringing with it a spate of new friction burns that will take four days and a pot of Sudocrem to soothe, when you can finally say, 'I've got an early breakfast meeting to get to – I'll text you.'

He kissed me goodbye slowly, with gusto. Meaning I felt nauseous all the way home.

\*

'Let's do some Googling,' Calum said. 'See where you're going, shall we? I know bugger all about American geography, and from what you've said, I'm not convinced you even know which coast you're flying to.'

'I'd be thrilled to argue with you,' I replied. 'But you're right. I don't actually know much about Detroit. Or America. I've never been before! How can that even be? I LOVE Americans!' I made the tea this time. Despite being in Calum's kitchen, I'd relegated him to spectator. I wasn't in the mood for bad tea today – I had twenty-four more hours in England, and I wasn't going to waste them supping a below-par brew. 'I'll be just outside of the city near this artsy town called Ann Arbor, and beyond that I've got no idea, really.' The kettle flicked off the boil and I poured water into the pot to warm it. I swilled it out, threw in some bags, and filled it up.

Whilst it stewed, I lay out on the floor to stretch. Calum turned on his laptop and clicked and tapped and researched my new home.

'Is Jay The DJ still texting on the hour, every hour?' he asked, only half-interested, as the machine fired up.

I winced. 'Almost. He's eased up a bit, but, urm, yes. He still texts me. I feel like a grade-A dickhead for not messaging back, but what can I say?' The picture of a naked teen celeb flooded Calum's computer. 'Nice,' I noted, and he grinned.

'Babe, just tell him the truth.'

My insides churned. 'The truth is that I shagged him to feel better about myself, Calum, and now I feel worse.'

'You should've broken yourself back in with Pete.' He pulled up Google and typed in the name of my future home. 'I said from the beginning he'd be your man.'

'Have you noticed how Pete has started to take his smoke breaks somewhere else lately? Instead of where we'd normally go?' Calum was busy gasping and shaking his head. 'I think he's avoiding me.' At first I thought he was just winding me up with his dramatic breathing, and then I realised that he was genuinely finding information that wasn't pleasing him. 'Calum?'

'Laura, it says here that Lonely Planet voted Detroit as the worst city in the world.'

'Detroit is the worst city in the world-world, as in *all* of the world?' I questioned. 'Or in the Western world? Do you think Pete *is* ignoring me?'

'No. Literally. The whole world. And Pete adores you. Stop being a twat.'

'Worse than Kabul? Maybe I am being a twat. He gave me the loveliest haiku in a "goodbye and good luck" note on Monday.'

'It would seem so.'

'That he adores me? Yes. Yeah, I guess. He checks in with me to see how I'm doing quite a lot.'

'Focus, Laura. I'm talking about this article. Detroit doesn't get a favourable review. All the articles say the same, in fact.'

'So, what?' I said. 'Detroit, a huge American metropolis, is worse to live in than Khartoum?'

'Uh-huh. Apparently.'

'Detroit is worse than Derby?'

Calum laughed. 'Apparently Detroit is even worse than Wolverhampton. That place comes in at number five.'

'Let me see that.'

'Listen to this,' Calum said, as I climbed up from a downward-facing dog and hovered near his workstation, adjusting the laptop to face me in order to follow the words myself. 'Apparently, says LP, "*Tell any American you're planning to visit Detroit, then watch their eyebrows shoot up quizzically. 'Why?' they'll ask, and warn you about the off-the-chart homicide rates and boarded-up buildings with trash swirling at their bases . . . 'Detroit's a crap-hole. You'll get killed there.'*"'

'Excellent,' I said. I crossed my legs at the ankle and collapsed my legs to sitting, ready to rest my head in Calum's lap. 'Sounds like I'm in for the ride of my life, then.'

'Hey – don't go getting comfy, duck.' He jiggled his knee. 'Can you pour the tea now you've rolled around on the floor?'

I obliged, sullenly. 'I'm gonna pay for how I treated Jay with a big old whack of karma coming back around, aren't I?' I said, waddling to the stove. Tea leaked from the spout on to the plastic worktop as I poured, and I pulled a dirty tea towel from the oven handle to mop it up. 'Shit.'

'I was a bit envious before, if I'm honest,' said Calum. 'But now? I'll stop here, I reckon. Good luck.'

I launched the tea towel at him. 'Don't! I thought Detroit was home to Motown and Ford Motors, all urban glamour.'

'Everything you'd expect from the place Eminem was raised.'

I laughed. 'Yes. Well. I suppose there's that.'

'And, no, you're not going to "pay" for anything, missus. You had a bad one-night stand. I hate to break it to you, but you're not special in that regard. I think they design them that way, to be honest.'

'They do?'

'I don't want to shatter the illusion of my love god status in your mind, but the first time Liam and I got naked I couldn't even get it up. But now? Now he says it's the best sex he's ever had.'

'Do you think that's because you're in love?' I asked.

Calum shrugged. 'Maybe. Or maybe we're in love because we fuck like we're feral. Who knows?'

'I'm gonna miss you in Detroit,' I said.

'I'd miss me, too,' he said, winking. 'Go do what you've gotta do, baby girl.'

# TEN

He'd been told all of his life that he was special, and so special he became. You could tell by the way every last person was with him: deferential, silently seeking his approval. Laughing a little too long and hard at his jokes, leaning a smidge too intently into his anecdotes – both of which were always measured just right. He was self-aware. Not self-consciously so – more like a guy who had done the work. Who knew what the trenches of self-loathing and uncertainty looked like, and the effort – the constant awareness – it takes to keep your head above water. Evolved. He was special, and he was evolved. He was also stunning. He had a flawed handsomeness that was very much on trend; he looked not dissimilar to a taller, broader, washed-out but very hot vampire currently on billboards across the city. Across the *world*. And he seldom spoke directly to me. But – he watched me. Oh, did Chad watch me.

He did it from afar to begin with. I knew when his eyes were on me. The first time it happened, at our earliest rehearsal, my whole body flushed warm, hurriedly and urgent – without warning – the hairs on the back of my neck rising in curious attention. To say my physical self caught on at a pace neither my brain nor peripheral vision could match sounds like an exaggeration, but it's not. My body was blind-sided. My reaction to him was corporal before it was anything else. My cells responded before my wits.

Had it been the other way around – if I'd been able to give way to reason before inexplicable biology – he'd have pissed me off. He was weighing me up, you see. That was flattering, and it was obnoxious. I should have reasoned, known, that he made everyone feel that way. Seen. I'd heard the way he was spoken about. Why he was so popular. So liked. It was because he made you believe you were the only one in his orbit, male or female. Charismatic. He was the very definition of it.

*Oh God,* wrote Calum in an email. *You've been in Detroit three minutes, you randy cow. Calm down.*

I wrote back, *\*HE\* keeps looking at \*ME\*, dude. I'm busy trying to pass myself off as an actor for college credit. I'm the innocent party! I am!*

Calum was having none of it. *I'm calling shenanigans*, he said – and, of course, he was totally right. If Chad was staring, it was because I was giving him reason to.

Eastern Michigan University – EMU – was a campus unlike anything I'd known on British shores. Set in acres and acres, old, turn-of-the-century buildings sat proud alongside brand-new, chrome-and-glass builds, and it felt like room to breathe. The thing about the States is the space; the vastness of it. At least, in the Midwest it felt that way. There were blankets of landscaped grass, water fountains and made-to-measure car parks. Brits are superb at making do, at improvising and settling, but Americans – they expect the best, and have the best. Consumerism reigned supreme. From the student centre to the on-campus accommodation I was staying in, from the post office to the supermarket, I wanted for nothing. I was provided for, and comfortable. I liked it a lot, and didn't get homesick once. It felt like coming home, mostly. I had sensed that a big part of my jigsaw puzzle was hiding out in the United States, and it was going to be one hell of a game to find it. I was ready. I promised myself I would keep saying *yes*. I wouldn't waste this opportunity, the one I'd forced myself to find. I wouldn't be shy about figuring out how to be. How to stop feeling so removed from who I knew I had inside of me, somewhere.

I was taking writing workshops for the most part, but had also secured a role in a touring production of *Antigone*, the Greek tragedy of family and power and standing up for what is right – a class that would never have been offered at Derby but at EMU was open, in variation, every semester. It was part of a programme called *Theatre For Young Audiences*, and I figured I might learn something. I'd worked as an English tutor the past few summers in Italy – it was a teaching job and we were encouraged to use as much drama as possible. It was a gig almost too good to be true: one week on the Italian Riviera in a place so beautiful it had featured in *The Talented Mr Ripley*, its grandness showing even the actors up, and then teaching placements at towns across the country. It was a job I'd go back to again, and again, and again, especially after being invited to become one of the orientation staff used to train up the newbies. It was my brother who found the company – essentially they gave jobs to people who could make children laugh. I'd probably end up there this summer, too – I was all for adding to my toolbox so I could keep getting paid to live *la dolce vita* in between uni semesters. I was in a cast of fifteen, travelling from high school to high school in the greater Michigan area, spreading the art, the words, of Sophocles, for the purpose of an assigned high school curriculum. It built my confidence and taught me communication skills that I knew would come in handy. Plus, like every prig who did A-Level Drama, I still harboured the odd longing for performance, even though my teacher had said, in no uncertain terms, that I was not destined for the stage.

It was that which gave me an element of Imposter Syndrome – whilst I hadn't had to audition for a spot in the cast, it occured to me that I could be wildly out of my depth with degree students who took acting as seriously as I took writing. The prospect was heady, though: I was terrified of making a fool of myself, but suspected, too, that in pushing what I thought I was capable of, I might very well discover a clue for my jigsaw; the glue that would help piece parts of what I was building together. At the first rehearsal I slipped into the space as innocuously as possible, hoping to keep my mouth closed and my eyes open. I was primed to push myself, to rise to the occasion, and I'm smart enough to know that that begins with reacting rather than acting. That's where so many people go wrong: not knowing when to shut up.

The night before I'd had an apartment meeting for my campus condo, and learned quickly my humour wasn't much in line with what they – the Americans – were used to. With about thirty of us in total, we'd been led by a small Chinese girl in introducing ourselves – a complicated feat of inventing an interesting and unique personal fact as a way to stand out from everybody else, whilst remaining person-able and likeable, warm and funny. One guy said, 'I have one attached, and one unattached, earlobe.' The person next to me introduced himself by saying, 'I've lived with this asshole for four years, now.' His friend punched him on the arm.

I said to the room, 'My name is Laura Jane Williams, and I've lived with this asshole,' I pointed to my bum, 'for my whole life.'

The silence had been deafening. The silence had been a reminder about shutting up.

I often get asked about travel. About how I do it, if I'm scared, how I manage to make friends and navigate strangers, and it comes back to that feeling of wanting to see what else I can do. Of surprising myself, of being the master of myself. I was that way even as a three-year-old. My mother tells a story about me refusing to wear the dresses and tights she had chosen for me as a toddler, waltzing upstairs at will to slip into clothes I chose for myself: trousers. I wore the pants in every relationship I had in my life because 1) control, and 2) I'm pig-headed and self-sufficient as all hell. My friend Amy says you could tell me that the hob on the cooker was hot, but that I wouldn't believe you until I'd touched it myself and come away burned. 'The hob on the cooker is hot,' I'd say. It makes everyone else throw up their hands in frustration that I won't ever simply be told. That I have to do, first. I'm built to go over my edge so that I might learn *exactly* where my edge is: a bit like how you have to fall over when practising headstands, until you learn where the tipping point is. I learn by tipping. By falling over. I always have. I go over the edge, and then I reel myself back. And on, and on.

*

As I smiled and said polite hellos as other folks entered the space, my skin tingled with the anticipation of *I don't know what comes next, but I trust it*. That became a mantra to me in Detroit. In those classes. As part of that team. *Trust the process. This feels good.*

The director of *Antigone* was a smiling, petite and assertive power-house who I felt understood me right away. She spoke in the same language I did – recognised the spaces between my words. Recognised the space between all of our words, such was her intu-ition. Her assistant scared the hell out of me, as all good assistant directors probably should do. There was a blonde, French-speaking dancer who played mother to everyone in between playing the African drum, and a guy of about thirty-five who had a friendly chuckle and worked on the logistics of the tour from an office across the hall. I understood quickly that the course was available for both under-graduate and postgraduate credit, so we had a mix of ages in the cast, from freshman to forty.

'Nice accent you've got there,' whispered an African-American woman with incredible teeth, during the warm-up. We'd just intro-duced ourselves to the group, and my vowels forced every head in the room to crane in assessment of my foreign inflection. Betty would come to be one of my favourites in the cast, even though she seldom smiled and was scarily quick to call bollocks when she smelt it. The reason I adored her, really. She added, 'Is this the part where you tell us you're actually from Illinois?'

I had my head between my knees, limbering up the backs of my hamstrings. 'Only if it turns out that you're not really black,' I replied. She winked at me, and I'd made my first American friend.

There was a Korean student who didn't say much, but when she did she floored me with her insight, and a Woody-Allen-esque comic with his six-foot-five Mexican-heritage friend, both of whom were funny individually but together I could barely breathe. Nobody could. We made up a motley crew, and I loved it. I had an overwhelming sense of 'My people! These are my people!' Like I'd gotten lost on the way to the party but I'd arrived just in time for the food. I was really fucking happy to be there. To be *doing something* instead of waiting for something to happen.

Because during the initial read-through of the script my pronunci-ation stood out like food caught between teeth, in breaks and on the walk back through campus after class, it was the main source of discussion. *We have a Brit amongst us!* Amid my new cast-mates it was generally agreed that they all felt a responsibility to make sure my stay in Detroit was the very best it could be, and I was absolutely affable to that – the energy in the rehearsal room had me buzzing in anticipation of something special. I'd tell Calum later that night: *Mate! If all that heartache had to happen again to get me here, I'd sign up for it twice over. It was always leading to this.* He'd said: *Did you just call me 'mate'?*

\*

After deliberately contrived personalities with ill-advised boys on ill-advised encounters, it took decidedly little effort to begin enjoying who I was in the cast, even when Chad made me self-conscious with his silent, cautious assessment. I didn't force anything; didn't will anything to change. In inadvertently being myself, I was responded to as authentically as I presented and, after only one day's rehearsal, my 'like' for me seemed apparent to everyone else. I didn't know whether it was because they were American, or actors, or I'd just gotten lucky to be exposed to such an open, willing group of people, but I felt welcomed by my new gang – as much of a misfit as they each were, in a kooky, 'cast of a sitcom' sort of a way. I love that about performance – everyone is equal, everyone is in it together. I got to be part of a team I didn't know I needed, and there wasn't even an initiation process: being willing to show up was the only prerequisite.

As I peeled off to head back to my place after the first session, Chad said to me – in amongst the hugs and promises to call and enthusiasm for the next run-through – 'a pleasure to meet you.' Five words. No smile. His seriousness made him intense. He held eye contact with purpose and it exposed every part of me. Mr Charisma.

I flushed, meeting his look for the briefest second before I was grabbed for a hug by somebody else, another person promising to add me on Facebook, to be in touch about lunch or dinner or beers, and I held on to that embrace for longer than polite as an excuse to recover myself.

He was still looking as I freed my arms.

*I get it,* I thought. *I fucking get it.*

# ELEVEN

I'd had a layover in New York before my transfer to Detroit, and stayed with my friend Andrea. Two years ago we'd met in a beach town in Italy, where we'd both headed to train as English teachers in the months before university began.

Andrea and I had bonded over the fact that he had thought me to be a spoilt little princess when he first met me, and as I proved myself otherwise as the days unfolded, he couldn't help but marvel at his incorrect assumption out loud. I was flattered. I think. We drank together every night and attached to one another in the hard and fast way summer friendships encourage: everything was a memory slipping by too fast, and we were in awe of it. It had only surprised me mildly when he'd whispered to me during a slightly drunken, late afternoon dip in the sea that he was gay, and that gave us room to become even more intoxicated with our summer romance.

Andrea had delivered me booze and a cheese sandwich in his Brooklyn brownstone, letting me sleep with his dog and feeding me truffle mac'n'cheese in a Greenwich restaurant that he then picked up the bill for, reliving memories that only the other knew. I filled him in on my life since we'd last seen each other: about the break-up, David's engagement, my shaky forays into new men.

'Oh man,' he'd said to me as he loaded me on to the train to the airport. 'Laura, those nice Midwestern men won't know what's hit them. Go easy, okay?'

I'd kissed him on the cheek after my millionth 'Thank you, it's been so incredible to catch up!' of the hour. 'I'm sure that's a compliment,' I laughed, finally letting go of his shoulders.

He touched my cheek. 'I'm not sure if it is,' he teased.

'Be nice!'

Andrea sighed, and went to say something, then thought better of it.

'Go on,' I said. 'Say the difficult thing.'

Hanging out with him, even just for twenty-four hours, we'd happily slipped into the confiding, hushed roles we'd played in Sanremo.

'You're walking wounded, you know? Injured in battle and bitter about the enemy. Don't let it eat you alive, Laura Jane. Be smart with how you let yourself heal, okay? And I'm only saying that because I like you.'

Sometimes it takes somebody else, standing far, far away, to see you more closely than you see yourself – just like Mary-Kate had in Paris. I didn't say anything to him in return, just nodded.

'Come back soon. And next time for longer.' He kissed my forehead. 'You're gonna be okay, if only you let yourself.'

*

Chad had all-American football player shoulders and easy confidence. He brought a quiet determination to acting, his craft – his degree major – and in genuinely impressive spades. But, it felt like he was proving some kind of point to me. Outwardly, he was as friendly as everybody else, but somehow he wasn't as forthcoming. It was uncomfortable to be brave with him, because it felt like a small test even to simply say hello. He was sizing me up against criteria I wasn't sure of.

'Good morning,' he replied to my own salutation, between mouthfuls of yoghurt.

'Oh,' I said. 'I'm terribly sorry, I didn't see you were eating.' I spoke more 'British' with him than with anybody else. Not on purpose – it just came out that way. As if I'd decided to take up as much space as possible against him in protest; to wear my difference to him as a point of pride. I sensed he liked that.

He went to say something, but we were interrupted by the two guards in the play – the Woody-Allen-esque brainbox and his Mexican sidekick, who towered over him by half a metre, all limbs and moustache and teeth.

'Laura,' said Woody, 'Been meaning to ask: you ever stood on your soapbox in The Hyde Park? When I was in London I used to go every Sunday and *talktalktalk*. There was some real interesting stuff going on in those parts. Don't have anything like it around here.'

Chad spooned the last mouthful of breakfast into his perfect Cupid's bow and, almost imperceptibly, cocked an eyebrow at me before floating off to the trashcan.

'Laura, hello? Gee, I guess they don't breed 'em very talkative in old England,' Woody said.

'No, I've never stood on my soapbox in Hyde Park,' I said, coming to. 'I'm not from London. I'm from Derby – about two hundred miles north.'

Woody Allen laughed. 'Two hundred miles? Why, that's right next door if you're from Michigan! You don't head on down there most weekends? I would, if I were only a couple of hours drive.'

'A couple of hours drive is a schlep where I'm from,' I explained. 'And I'm so busy, you know? I write a lot. I want to be a writer.'

Woody Allen pulled up a chair next to me and motioned for me to sit down too. 'Oh yeah? You write? I majored in creative writing. I'd

88

love to see some of your stuff. I'm always looking to see people's stuff.'

The Mexican continued to hover over us. 'I . . . you have a nice dress,' he said, in between Woody's breaths. I didn't register his compliment until the conversation was over. I'd barely heard him. I was watching Chad with the woman who played his mother over Woody's shoulder. She was touching his arm in laughter, but his eyes were, I'd already felt, on me. I smiled at him, unsure. His face cracked in return.

The story with him does not end well, that's the spoiler. It doesn't end well with Chad, even though that cast made me feel more positive about myself than I had done ever, in my life. I wish there was a way to say sorry from the future. I don't think it's fair to reach out after all this time but, if I could, I'd tell Chad I was still learning, then, and there's no excuse for using him – for using him to figure out where my edge was. I was looking for myself in all of them, all the men I spent my time with, and he would be another on the list. I should've known better – especially since he was only eighteen. I didn't, and I'm embarrassed by it.

The play had been designed by the director as 'in the round', meaning that the audience circled the entirety of the stage, and when it wasn't your scene you stood within the audience, watching what was happening along with everyone else. Chad and I had only a single scene together, so it thrilled me to learn I could watch him as well, for swathes of uninterrupted time, and in a legitimate way. The reciprocal scrutiny was heady.

Rehearsals became a sort of performance-in-a-performance, where I was throwing myself into the role of Ismene (blonde, full-figured and radiantly cheeky; the laughing, talkative Ismene is the good girl of the family, apparently . . .) but more out of a weird desire to portray myself in a particular way to him. To be as committed as he was. To impress by mirroring his values. I'd monitor him, too – this bold, magnetic boy who seemed more like a man than most of the supposedly grown men I knew. He was gracious and kind, supportive to the other cast members and generous with his praise. And he was generous with me, as well, in the brief moments we did exchange words. He'd make comments and observations, ask questions, consider their answers. But his behaviour indicated one very important thing: he wouldn't compete for my attention.

It was the single most intoxicating thing about him. Throughout my twenties – my whole life – I've only ever met a handful of people who can so readily declare, with their actions, with their own demonstrated self-respect, that the terms of their relationship with you are that you 'meet them on the bridge': that they'll show up fully only if you show up fully. He demanded to be taken seriously by me – for me to focus my energy on him if I was going to let him cross my mind at all. It forced me to really understand when I was being 'present', and when I wasn't. It was confronting, and made me feel like he had the upper hand. I had to grapple with discomfort to be my best self for him, and it was maddeningly worth it.

When other people were around, when we were in a big group at lunch, say, or shooting the shit before the director arrived, he'd sidle away and watch from the sidelines as I put on 'The Laura Show' for my new friends, sharing anecdotes and stories about my life and what I thought about the States. I was happy, in those moments. Silly and myself. Proud.

When one of them commented to me, 'God, what confidence! Coming all this way, alone, just for the sheer hell of it!' I said, 'Well, I didn't come all this way to sit mute in a corner.' And he, Chad, laughed in spite of himself, catching my eye. It felt like his approval, for the very first time, and I hadn't realised how much I craved it. I hated that I did. I hated how I treasured being the one to make him laugh.

\*

Before I left for America, I'd spent the afternoon at my parents' house, up in the Peak District. Dad woke me up from where I'd fallen asleep after a boozy lunch, gently shaking my arm, saying, 'Looby. Looby?' He is the only person in the world who calls me Looby. He rubbed the bridge of my nose with his pinkie finger, something he has done since I was a babe in arms, and said, 'Stay soft, won't you?'

'You what?' I mumbled, opening one eye. 'I was sleeping.'

Dad pulled up the fleece blanket I'd yanked off the back of the settee so that he could tuck me in properly, like I was tiny again. 'You're so beautiful, and clever, and funny. Don't forget that, will you? Be kind to the people who want to love you.' He stroked my hair and I closed my eyes again. 'I don't know what we did wrong, but you never believe us when we tell you how loved you are.'

I thought about that as I ate dinner in a café and fiddled on my laptop with a short story for another class. I wished I had somebody to tell about my day. Not just Calum, or my parents, but somebody to lie down beside to tell about the adventure I was having. Being strong was lonely before I knew how to be alone.

# TWELVE

His message said: 'Hey, wanna come work out with me?' My stomach seized into knots. I could recognise the gauntlet when it was cast before me. I'd been hoping it would, but couldn't imagine how. *Sure!* I replied, agonising whether or not to keep the exclamation mark. *Come get me in about an hour?*

I'd wondered how and when we'd be alone, if even we would. Small discussions about the play, the script, aside, we seldom spoke directly to one another. The cast travelled en masse, never apart, and it had grown into a kind of game, really, in that we focused our energy on everyone else in the group whilst orbiting the same physical space; a wordless game of push-and-pull.

*Are you sure this isn't all in your head?* Calum emailed. *Are you having dangerous liaisons with a near-on-minor only in the corners of your mind? It's okay if you are. I can play along.*

I tried to explain that what Chad and I said by not speaking was more than what any actual words could articulate, almost doubting my sanity as my email response dragged on. *Maybe I'll just fucking-fuck-fuckity ask him out and get it over with,* I concluded. Calum replied, *In my imagination, he says yes.*

It was a coup, a win, that Chad had broken the fourth wall first. *FUCKING TOLD YOU SO,* my brief note across the ocean would later read. I barely had time to make myself nervous when he texted to say he wouldn't pick me up in a hour, but rather in thirty minutes. I pissed about in the bathroom, applying many thin layers of make-up so as to look as naturally fresh-faced as possible, adding a sweep of blusher to give me a pre-exercise glow, and took my remaining thirteen minutes to assemble a loose, half-ponytail that gave an affected air of having not considered my hair at all. So often it takes more time to make yourself look like you have made next to zero effort than it does to go full warpaint. Before I knew it, there were three taps on my front door. My chest tightened and I let out an exaggerated exhale.

'Good afternoon,' I said, hamming up the Britishness, as ever.

He smiled widely, perfect American teeth pearly white and lined up like soldiers. 'Ready?' He was dressed in fleeced jogger bottoms and an EMU hoodie with an eagle on the arm, everything baggy and nonchalant and suggestive in that way sportswear can be only on a young man with tight arse cheeks.

'Made ready,' I replied. 'Let me just grab my keys.'

'Bring another layer for later,' he yelled to my back as I re-entered the house. 'It's going to get super cold. You'll need it.'

We fell into step beside each other as we headed to the campus sports centre – a huge four-storey building that we got access to for free. There had been many moments in the few short weeks I'd known Chad where I'd thought his attention elsewhere. That although he was close by he was uninterested in the conversation I was conducting with Betty, or the director, or heaven forbid the director's assistant. But then he'd quote something back to me, later, in passing, repeating what I'd said or picking up to develop a point I'd made previously. I was at the beginnings of suspecting I'd been working too hard for attention I already had, like a cocker spaniel to his master. Hotfooting it across campus together Chad talked with little to no pause about a debating competition he had coming up and it occurred to me as he opened the red double doors, a lady to his gentleman, that this disarmingly attractive, thoughtful, talented boy was trying to impress me. The penny cracked the cistern as it dropped heavily: he was nervous.

I do that. Did that. Struggle to truly believe, when it comes down to it, that they do actually fancy me. I tread this bizarre, dizzying line between utter confidence and abject fear. There's no safe middle ground. No happy medium. Agreeing to meet in the main sports hall in five minutes as we entered separate gendered changing rooms, I wasn't sure which camp his anxiousness put me in. I had no armour; no defence; no plan for seduction. I'd just have to, I resolved, horrified, enjoy myself. And to do that, I couldn't have an agenda. I had to free-fall.

\*

'Listen, beautiful,' Pete had said as he'd walked me to the bus stop, that night we'd shared cigarettes outside the pub and I'd cried and cried and cried. 'I know you pretend you're not as soft on me as you are, but let me tell you: you're allowed to hurt. It's painful to watch you beat yourself up, like you reckon being upset is a character flaw.'

He had his arm around me, and I nestled into the space under his armpit so that he couldn't see my face.

'You're a lovely lass, your arse is perfection, and you write bloody good stories as well.'

'Thank you,' I said, muffled by my proximity to his adrenal glands.

'But, you've got to stop it. Stop believing some fella is gonna save you from being upset. You've just gotta ride it out, solo-style. You and the tears, and your mates when you need 'em.'

'Okay,' I said.

'It only hurts until it doesn't, I promise you that much.'

'Okay,' I repeated.

'You'll end up on dangerous ground if you reckon you'll love your-self only once another boy does.'

'Okay.'

*

Stealing sideways glances at Chad, I tried, probably unsuccessfully, not to disclose my own butterflies. Underneath his joggers he'd been wearing knee-length shorts and a vest top that gave way to strong, impressive arms. He threw his gym towel and water bottle on a nearby bench, causing the muscles to ripple, and I followed suit, before he said: 'So – capoeira. You down to learn some moves?'

He'd told us in rehearsal about this Brazilian martial art he'd been learning on campus, and I'd Googled it when I got home. I Googled everything he mentioned, all the hints he left. It seemed slow moving and considered, the fight technique, but with a rhythm: sort of like Tai Chi to a beat. 'You are my teacher, and I am but your humble student,' I said. 'I'm down.'

'Cool. Really cool. Urm – let's warm up a bit first. Laps are probably best.'

I trailed him around the sports hall where tall, leggy, black men in sweatbands were playing basketball. Chad was muscular and lean and tight, a real sportsman to look at. I, by contrast, was none of those things. Never have been. I let him lead a few laps at jogging pace, a few at sprint, some burpees and star jumps and stops and starts, trying to keep up. And I did – I did keep up. But then, void of exercise for an awfully long time – possibly, even, ever, though I wouldn't admit that to him – all the blood rushed to my head. I wooz-ily noticed small beads of sweat appear on the back of his hard, sculpted neck, colour mildly flushing his serious cheeks, and the light-headedness gave way to nausea. Suddenly he was asking me if I was okay, and pointing out the bench across the hall, the one with our stuff on.

Stumbling across the ball game I closed my eyes as we sat, the weight of his hand boring down on my damp back as I focussed on the in-and-out, in-and-out of my uneven breath. I thought I might throw up, but couldn't decide whether it was from my burst of energy, or his touch.

'Okay?' he said, leaning in close to my face, and when I looked across in surprise that he was there, beside me, our noses were close and my eye caught his and my tummy lurched again. 'You got this,' he told me, smiling. Amused. Caring. Chad.

'Yes,' I said. 'I don't think I ate enough today.'

'We'll go grab some food after, if you want.'

'Yeah, I do want.'

We sat on the sidelines of the gym hall and, as I got my breath back, we watched the ten sporty black guys play their game at a speed and with a skill I'd never seen before. It took me fifteen minutes to recover from our warm-up, and that could've been me done – I was sure my blusher had streaked and I could feel my loose ponytail sticking in clumps to the sides of my face.

'I promise,' Chad intoned, 'that I will go very slowly with you. You can help make me a better teacher. You're really doing *me* the favour.'

That boy knew *exactly* what he was doing. He showed his age that way. The older we get the less certain we become, I think, and Chad was absolutely sure of himself in the gym. He was in his comfort zone. He was in his comfort zone and sensed that somehow I was not, and so relished playing professor. His previous uncertainty had vanished. He knew he was in charge – but to let him felt a small personal triumph. I didn't have to be in control, operating at a secure pace, all the time. Isn't this how people learned and grew? I could be both self-sufficient *and* humble enough to be taught.

I acquiesced to being educated on some basic capoeira moves. The rules determine that one must maintain fixed eye contact with one's partner at all times, so we moved and swayed and sidestepped across a corner of the gym, never once touching but looking into one another's eyes deeply. I watched him for guidance, and he watched me to ensure I was following him properly, and for an hour we ducked and weaved and moved and looked at each other. Looking, looking, looking: the cornerstone of our whole dynamic. I anticipated his moves and stretched to make my own – another cornerstone of our interactions.

Afterwards we sat at a window table in the cafeteria with salad and waffles, where he unwound into listening. I told him about England and my writing; he told me about high school and how he was thinking about becoming something in the church – a minister, maybe. A pastor. It wasn't until I visited the bathroom that I figured I should be embarrassed by my now-make-up-less face, brow crusty where the sweat had dried, but my eyes were bright. I was smiling. As I watched him across the cafeteria, he smoothed down his hair using the reflection in the window. In that gesture I knew I wasn't alone. We headed to his apartment because I'd asked, sometime, to hear songs of his he'd told me about, that he'd written, and I lay on the floor of his living room as he sat in a chair by the kitchen table, and he played one song after another and I focused on the ceiling and his lyrics. Six hours since he'd picked me up – three weeks and a bit since we first met – we relaxed.

'Play just one more,' I said. 'I don't want you to stop. Not yet.'

\*

Weeks later, we'd lie in bed together and he'd tell me that was the moment he'd fallen for me properly. 'I suspected I had, but that – that was the exact moment there was no going back. You were such an interesting listener,' he'd say. But, for now, I didn't know. I didn't know that he'd start to meet me before rehearsals for breakfast, or come over to my apartment to watch comedy series on my laptop before I fell asleep, 3 a.m. coming too soon, and that he'd cover me with a blanket and lie beside me and we'd snooze together, barely touching, but electricity brimming. I didn't know that we'd all go to karaoke and I'd rap 'Gangsta's Paradise' to a room full of strangers, and when I sat down again he'd say, mockingly, 'Wow. Will you marry me?' I didn't know he'd bring over poetry books that he'd read in Spanish, or that I'd meet his mother.

'I'm . . . I'm in so much trouble,' I said to Nancy, my American roommate, the morning after our first date. 'I'm truly bollocksed. This is a disaster. I . . . I think I really like him.'

Calum wrote: *Laura? For the love of all that is unholy, please do not over-think this. Just have fun. That light fluttery feeling in your chest? That's what they call it: fun. I promise you, you'll like it.*

He'd texted me when I got home, to say what a beautiful day he'd had. The next day, he stopped by with some books he thought I might like – and I did. The day after that he asked to come by to run through some lines for a project he was working on, and when we'd finished he played guitar for me again, saying, 'I like watching you listen, is all.' He totally threw himself, unabashedly, into getting to know me, and the feeling of it was giddy. We left rehearsal one day to find it snowing heavily, and he walked me home, stopping on the stoop to wrap his scarf around us both. He said, 'Out of everyone, it's you.' I liked myself more when I was with him. I liked myself more when I wasn't, knowing that he thought I was great.

That he was great. That whatever this thing was – this 'fun' – it was great.

We'd swap loaded glances across the rehearsal space as we came closer to the opening of the tour; accidentally bump into each other at our usual lunch spots, when really it was absolutely purposeful; often he'd come over to say hi when I was writing at my favourite table in the café, pretending he only had five minutes to spare and then hours later we'd be laughing at how the time escaped and slowed down, all at once, when we were together.

When we had sex, finally, we made love: it was sweet and tender. Chaste. I was his girlfriend, I guess. And that's when it began to unravel.

# THIRTEEN

What had been the thrill of the chase for Chad became a game of possession for me. I was happy, but also insecure and uncertain in this relationship that had accidentally blossomed: my first relationship after David. But, instead of saying so out loud – instead of being a grown-up and acknowledging that I was petrified – I acted out. I treated the eighteen-year-old like a piece of shit, and he didn't know, in his youth, in his wholesomeness, how to stand up to me. I wonder now if I wanted, on some level, to stomp his confidence out of him right from the start. That it was that – his okay-ness – that I envied.

I wanted him to come over to my place almost every night. I got antsy when he didn't text. If he took too long to initiate sex when we were together I'd get weird and uneasy, my mental dialogue switching to, 'This is the night he's going to break up with you, Laura. It was only a matter of time.' I had no control over how I felt, and it was nothing, really, that he did or didn't do that set me off. A switch had been flicked once we consummated our romance. I didn't know how to be in the beginnings of a relationship with him. How to have sex with somebody I liked. I was unable to relish it, the falling, because I was panicked about who would catch me. I couldn't luxuriate in the early unsureness of something that could become love, I could only tense and make it painful.

I have a friend who once thought she was going to drown. Her canoe capsized, and she was strapped into her seat. By the time she'd freed herself she was trapped under the upturned boat. She struggled, she says, fought and kicked and desperately tried to find a way to get to the water's surface again. She couldn't. *I'm going to die,* she concluded. *I'm going to die.* When she surrendered, gave way, she floated upward and became free. If she'd kept fighting, she told me, she would've drowned.

With Chad, I was drowning.

Maybe six weeks after we started sleeping together, I walked across campus after a writing workshop and spotted him in the distance, lying on the early spring grass, on his belly, talking with a blonde girl I didn't recognise. He was using his hands to talk, and she was laughing. Jealousy seared through my veins like a match held to oil at my wrist. By the time he eventually got to my apartment, not even minutes later, I'd worked myself into some kind of stupor: I opened the door, pulled him into my bedroom, and threw him down on to the bed. Straddling him, I said, 'I want you to fuck me hard, like I am your whore, okay?' I talked slowly and deliberately. 'Fuck me and don't stop until you've cum inside me.'

He pulled away and stared at me, questions etched in his face. I kissed him. He pulled away. I grabbed his jaw and tugged his face back to mine. I felt him resist until I pulled off his shirt and kissed his neck and said once more, 'Fuck me, and hard.' He exhaled deeply. Sadly. He called me his whore and we didn't speak before going to sleep, not touching, the distance between us a valley, even in my single bed.

We had a month of meanness and wilful misunderstandings after that. We hadn't told the rest of the cast about our relationship, valuing the dynamics of the group too much to alter them by attaching our names to one another. Betty knew. I knew Betty knew by the simple, 'You did good with that boy' she gave me the night after group karaoke. But, largely, we went unnoticed. I was relieved. It meant our demise went unnoticed, too.

It was convenient for me because I was different with them. They liked me, and I liked being around them. Everything was light, focussed on the work, an all-hands-on-deck scenario. And then behind closed doors Chad and I had stopped talking. We'd begun hate-fucking, going days with no contact between wordless shagging. It was my fault. I'd taken something good and ruined it, on purpose, because I didn't trust myself after all. His only mistake was to follow my lead.

Four months in the States was enough – I'd decided not to pass another semester there because I'd fuck that up, too. I'd made ghosts out of the city too soon. So, I did what I excelled at: I bolted. I told myself this next do-over would be the real do-over. I'd do better next time.

# FOURTEEN

When I got back from the US, there was a long list of men that happened in quick succession. I couldn't process Chad – the closeness of it. The vulnerability. I headed back to Derby, via some teaching over the summer in Italy, and threw myself into promiscuity partly out of shame, and partly because it felt good, reassuring, to remember I could be in control. It was always about the fucking *control.*

'So, you're over him? Are you pretending to be fixed, or are you really fixed?' Calum levelled at me in the toilets of The Cottage.

'Fuck off!' I said, swaying to my reflection at the sink. 'I'm not a fucking problem that needs a solution.'

'That's not what I said.' He dried his hands on a paper towel, aiming for the bin and missing.

I walked to pick it up for him. 'Yes it is.'

He sighed. 'Do you want another drink?'

'Yes. And a shag.'

'That was never a question.'

'Stop trying to riddle me a fucking answer, then.'

I drank a lot because if I danced until I sweated, with my eyes closed, in amongst a crowd of strangers, I didn't have to think. I sat with an unease, a discomfort I couldn't yet put my finger on. In the club, it didn't beat as hard, wasn't as loud, demanding. Then I'd take a bathroom break or trip to the bar and the edges of a reality would come back to me, and I'd procure somebody to take home to stem the flow. I thought it was exotic and daring of me, knowing the answer to sleeping with any man you want. But once the truth of it became obvious, it wasn't an achievement any more. The secret to sleeping with any bloke you want is simple: just ask. Anyone can do that.

*

'Your friend said you've been dumped,' I said. 'Y'okay?'

He was a schoolteacher, and we were at the front of the line at the chip shop. In lieu of a man, that night I'd sought consolation in a bag of Derby's finest carbohydrates; on this particular night, with added shredded Cheddar.

'I don't mean to pry, it's just he told me when I was getting the vinegar. That you're sad. Because you've been dumped.'

The five-foot-six, rugby-player-built English teacher didn't say much in reply.

'I got dumped, too. I'm not okay. In fact, I don't know if I'll ever feel okay again.' I was, it seemed, incredibly verbose about my feelings when under the influence, and to people I'd never see again. 'I hurt so bad that sometimes I think it would be easier to die. I replay every interaction we had in the months before he finished it and I wonder if I could have stopped it. Prevented it. Reacted differently at some point and steered him away from not loving me any more. I don't know. Love fucking sucks.'

The guy made eye contact. 'You're the only person who has had the balls to say that kinda stuff to me,' he said, and I saw that he was crying.

We looked at each other for a long time.

'Would you like to go for a walk with me?' I said.

He looked to his friends, who were over in the corner amusing themselves with the girls I'd gone out with. He nodded.

'Come on.' I took his arm in one hand and my cheesy chips in the other. When I was down on my knees for him not long after, in my flat, he said to me and my British self, 'So, what part of Australia are you from?' He didn't stay the night.

\*

I had one semester left at university, and began it shagging a semi-committed teenage father-of-one. In addition to the toyshop, which I'd gone back to for one last stint, I was working as a study advisor in the library, and as a note-taker for disabled students unable to make their own class notes. Both of these roles relied heavily on academic achievement, and mine had surprisingly not wavered. I operated at the top of my class and was on course for a first-class honours degree.

A student – the father-of-one – in one of the classes I worked in somehow got my number. The first night he texted I went to his house and we had sex. Just like that. I continued to go to his house for sex every night for a month, even though he snored like a tiger and didn't eat pussy. I treated him like dirt, like less than dirt, and when I ended it he chased me down his road in his pyjamas to tell me he loved me.

At 1 a.m. on a training weekend away, for work, I knocked on the door of a guest – a fellow trainee – I'd had my eye on and said, 'Hello. I've been watching you, and I think you should pay me a visit. In my room. Room three four two.'

He said, 'I'll be right there.'

There was a female friend who wore fangs and fingered me on a bus, but wouldn't let me touch her. We had a bizarre, confused relationship for about six weeks, whilst I was shagging men as well, that revolved around her being able to do whatever she wanted to me, and yet I never saw her naked. Not once. Wasn't allowed to touch her. We don't talk any more.

There'd been a string of men in Italy, right after Detroit, including a colleague who loved to fuck a girl on her period. I'd 'borrowed' the key to the school we worked in for the week and we'd sneak in after dark to shag on the desks. When there was confusion one morning over why there was blood smeared on the floor by the headmaster's office I had to feign total puzzlement.

Peers from my teacher training sessions. Colleagues from work: the toyshop, the note-taking, the Italy job. Strangers. Friends. Nothing was sacred; nothing was off-limits. I was forever looking for some-body else. One man was too much and a stream of them never enough. And then I started to see Big Dick. Never before 10 p.m., only sporadically and always on his terms.

'So it's . . . it's good? Like, rough but good?' Calum said to me as we walked to a workshop session together – one of the last of the year. Of the degree. We'd graduate soon, and I'd say my goodbyes to go teach English in Rome. I was one foot out of the door already.

'It's like nothing I've ever had before,' I said. 'Yeah. Good. Dirty. Filthy.'

Calum nodded slowly. 'Okay. Well. If you're being safe . . .'

'Oh God, yeah, totally,' I replied, knowing that we hadn't been safe. Not totally. I was on the pill and he'd never cum inside me – but he had penetrated me without a condom, which was stupid and I knew it. But. But I didn't have the confidence to insist to him that he wear one. I felt like it would ruin the moment, and that it would make him mad – or not want to see me again. So I let whatever happened, happen, without challenging it too much and . . .

'Laura, are you sure?'

I burned. I couldn't lie to my best friend, and I felt like an idiot for not being able to explain just how much I needed Big Dick to . . . use me? Keep me in my place?

I was missing something, and needed him to fill the hole. Literally. I wanted him to cum, patch up the wound with his body, because he did something I couldn't do alone. Being with him helped me to feel . . . less. More. Something different.

With all of them, it wasn't the act so much as what it was doing to my ego to get there. That I could control somebody, get them naked with me. I'd had no control over David leaving. The way he cried when he left but left all the same. I had no control over him and Gwen, and no control about how long it had been going on. Whether she and I crossed over. If I'd been made a fool of in a bigger way than I dared consider.

I'd needed David to be a faithful man so that I could believe that faithful men existed. I had zero examples in my life of what a faithful man looked like. David had, in many, many ways, been a safety blanket through that. A relief. Positive evidence. And somehow . . . I don't know. Somehow, because David probably had done it, too, just like every other man I knew, all bets were off, because obviously it was true: men were cheats. And so it was balm for the ego, locking eyes across a bar. Salve for the dented spirit when I got up the confidence to approach. If all men cheat, I thought, I'd rather be the one they're cheating *with* than *on*.

I liked how it felt; that men loved the pursuit and I could make them think it was their idea. That I could fuck any man I wanted as long as I had the balls to suggest it. There was a way of being just the right amount of provocative, mastering how to make pupils dilate in shock. I enjoyed manipulating language in order to say the unsayable as code for what else I'd do, too.

We're taught that sluts are bad people. Broken. Desperate. But in no other aspect of my life did I act 'bad' or 'broken' or 'desperate'. I was no madonna – even my parents knew that – but nor was I cast as the whore. I had friends, workshop peers, three jobs; I was liked and respected and popular enough. I never doubted the love Calum had for me, say, or Mary-Kate. I've always happily taken centre stage – I'm naturally domineering and so assume a leadership role in most situations. I commanded attention because, to others, especially those who didn't know my history, I seemed in control. Measured. A lot of people marvelled at my 'go for it' attitude. Whenever my single status came up, the overall analysis was that I'd need one hell of a man to keep up with me. I was unstoppable.

But then there was Pete. 'There's something different about you since you got back from the States,' he said to me, during a cigarette break. Our paths didn't cross as much as they used to. We took different modules and our timetables didn't match up anymore. He eyed me with caution these days. I was defensive, hating that he knew enough to search for the cracks.

'There is?' I said, not wanting to be drawn in.

'Yeah – even in saying that. "There is?" All mysterious and shit.' I didn't respond. 'You seem a bit steadier and that, but . . . I think I preferred you with your heart on your sleeve, to be honest.'

His comment bothered me for two weeks.

I needed to feel wanted. Had to remind myself that I could. That there were other men out there. That I could feel lonely, but I didn't have to be alone. I didn't want any of them to love me. To call. To treat me with any semblance of respect, because I didn't respect myself. I truly believed that if the one I gave everything to still wanted to walk away – and for my friend, to boot – I couldn't have much to offer in the first place. I could be a funny mate, an insightful shoulder to cry on, an honest employee and an attentive, well-meaning daughter, but a wife? Nope. Nobody wanted me as a wife. It was the one 'status symbol', the one arbitary measure of my worth, I didn't think I had in me, so I lashed out.

And so I fucked 'em. That one, and that one. And that one – and that one. One after the other, filling up and filling up but never being full. I started to pride myself on "not being like other girls". Of keeping everyone at a distance. Ignoring them, mostly, as they peeled off the condom. I was a slut because none of them were the answer. As I learned to cling to my gaze a little longer than necessary, resting my hand on a knee a little too high to be only friendly, there was always a question in my eyes. In my heart. And the moment I let myself be kissed – rough, and fast, always too fast – the tiny speckle of hope that I had would be quashed. *This one won't be my knight in shining armour.* Let's just fuck, then. Get fucked.

I could get wet for them. Turned on as all hell, sometimes. Sometimes I faked it, and sometimes they made me cum. But it was never from being inside me. It was never where they could see me. They'd slip a hand into my knickers from behind or go down on me in the dark. From there, they could've been anybody. Nobody. Him.

I lost two years, almost three, to the pursuit of refusing to take my heartache lying down. I couldn't go to the pub or a party, a work event, even, without saying to myself, *There. That one.* There always had to be somebody to take home. A conquest. A concrete way to say to myself: *See! I won't ever let anybody do that to me again! I am an emotionally detached and liberated woman, and so I win!*

Every time I threw a guy out of my bed at 4 a.m. I strengthened something inside of myself that had promised – pledged – to never get hurt again. To never invest in somebody again.

I was never valued. I gave it away too easily. I used and was used in a way that can't be undone. I noted their attitude, the way the texts were short and explicit, everything void of emotion, following my lead, all of it confirmation that men are sexual predators. Easily led. Emotionally stunted. Depending on when you asked me I'd tell you I was the predator, or I was the prey. I oscillated between the two, losing my navigation entirely, until I was a kid kicking and screaming and not quite sure what for. I hadn't learned yet that dating, couple-dom, relationships – they take trust. And because I didn't trust myself, I couldn't extend that courtesy to another.

I never felt bad about moving on to the next, because it didn't mean anything anyway. That's why I was a slut. I'm not afraid of that word. That isn't loaded language for me; just fact. I was a slut because not one of those men could disprove my theory. Nobody saved me from myself. I had to learn that there was only one person for that job: me.

# FIFTEEN

'Celibacy,' I said.

'Celibacy,' he repeated back.

'For one year.'

'Bullshit.'

'I don't know how to . . . love. How to do this.' I said through my webcam. 'Look. I'm reading this book.' Our relationship was mostly conducted over Skype these days. I was in Rome. My feet were itchy, and I needed to keep moving. Needed to keep reinventing. See what fit. 'I'm reading Milan Kundera's *The Unbearable Lightness of Being.*'

'Never heard of it,' Calum said, opening a pot of curry he'd just had delivered and sniffing it with nose crinkled. I watched the steam waft up through the camera of my Mac and regretted that Trastevere didn't have a decent Indian on offer.

'Well, that's because you are a writer who doesn't fucking *read.*' I rolled my eyes and picked up my paperback, holding up the cover for display. 'I'm embarrassed for you.'

Calum imitated me and then said, 'I read, Laura, just not the wanky, shitty stuff that depresses the bejesus out of everyone, like you do. Look – I've got Dawn French's autobiography right here. Even that cover on yours, to look at – I mean, it's *brown.*'

Waving my hand, dismissing his commentary, I accused: 'Can you swallow before you speak, you heathen? And use a fork.' Watching him lick his fingers, I carried on before he could respond. 'You'd hate this book, it's true. But it is really important to me. So, eat your curry and let me talk for a minute.'

He picked up his cutlery, tucking his napkin into his collar. 'I know the rules of this friendship,' he said, darkly.

I explained that the story focuses on a young woman in love with a man torn between his love for her and his incorrigible womanising. One of his mistresses, in turn, actually has a lover who is faithful to her, and the narrative of the two couples highlights how our individual worlds are shaped by chance and fortuitous events, and ultimately we often fuck it all up – sometimes on purpose – because we don't know how to love.

'So,' said Calum, brandishing a poppadom. 'Everyone sucks at everything and so what's the point, there isn't one, the end?'

'No!' I said. 'The opposite! Kind of like . . . I don't know. I'm figuring it out, still. But, I think it's along the lines of: sex is easy and love is hard. Maybe. Maybe I've sort of . . . I don't know. Been choosing emotion free sex over emotionally draining love,' I concluded. 'Like, this book – it was somebody else putting into words the thoughts I have, but haven't been articulating to myself.'

'That love is awful?' Calum said.

'Stop poking fun at me!'

'I'm not poking fun at you! I'm just saying – yeah, you've had a lot of sex. But you've done it because you wanted to. Right?'

'Right,' I said.

'So. Your question is now . . . why did you want to.'

'Right.'

'And the answer definitely is not, as we earlier presumed, "Because you were horny and needed to rub up against somebody"?'

'I don't think so. I want to be kinder to the ones I rub up against.'

He exhaled loudly, putting the last of the cracker in his mouth. 'Well then, shit, baby girl. We've got some work to do.'

*

I was living in Rome's oldest neighbourhood, Trastevere – literally 'across the river'. I'd read *Eat, Pray, Love* – and, from the mass of single foreign women clutching guidebooks in every museum, restaurant and park, I wasn't the only one. We knew, collectively, these single foreign women and me, how our *healing* was going to work: as chicks, via ethereal sunsets and a smile as wide as Julia Roberts's, we'd been given a free pass to travel the world so that we might *find ourselves* – and, hopefully, a new man, too. I don't know if I was buoyed not to be alone in my pursuit, or devastated by it. Clichés are well worn for a depressingly common reason.

The city did not disappoint, though: low-dappled sunlight, shining through curious vines seeking the approval of better light, higher up, casting shadows on lovers' flawless shoulders, all hands and teasing and passion, their *aperitivo* waiting on white-clothed outdoor tables beside them. There were cobblestones and brick in every possible shade of terracotta. The occasional nun flâneur-ing by in full habit and Velcro sandals. *Carabinieri* in dark blue uniforms that caressed the bottom like a mother's gentle hand, gracing, fortuitously, most street corners. Every twist and turn was an opportunity to get lost and then found again in more magic, vowels trilling and tongues rolling in the music of a language designed to woo. Elizabeth Gilbert knew exactly what she was doing when she issued the unwitting instruction for all broken hearts to head to the Eternal City. It was hard not to believe in the beauty of life when it confronted you, unforgiving, at every fork in the road.

I'd moved here to write. To write properly. I'd had €400 to my name and was waiting for my first pay cheque from my summer teaching job to come through, and wanted a gig that left me a lot of spare time to write my book, instead of just talking about writing my book. That was what I'd gone to university for, after all, and I thought I'd like to be in the one per cent who use their degree to get a job in a related field. I'd jumped at the offer of a six-hour day when a friend-of-a-friend-of-a-friend posted a Facebook status about needing a replacement for her role. Reassuring her of my TEFL qualifications over a quick Skype interview from my summer teaching job in Sanremo, I was officially offered the job. It happened even quicker than the Detroit adventure: within the week I had a budget airline's one-way ticket to Ciampino. It never occurred to me to be alarmed that she was shipping out, and so shipping me in, so fast. I just needed an income.

I'd been writing since I was eight. I remember designing a story about princesses and their fates, illustrations included, and pushing it into the hip of the work experience girl in the playground at school. She'd been the grown-up of the grown-up-est to my mind but, thinking about it now, she will only have been fifteen or sixteen. She didn't understand what I'd written, she said, and I was devastated, stuffing the story away never to be sought out again – but in one way or another I'd been honing my storytelling proclivities ever since.

'Oh yeah, this is definitely a story you need to write,' Calum had said as we sat watching reality TV on his sofa. 'You've shagged enough blokes to fill a few hundred pages, and heartbreak is the most universal theme there is. You've got my vote: get to it! And pass me the pick 'n' mix, please.'

And so, in Rome, with my headscarf knotted high and some exotic

– and erotic – ideas in my head, I'd begun reliving the nights with men whose names I mostly did not remember. And in those first few months, it felt, as an outsider looking in, very *bourgeoisie-bohemian*. I didn't start until 2 p.m. at the school, since it was an after-hours programme that I 'taught' – I use the term loosely because I was so uninvested in my class – so I'd spend mornings wearing red lipstick and dragging on roll-up cigarettes and drinking coffee, penning chapters about what I thought were the shocking, real-life adventures of my vagina. And I'd get off on it, too, when people asked. I'd shrug, smiling coyly, and say, 'Well, it's a sex memoir.' I found, quickly, that it was a great way to seduce fellow expats. Not into a shag, but seduce them into the idea of me – the notion of me as a writer. I could almost believe that fate myself, then. Looking somebody in the eye to say 'sex' and 'memoir' floored even the sturdiest of constitutions, and the kind of men I favoured – the peacocks, who like the spotlight and attention – often suggested that perhaps they, too, could get a mention. That was enough to satiate my appetite. I was sleeping around less (comparatively, anyway), since I spent all the energy I had on hitting a daily word count. I suppose it felt like the unabashed shagging had been worth it, if I got a story out of it.

Take it as testament to how utterly, totally without other purpose I felt when I say: I really did think I was going to astonish the masses with tales of seduction. With blow-by-blow (*womp*) accounts of many nights with many men. I had this idea of penning my own version of *The Sexual Life of Catherine M*, a book I'd never let my parents read but that would mark me as a sexual adventuress. I prided myself on how outrageous I was, how easy it had been to lure a man into bed. I bought into the myth I'd been expertly crafting for so long – that my sexuality was my identity, and that my value was based on how much any given man wanted to fuck me.

*Write what you know*, they tell wannabe, first-time authors, and so I began writing about sex.

\*

His name was Bobby, and I met him through my colleagues. It's funny, the people who form an expat community – by common language and circumstance, bodies gravitate toward each other; people who, otherwise, in more native settings, wouldn't deign to pass time nor air with one another. Shared experience is the fastest and most sure-fire way to bond, though, and swapping notes on where to get the best American branded peanut butter or putting in Cadbury requests with whoever was visiting home next was a way to ensure friends for life – or at least for as long as you both lived in the same overseas city.

I'd avoided socialising with folks from work, mostly because I didn't want to get 'found out' – I was a schoolteacher blogging and writing about sex and relationships. I needed the two things to remain separate. I wanted work to be my safe haven from myself, where I could be professional and not shag anybody and get praise for a job well done and not because I had the most ridiculous dating stories over lunch. I was the definition of split personality. As further excuse, I was broke. I could barely afford food, let alone fun.

'You never come out with us,' Sarah said one evening, as I rebuffed the offer of a beer at the Irish pub once again. 'You really should.'

My absence was conspicuous.

'Don't you like us?' she pushed.

I made different excuses every time. 'Oh, you know me,' I'd say. 'Always eager to get home and write!' Or, 'I'm just so tired today! Those kids *killed me.*' Two months in and it was weird that I didn't join the gang at the bar. I was in need of friends, after all, and there was only so much Skyping Calum could commit to.

'I'll come,' I said. 'One weekend, I'll come.'

That Saturday night I did, and that was how I met him.

I'd heard the others talk about him, this mythical Bobby. When he walked into the bar, all long limbs and full lips and pulled down baseball cap, I saw it. The authority in his walk. The self-assuredness. He was an easy leader, alpha. Confident, borderline cocky: my favourite type.

The last thing this book needs is *another* breakdown of how I saw a man, wanted the man, and debased myself in order to fuck the man. I'm boring myself, now, by retelling the same misadventure but with a different antagonist. The long and short is that I made sure, two bars, one three-course meal and a *digestivo* later, that it was he and I who naturally fell to the back of the large group we were with as we headed for a final nightcap. I said something inflammatory, pulled him towards me as I leaned against a wall, and willed him to kiss me. I ignored him at the bar ten minutes later, but as he drained his glass and bid everyone goodnight, I followed him and silently walked back to his apartment by his side.

The sex was fine. Perfunctory. What you can expect from two drunk people who don't know each other at all. He surprised me when he asked me, the next morning, not to leave so early but to stay and hang out. I was rude and made my excuses. I felt worthless, I know that much. That book – the Milan Kundera I'd told Calum about – it had already sprouted discontent with this arrangement I had with myself. The sex. And yet, no sooner had I left him than I'd messaged Sarah to get his number, and then texted to say *Hey, it's Laura. Do you wanna hang out this week? And by hang out, I mean have sex again.*

I see now, on reflection, how that would have made him feel worth-less, too.

He said yes.

The week after finishing the first draft of what became known to Calum and me as The Sex Memoir – capital letters always inferred, even in speech – and just before announcing to him my notion of celibacy, I found myself in my tiny Roman room, music drifting through the windows from the cellist touting for tourists' loose change, staring at the beams above with the pages I'd penned all around me. I was trying not to cry. Those pages – the ones I had convinced myself marked me out as *special* and *bohemian* and *achingly interesting* – they were a mirror to a truth that was undoing me and only three minutes previously had I fully realised it: I was a common whore.

I didn't like the woman I saw in those words. I'd set out to be confrontational and self-assured, but as I continued to sleep with Bobby, my shamelessness was reaching a peak – if it hadn't already. I'd tried not to worry too much about getting a first draft that was 'perfect'. I've written long enough to know that any first attempt at anything is basically an exercise in getting words out of your mind and on to the page. A sort of verbal projectile vomit – better out than in. *You can't edit a blank page*, Calum and I would tell each other, as we competed over who could reach any given word count quickest. The real work, with writing, begins after you've written. It's the editing, the restructuring, the adding and deleting and changes that make you sweat, that make a piece finally come together. But I wasn't going to get that far with what I had. The Sex

Memoir, in its stream-of-consciousness, run on and unedited form, was simply a series of the same bullshit over and over again. Just like with Bobby, all the men in the book served the same purpose to the plot. And the plot was: girl hates men. Girl hates self. Girl has empty, meaningless sex to prove a moveable point. It was dull. So void of the sexy life and erotica I thought it would have – and that was nothing to do with my actual writing (well, perhaps it was in small part to do with my writing). It was everything to do with the fact that the woman in the book – me – was apparently so very soulless. She was a shell. Seeing myself objectively like that, as a character on the page, it crippled me how two-dimensional and grey I was. Having spent the past few days rereading what I'd gotten down so far, there was a feeling in my stomach, a sort of knot, tugging hard at my core, that grew in strength the more I digested my own paragraphs. For the most part, I literally did not recognise myself. And the bits I did recognise I wasn't one bit proud of.

It's a fucker, the moment you understand how little of yourself you've come to like.

*

Bobby and I seldom addressed each other in public, but after a night out I would always wake up in his bed. Most of the time I'd sneak out before he was awake, but on occasion I'd sleep in a little and play make-believe. Pretend that it was more than it was. It was as his alarm went off for work early one morning that I uncharacteristically leaned into his neck and breathed, *Make me cum.* I was trying to be playful and light, to make a something out of a not-very-much-at-all. And so, when he pulled away and looked at his watch, deeming time to be of the essence and barely addressing my request, the last part of me

available to die inside did. It wasn't about the sex. It was about . . .
everything else.

'What a twat,' Calum would later say, via a shaky Wi-Fi connection.
'Didn't he read the handbook that decrees he has to finish the job he
started if there is a beautiful naked woman in his bed?'

I laughed, but half-heartedly. 'I dunno . . . it's weird. I couldn't
shake the feeling that if he was my boyfriend – and, I mean, don't get
me wrong, I do not want this man as my boyfriend, not one bit, that's
not the thing – but if he were my boyfriend it wouldn't have hurt as
much. Because. Huh. Because I don't know why, actually.'

'I think I understand,' Calum said. 'Kind of like, if you're just there
for sex, but then he doesn't want sex, then what's the point of being
there at all?'

That was exactly it.

As Bobby showered I, sort of . . . fought back tears. Swallowed
them in a way that was big and deliberate and painful. Something
was happening but I didn't have words for it. I was sinking into something, grasping with humiliating clarity that this – this display, this life
– was not what I wanted. It had been my doing, my own creation, and
I had needed it, for a time. But now, I had had enough. I needed
something else. Needed to feel a different way. I was done being
detached and holding back. I wanted love. I wanted love to wash over
me and heal me and be me and become me.

I wanted to love myself.

That was it.

A voice raged inside me as the thought wandered across my mind.

YES! she screamed, uncompromising and forcefully. YES, YOU
DO! THAT IS WHAT YOU WANT!

I let that sit with me. I wanted to love myself. Wholly, for better and for worse, without restriction or excuse, I wanted to love myself. I didn't know how to get there, to that. How it looked. But I knew how it would feel.

It would feel like enough. And I – I desperately wanted to feel like enough.

# SIXTEEN

It took four weeks before I wrote the letter. I carried my satchel with me everywhere, the notebook nestled in amongst lesson plans and children's books; my buried secret. The beating heart under the floorboards. There were things I wanted to articulate that were taking time to build courage for. Truth steeps like tea – the longer you wait, the stronger it tastes.

One night, a Tuesday, I couldn't sleep. I'd been Skyping with Calum, again, and we'd talked about the celibacy, again. I'd said, *I'm going to do it. I have to.*

'A year of celibacy.' Calum said. 'And on purpose.'

'On purpose,' I said. 'Just to see.'

'Well, baby girl – if you think it will help . . .' I didn't know what to say to fill the silence of his incomplete sentence.

'I don't think anything,' I answered, finally. 'I just know that I'm really, really tired of myself. Aren't you?'

He hadn't responded.

'It's been a month already. I feel good. Not much different, but – empowered? It's not like I haven't gone four weeks without sex before – I'm not an addict – but to have this be a choice feels . . . yeah: empowering. Purposeful.'

'You're an everyday Spice Girl,' he said.

I needed to work this out with myself. Needed to get to the root of why I felt incapable. So 'other' than everyone else. So unlike who I was supposed to be.

I flicked on my desk lamp, rubbing my eyes as they adjusted to the light. I didn't remember putting the notebook out on the table, but there it was, pen beside it, waiting. Like I said, sometimes we know stuff before we know stuff.

*Dear Laura*, I wrote. And then: nothing. *This is stupid*, I scolded. *No, it's not*, I reasoned. *Fucking dumb*, I thought. *Fucking do it. Write, say things*, I intoned. I let the pen nib hit the blank page, deciding that once I started, I wouldn't stop until I'd finished. They say 'die empty'. I wanted to write myself empty. I wanted to be empty to make room for all the other stuff I didn't yet have words for but that was there, just under the surface, the first signs of a simmer that would tip over into boil.

*Dear Laura,*

*Single doesn't mean less-than. Single is whole. You are every-thing, now, in this moment: fully formed, a force to be reckoned with, all you need to be – and will ever need to be – in one perfect soul. One is a round number, remember.*

*Also remember that you are enough.*

*You are complete.*

*You are loved.*

*He was just one person, Laura. One man. And if you are totally honest – utterly brutal in your truth – you know it was never he who you would marry. It was baby love. First love. Permit him his happiness with somebody else. Acknowledge that he went about the whole sorry mess in a clumsy and thoughtless way, but that ultimately, it is for the best. For him. For her. For you.*

*You're not a victim.*

*You're the heroine of your own life.*

*Act like it.*

*They're on their way. Your person. It might not be today, though – in fact, it's probably not today, or even tomorrow – and that's exactly how it should be. You're not with the person of your life because you are the person of your life. They are extra. It will happen when it happens. But it will happen.*

*You can admit that life seems better as part of a two, if you want. But don't sit and wait. Don't simply pass the time until they arrive. You are worth a thousand more dreams than that. Continue, with full speed ahead, to be wonderful, to be you, to live, because your one? They need you to have stories. To be in full colour, already, without them, so that they can spot you in the otherwise black and white crowd.*

*And then, when you meet, finally, there'll be so very much to say.*

*You'll need days, weeks, years, a lifetime, to fill each other in on the details you have missed. And still it won't be enough. Store up your stories for late-night pillow talk and early-morning murmurs. Know that you'll understand their life so much more, because you understand your own. You did the work to be your best self. You'll know how to fill the spaces in your togetherness because you learned to be comfortable with your aloneness. You'll never need them to survive.*

*Appreciate your solo status. What you learn now will make you even better for them. Weathering a storm of uncertainty will make you a stronger anchor for when they lose their job, or your kid gets sick, or depression sets in and they need you to be the strong one for a while. If you pay attention to the beauty of your journey – to work, through life – you'll never be short on ways to* brighten their day. Master your favourite meals to one day share, take the trips so you know where the best, hidden away spots are, look after the relationships that you do have.

Be the one you want to find, so that when the right mix of luck and serendipity explodes into a romance that you didn't dare hope would look like this, they can marvel at your braveness. Revel in your adventure. Laugh at your worry that you thought this might not ever happen for you.

This was always going to happen for you. You were always going to go a little bit longer, a little bit further, alone, without them, in order to be ready for the love coming your way. Don't, for one second, think that it might not happen for you. Don't build that kind of energy around yourself, because then your person might miss you. Even the right people can fail to see through the clouds of 'I'm not even looking for love, anyway.' Yes you are. Own it. Own the fact that you are so in love with your life that the only thing better than having these experiences alone would be to have these experiences to share with somebody who matters.

Admit it to yourself, and then out loud, to others. Yes, you can say, I'm not looking for love, I don't want to scare it away, but I'm open to it. Ready for it. I welcome love into my life. Like attracts like: when you say you're happier to be single, the universe will take you at your word. Make sure the universe knows that you're doing your best to become the person you need to be. For them. For yourself. For the love that will be your life.

And then, one day, at the grocery store or a friend's birthday, at a work function or at a wedding, you'll know. They will say hello, and it won't feel like the first time. It will be the kind of hello that means, 'I've missed you, and I don't even know you yet.' The kind of hello that isn't a question – it will be your answer. And slowly, *you'll unfold for them, and you'll see all the parts of them, and you'll say a prayer to the universe for ever blessing you with this much good fortune.*

*Your one will embrace you, and they will thank you. They will thank you for holding on in there, for waiting, for not settling with something less-than when they were right around your corner, prepared to be your more-than. They'll say thank you for trusting that it was they who would come. And every last moment of doubt will disappear like a cloudless vapour.*

I didn't reread what I wrote. I finished, put the pen down, and went back to sleep. In the morning the notepad was already back in my bag.

\*

'Don't make me,' I pleaded down the phone. 'Please don't guilt trip me.' I was talking to Leah, a teaching colleague who was based at a different school. Our paths crossed a few times a week and it was always a joy when she was in the building. She had the same sarcastic, British humour as me, even though she was from Pennsylvania, and so we riffed with each other like guitarists.

'Bitch, you've got approximately twenty-two minutes to brush your teeth, reapply some lipstick, and wear something that doesn't suck,' she snapped down the phone. 'I need a wingwoman tonight, and you've already said yes so you can't back out now.' I sighed. 'Great,' she said. 'Love you! Miss you! Byeeeeee!'

I arrived at the bar late and saw she was already sitting with two men. I knew exactly what that meant for my night and so ordered a double Tia Maria and Coke and hung on to a conversation being conducted in fast Italian that I struggled to keep up with, let alone contribute to.

*Do not leave my side,* I had instructed her, in between my third and fourth drinks.

I ended up leaving her side, to drink absinthe with Marta, a drunk girl I met in the loo whose state was matched only by my own, and with whom I was suddenly speaking quite fluently in her mother tongue, having a grand old time.

Marta put me on the back of a scooter belonging to a man I didn't know to get me home, long after I'd lost Leah, and he was lovely and attentive and I had this moment, on the back of his bike, as we waited at the traffic lights beside the Colosseum – *the goddamn Colesseo* – where he turned round just enough for his lips to brush past mine, and in that moment every fantasy to be had about Vespas and Rome and old buildings and Italian men came true.

But then.

As he delivered me home.

And got off his bike.

And kissed me again.

I simply said, *'Buona notte.'*

I didn't invite him in.

I don't even think I wanted to.

It wasn't until the next morning that I realised how big that was for me. That's pathetic, but it's true.

I obsessively reread the chapters I'd written, the story of the past three years, since the break-up, looking for clues in my own prose as to what to do next with my life. It was like having ants – my eye catching one on the floor, near the corner, shifting focus in alarm to realise there's a whole trail of the bastards. It's so easy to see now that I was infested with a hunger I was looking to fill in a very specific way but, at the time, I became a parody of myself. I was missing myself without

David because I'd never done the work to develop myself. We were so young when our worlds merged that I had no true sense of myself outside of him – of course his leaving left me bereft.

And so, when I realised my character could be one of rule and command – over, say, hurt and upset – I seized it. Then I became known for it. I did such a terrific job of throwing myself into my new role that I made almost everyone around me – even Calum – think that I was *having fun*. That I was a good-time girl. That my new independence was so dizzying that I was swimming in it whilst I could.

I became rude about the romance of others. Joked about how I was Girl Most Likely to return from a two-week yoga retreat married to a man I met on the first night, photographs proving how a chap dressed as Elvis told us to solemnly treasure each other til death (or the first signs of general inconvenience) did us part. I criticised friends, cousins, strangers, who I deemed to be chasing blood diamonds for their ring finger like hunting hounds, changing their name and character to get a joint bank account. I stopped taking any kind of commitment – marriage most of all – seriously.

Obviously, I was trying to take David and Gwen less seriously.

Why get married, I declared to anyone who would listen, when there is so much paperwork to file when you divorce. Girls like me dance in clubs with husbands like yours, I'd announce, illustrating my point with tales of men kissed in dark corners of bars who tell you about their wife at home only afterwards – if at all. *I've had colleagues sleeping with new fathers*, I'd say, *and seen domestic abuse too close to home.*

Little lies. Big deceptions.

'It's the hurt we cause each other,' I remember saying at one party where I found myself in the kitchen with two other expats, sloshing vodka into everyone's glass and hanging a cigarette out of the window. 'The things we're capable of doing. I just want no part in it – no part in it at all.'

The other girls chorused murmurs of imprecise agreement.

'Anyone who does is an idiot. A fucking idiot. Gambling your life on somebody else's fidelity are odds not even the biggest gambler would put his cash on. There's just too much evidence to the contrary. Too much evidence to the opposite.'

The girl in the pages was so obviously compensating. Hurting. Distracting herself – truths I had no idea about. She was giving away a treasured, sacred part of herself – her body – so that she didn't have to risk somebody taking, and breaking, other parts of herself. Like, say, her heart.

It was all so goddamn elementary, and I'd had no idea about any of it.

It was all so painfully obvious that I was mortified to think it had been apparent to everyone but me.

# SEVENTEEN

'I don't believe it,' Fern said, gulping Peroni straight from a large bottle with one hand, and running the other over the back of peroxide stubble high on her neck. 'Like, a whole year? A whole year without sex?'

Kane, more handsome than any thirty-year-old has the right to be, leant back against the wall to take in the view of the city, eyes sparkling, T-shirt riding up just enough to reveal a sliver of rock hard stomach. 'I'm with Fern, I'm afraid,' he said. 'I'll have to see this to believe it.'

I'd worked with the pair of them the past several summers. They both lived in Sanremo and worked full-time to my part. It was so wonderful to see them in Rome, to show them the life I had been building there. We walked the streets, *fare un giro*, and, in between mouthfuls of *gelato* and *pizza* and *arancini* and *caffè*, caught each other up on what had happened since we'd last said goodbye. I'd waited until the late afternoon to tell them that I hadn't had a bloke in two and a half months, and that my intention was to last until the end of the year.

'Whatever happened with Ross?' Fern asked, referring to the last boy of the last summer. The last time she'd seen me, actually. 'That seemed to get really intense, really fast.'

I kicked at a loose stone with my toe. 'Another disaster,' I said. 'I always go really intense, really fast. I didn't know I did, but.'

'But once the wind is in your hair it blows every suggestion that you shouldn't be doing it away,' offered Fern. 'I fucking knew it. I knew you were compensating for something. Nobody ever believed me, especially not you, but I knew.' She lowered her empty bottle to the ground behind her.

'I'll just never forget passing that big footballer guy after you'd had your way with him, a couple of years ago,' said Kane in his Australian drawl. 'What was his name? God, he was such a cocky shit – but walking home from your room he was like a little boy. You killed him!'

I furrowed my brow. 'Thanks, Kane.'

Fern added, 'Or the one with the back tattoos – you just knocked on his hotel room door like, "Yo? Wanna bang?"'

Kane laughed. 'It's a marvel, really. Like, hell. You got more pussy than us guys!'

I laughed in spite of myself. 'Did I ever tell you when Romina pulled me aside before one of the week's training sessions?' I said, referring to our collective boss. 'She said to me, *Laura. Do I need to have a chat with you about proper tutor conduct?* I had no idea she was on to me!'

'Laura, everyone was on to you.'

'What did you say to her?!'

'What do you think I said? I said, *Yes, Romina. Probably!*'

We laughed and settled into a companionable silence. Moving around so much, always travelling, it was nice to inhabit the shorthand of long-term friendship. The view was breathtaking as the sun started to lower. From Janiculum, the hill with the best vantage point over the whole of Rome, life seemed slow and steady and hazy with early spring goodness. That might've been the beer. I accepted it anyway.

'I joke, but . . . but this is important to me,' I said, finally. 'I don't want to be the slutty one anymore.'

Kane cracked the last large beer and took a long pull. 'Well, which one do you want to be?' he said, swallowing and passing the bottle to Fern.

Fern laughed. 'I know which one she is. The wanky one!' She forwarded me the bottle.

'I'll take it,' I said, picking at the Peroni label. And then, 'Something is changing. I feel it. I'm gonna rework the manuscript to tell a different story. I'm excited by that. It's sort of like . . . I dunno. If I can change the words on the page then maybe I can change my life. Like, literally, I have the chance to totally alter the story I tell myself, and – look, I know this is the wankiest of the wank, but – but if I tell myself a different story about all that happened, maybe I can write myself into a really cool future.'

Fern and Kane exchanged a look. 'See,' she said. 'I told you: wanky.' She winked at me. 'Wanky, but . . . good.' I handed the beer back to Kane, leaning across her.

'This summer will be a bit different, then,' he said. 'If you're off the fellas.'

'I know,' I said. 'Like, how will I even spend my time?!'

Fern put her arm around me. 'I'm excited,' she said. 'All of us, back together again, doing what we do best.'

'You mean drinking all night and then acting like we're not hungover as we tell a bunch of college kids that, under no circumstances, are they to go out drinking all night and then go to school the very next day? Do as we say, not as we do?'

'Exactly,' she said. 'We're so good at that.'

*Who do I want to be?* I pondered, stumbling the short way home at that lovely level of middle-class drunk – woozy, but not out of control

– that means sleep is imminent and dreamless. If I was no longer the hyper-sexualised one, the saucy one, if I didn't want my perceived 'outrageousness' or 'extreme liberalness' to define me, then where did I want to grow from? I was granting myself opportunity to build character – not personality, but solid, dependable *character* – from the ground up. To shatter the parts of foolish behaviour and unlearned lessons; sit in amongst the muck, and say, *Right then. What else can I make with this?* I didn't want to change myself. I feel that intrinsically, we are who we are. My blueprint was decided long before I had any say. The bits already exist. But I was absolutely in a position to alter the arrangement of those parts, to make something different, something that had an altered centre, a different north. I could chase excitement or love or spirituality or sensibility or intellect or anything I wanted.

I was giddy with the possibility of it all.

Who did I want to be?

Who was I already?

Outside of the sex, what did I already know about myself – about my hopes and dreams and needs and desires?

That seemed like a good place to start, answering that.

A terrifying place to start.

But a good one.

I needed to grapple with some answers. I had too many unsolved questions.

'Roberto,' I said, down the phone. 'It's Laura.'

'Laura! Hi! We were just talking about you in the office. How are you?'

'I want the convent job.'

'Oh! Straight to business. Okay then. Urm. You mean the one in Loano?'

'Yes. Fern told me about it. The three-month contract at the convent, teaching English. Can I go?'

'You know that it's in the arse-end of nowhere, right?'

'Right.'

'And it'll be just you, and one other teacher?'

'Yup.'

'. . . A female teacher.'

'I know, Roberto. I'll go and do the teaching training workshops, if you want me, but after that – will you let me go?'

I could hear him shrug down the phone.

'Sure,' he said. 'I thought I'd have to work really hard to convince somebody to do it, so you've just saved me a job. I'll send you over the details. But, you know, three months in the middle of nowhere, that's not the Laura I know . . .'

'Exactly,' I said.

And just like that I'd signed up to live in an Italian convent for twelve weeks. I'd have a few weeks left in Rome, a month in Sanremo, and then head on over to *Chiostro di Sant'Agostino*.

I thought the quiet might help.


On top of the hill, several beers in, Fern had said something, and it played in my mind, over and over, taking turns with the *why her and not me* monologue that still echoed there.

'Laura,' she said, 'You're . . . you were walking wounded. I saw it. I saw your bullshit.'

I didn't say anything. *That's exactly what Andrea said*, I thought.

'I love you, but you're full of shit. Were full of shit. And I knew it was because you were hurting. I know that. And that's why I'm still here – because. Because you're fucking awesome. But you just don't see it, do you?'

I continued to sit in silence, because Fern doesn't give compliments. Not like this. And her earnestness – the way she really meant it and had given no warning for it – was disarming.

'I want you to do something for me. Are you hearing me? I want you to do this one thing.'

'Okay,' I said, and my voice sounded far away.

'I want you to stop judging yourself.'

She saw me look confused in the moonlight, even though I refused to look directly at her. Kane was taking a leak in the darkened alley down some steps, and would be back at any moment. I didn't want him to bear witness to this conversation. He didn't know me like Fern did. With Fern it was different.

'You've gotta start being a bit kinder to yourself. It's like you made one bad decision, a really long time ago, and it made you feel shitty. So you've made more shitty decisions. And you hate yourself for it, and hate yourself for wanting something else, now.'

The honesty in her words smarted.

'I want you to love yourself like we love you. Because we do love you. Do you know that? Do you understand that we are all here for you?'

I stared at the blurring lights of the skyline.

'I want you to fight for yourself like we fight for you. Day after day, the blood, the sweat, the tears. The commitment of it all. I want you to start doing that for yourself, too. I see that you're turning a corner. Stop judging yourself and lean in to being a proper, feeling, messy human being again – but one who likes herself a bit more.'

She slid her arm around me. Kane reappeared beside us. 'What's going down?' he said, as I used my scarf to wipe my wet face.

'Laura is falling in love,' Fern said.

'What?!' said Kane. 'After all this talk of celibacy?'

I wiped my nose. The cold setting in.

'It's because of all this celibacy chat, innit? She's falling in love with herself.'

# EIGHTEEN

What I wish I'd been taught, but also realise is something we must learn for ourselves, is that it is never a breakdown – it's always a break-through. When I lay on my borrowed bed in that tiny Trastevere room and cried and cried and cried, confounded and finally startled by the woman reflected back at me in the first pages I'd written, the thought on repeat in my mind was, *Whatthefuckisallthisfor? Whatthefuckisall-thisfor? Whatthefuckisallthisfor?*

The tears, all of them, they were a beginning. I was wrong when I thought they were an end. I had to have everything I thought was real – David and Gwen, my role in my own life – smashed into a thousand pieces in order to let in light. And in the ruins, in the discarded shards of what I thought I wanted, slowly I started to see the glimmer of something else. Something better. Something more *me*. When you're down at the bottom of your own proverbial hole, face down in the dirt and choking, you cannot believe that it will ever be better. It takes all the energy you have to breathe. To hope is beyond comprehension. But, I saw, now: the suffering was finite. The suffering was within my control. The suffering had been at my own hand.

*Laura*, I wrote in my notebook. *Use this hurt to inform your next decisions. Focus on what feels good, and lean, unapologetically, into that. Wrestle for your happiness, but know that the best people aren't happy – they're whole. That means fighting the good fight, knowing*

*what you can change and what you can't, and having the good grace
to appreciate the difference.*

There was a moment in Rome, right after I'd asked Roberto to go
to the convent. A tangible, real, 3-D moment, when I felt it. In between
Skype chats with Calum and snatched conversations between lessons
at school; somewhere in amongst the reluctant nights out and the
books that shifted my feeling, visits from old friends and the aloneness of a room in the city's oldest neighbourhood; a shift. A change in
the pace of my heart.

*This is my becoming,* I understood.

\*

'You want this?' the guy behind the desk said, raising his dark caterpil-
lar brows. It was my last Roman weekend. My forearm was flung out in
front of his face, where a colleague had scrawled on me in biro three
days ago. On half the length of the underside of my forearm, starting
just below the wrist, was a semi-peeled banana wearing a top hat.
The banana was smiling.

'It's the funniest tattoo I have ever seen,' the guy with the eyebrows
said.

I said, 'What, today?'

He shook his head. 'No. Ever.'

I nodded solemnly.

Mary-Kate had come to visit from Paris, and stood beside me in
the lobby of the tattoo parlour. 'Do I really want to get a tattoo of a
banana in a hat?' I said, turning to her as Eyebrow Guy continued to
examine my arm.

'Yes,' she said, nudging me. 'You do. Obviously you do. Obviously
you want the tattoo of the banana in the hat.'

We'd had, of course, the loveliest few days together.

'I just can't believe this is the same woman sat before me,' she'd exclaimed, over blue cheese gnocchi at my favourite *osteria*. 'I mean. Of course I believe this is the same woman. You're a powerhouse. But . . . but you're also *glowing*. Like, you just look so . . . so *full*.'

'I do?' I said, not believing her, and yet hoping it true.

'You seem very much at peace,' Mary-Kate told me. 'Or, no. Not *there*. Not at the destination. But very much on the way. Nine months in Rome has done you so well.'

The tiramisu arrived, refocusing her attention. Picking up the spoon, she'd breezed: 'Now. What the hell have you got drawn on your arm?'

'There's this kid in class – Virginia.'

'Oh my God, this tiramisu is incredible.'

'I know! Like, how can it be so light, and so creamy, and so boozy, all at the same time, huh?'

'*Mamma mia.*'

'I so love that you understand food like I need you to,' I said.

Mary-Kate was almost done with her dessert already. 'So, this kid,' she said, scraping the sides of her glass bowl for the last two mouthfuls.

'Virginia.' I piled pudding into my gob greedily. 'Virginia is a pain in my asshole. Like, a reaaaaal little . . . cunt. She's a cunt.' Mary-Kate shrugged. She'd worked with kids. She got it. 'She looks like Drew Barrymore circa *E.T.*, except with jet black hair instead of blond. And she comes into class, all stripy tights and biker boots and ballet tutus, attitude for days like only a five-year-old can do. She won't sit still. When she does the work she's top dog, but she likes to sing and dance and put on a show for everyone.'

'Basically she's you, then,' Mary-Kate noted.

'Fuck off,' I laughed, 'Anyway, we were playing Pictionary in class to kill the ten minutes before home.' I dipped my finger in the last of the mascarpone, then licked it. 'And it was Virginia's turn to go – URGH I COULD EAT THAT AGAIN. COULDN'T YOU EAT THAT AGAIN?! She scribbled on the board, Virginia, and scribbled some more, tongue out, no detail too tiny, drawing and drawing and drawing, on and on.' I shook my head at the thought of it, wiping my dirty hands on a napkin. 'And when she finally finished, she spun on her heel and looked at the class, who didn't have a clue what she'd drawn and so who were all looking at me, and I was looking at the board desperately trying to hazard at least an approximation of a guess. Virginia got a good sense of the room, just like I would,' I winked, 'and she sighed dramatically, flinging her arms in the direction of the drawing and saying, totally exasperated: *banana, con capello!* It's a banana, with a hat!'

'Did it look like a banana with a hat?'

I snorted. 'Not one bit,' I said. 'But to her it didn't matter. She realised nobody else saw what she saw, but instead of getting upset by that, like most kids would, she celebrated it. She danced around the classroom singing, *Banana, con capello!* and generally acted as though it was sad the others couldn't see the magic she had created.'

'Cute kid,' Mary-Kate said.

'More than cute!' I said. 'It was such a beautiful moment, and she was so secure in herself. It just made me think, yeah. A banana in a hat. It doesn't matter what anyone else thinks – as long as I know what I've created, and the intention behind it – it's a banana in a hat.'

'And so,' Mary-Kate said, 'you're going to get a banana in a hat tattooed on you.'

'I thought we could go tomorrow.'

The receptionist at work had reasoned, 'But, what about when you are eighty years old? What then?'

To me, that was a non-issue. 'Are you kidding me?' I said. 'If an eighty-year-old dressed in neon and red lipstick came to ask a question at this desk, you'd scurry back into the staff room quicker than a bad smell to tell us about the banana in a hat tattoo she had. You'd be all, *The old lady has a tattoo of a banana in hat! I wonder what the story is! I bet she's had some life!'*

'No,' the receptionist told me. 'I'd say, why didn't she have friends kind enough to stop her getting a tattoo of a banana in a hat?'

The more people questioned the tattoo, the more it cemented my desire to get it. Because, not everyone will understand. And the more people who didn't understand the banana in a hat the more I absolutely did. I got it.

Those short months in Rome – nine, in total, four of them celibate – made my desire to create things, to create myself, stronger. I wanted to be more sure of my capabilities, of what I could do. Life doesn't have an instruction manual, or guide, or map, and we can only ever do our best. And if our best comes from our hearts, from our truth, then it can't be wrong. But. We have to give *ourselves* permission. It can't come from anybody else. And that's what struck me about Virginia: she gave *herself* permission to be incredible. That's what the tattoo was. My permission slip to be my best self, for myself.

Mary-Kate said, as we celebrated my new permanent accessorised banana, 'The thing is, we've all been hurt before, Laura. It doesn't make you special.'

As I'd been tattooed she'd held my hand, and I'd winced at the pain until she said, *Talk to me. Tell me what is on your mind. Just say words, Laura. Say words and verbal vomit all over me until that rattling noise stops.* And I guess because the last time I'd seen her was right after the break-up, and we'd sort of skirted around saying his name, he was on my mind. So I'd said the words that were on the tip of my tongue anyway, and just like that we were back talking about my achy breaky heart.

'I don't mean that horribly. I actually sort of think the opposite. That thank GOD we've all been hurt before. Because then nobody comes to us whole and perfect, and so we don't have to be whole and perfect.' She stirred her drink, pushing the orange slice to the bottom of her glass with the straw. 'It's the specific experience of two people that can make or break a union. But, like, the experience should be welcomed. Needs to be welcomed.'

We were in Campo dei Fiori – field of flowers – a touristy piazza in the historical centre. We had four glasses of *spritz Aperol* in front of us because it was happy hour and we got a deal, and I took the clingfilm off the tattoo to rub on some cream we'd picked up at the pharmacy.

'Feeling bruised, Laura. It means you tried. That it didn't work out is almost irrelevant now: it doesn't work for a lot of people. But that you tried for love at all means that you understand love. You understand what it means. To fall, to hope, to surrender control. You'll love better next time because of that. And your one? They'll be so thankful for that. So sorry you were ever hurt, but so grateful for who it made you: theirs.'

I rewrapped my banana and picked up a glass. 'I'm doing my best,' I said, raising it in salute. 'Now that I see it, you know – how I wore my scars as armour or whatever – I'm doing my best to undo that.' I slurped up my drink.

'I know. And it suits you! You seem well. Stay that way. I wish I could promise you that this won't happen again, that you won't ever be hurt again, but I can't. But this work that you're doing – this time that you're taking to really get to grips with who you are and what you want and what it means to be fucking human, even – it means you're not just surviving. You're thriving. You risked it all for love and it was worth it because it made you who you are now. And who you are now is the perfect piece of the puzzle for somebody else who also hurt once.'

'I don't know if I can even *think* about being with somebody else just yet,' I said, squeezing a wedge of orange into my second *spritz*. 'I don't think it will happen for a long time.'

'Well, when it happens – and it will, eventually – whoever you are with, they'll know how to be gentle with you. And you'll know how to be honest. And together you'll hesitate and wonder and be uncertain, and probably think about not doing it altogether. The biggest equation any of us face in love is figuring out whether the pain of losing somebody will be greater than never having known them at all.'

'I think,' I said. 'The biggest thing I've learned is that nobody can promise you everything. They can only promise you they'll try. And that was the thing with David, with the whole sorry thing: he stopped trying. He stopped trying and before I had a chance to figure it out, he'd changed his mind.'

Mary-Kate put her hand on my arm. 'And the thing is,' she said, 'by your own rules, he's allowed to do that.'

I sighed.

'What I want to say to you is this: when you decide to try again, you can't do it in halves. It doesn't work. I want you to go balls deep, and give everything to the next one. So that you remember you can. So you're reminded of what you're capable of. Okay?'

'Okay.'

'I'm serious! Dating sucks, and is basically a game of who-can-care-less. Don't play that game. Play a different game, with different rules.' She signalled to the waiter for the bill. 'We're all so busy walking away from each other because we're special in our pain, and it denies us a new story to tell ourselves about love. It denies us the chance to share our hurt, and to make something new – better – out of it.'

'You're being very wise this evening,' I said, draining my second glass.

'It's Rome,' she said. 'It brings out the passionate romantic in us all, doesn't it?'

'It brings out the celibate old maid in me, actually.'

'Well. Yes. That's a banana-in-a-hat situation. Whatever you think is best for you. I'm just over here getting a little too drunk as the sun sets on the Eternal City, with my old friend Laura, who I love, and who deserves to be loved and in love, saying bleed in the name of love, *ma belle*. Lead by example. The rest of us need you to.'

\*

I slept heavily and with wild dreams that night. I stood in a restaurant, talking with my aunt, and Gwen walked in wearing a big, billowing wedding dress. She snaked through the pillars of the old, dimly lit converted barn, around waiters and tables who told her she looked beautiful. *Oh, you didn't know?* my aunt said. *They're getting married today.* A faceless bridal party marched through the restaurant, and then David burst through the doors saying, *Have you seen her? Have you seen her?* My aunt laughed lightly, happy for them, and continued to chat with me, and the diners persisted in eating and drinking and being merry, and in amongst it all a wedding happened. *So sorry to hear your news,* my aunt then said to me. *Death is a terrible thing.*

*Death?* I said to her.

*You'll be so fondly remembered,* she continued, *after you've gone. I just hope it doesn't cause you too much pain.*

# NINETEEN

'You've got to be FUCKING KIDDING ME,' I squealed, throwing my bags to the floor and allowing myself to be rugby tackled by their love. 'Fruit with hats?'

Amy cackled from her diaphragm like a drunk horse. 'Well, we missed you last night! So we did it your honour.' She held her arm aloft, a fuzzy picture of a strawberry wearing a sombrero etched on to it in marker.

Jo pulled up the sleeve of her hangover hoodie. 'Mine's a grape,' she said, showing me a wonky oval with a beret.

'You're assholes,' I laughed, pulling them in for a three-way hug again. 'You're drunken, piss-taking assholes. I've missed you.'

I'd travelled on the overnight train from Rome up the coast of Liguria to Sanremo. It's the pilgrimage I'd made every summer for most of my twenties, first as a wide-eyed newbie English teacher, just before university, and later as a wide-eyed newbie teacher of English teachers. This would be my umpteenth summer working as part of the same team, running workshops for fellow twenty-somethings on how to teach Italian kids, and games for high schoolers, and ways to use digital media in the classroom. After this month I'd head to the convent. It felt like the last year of university – we knew that, for most of us, this would be the last hoorah. Summer camp is a kid's game, and we were all in our late twenties now: it was time to pass over the reins. I was part of a crazy, disparate, loud and proud cluster of world travellers who scrambled together once a year for a few months of work-hard-play-hard, and I adored it – but I was growing up. We all were.

'Paul's here,' Jo told me, as she picked up my suitcase before I could protest that I'd manage alone. 'And he's pissed off Romina already, so he'll be at Camp Trotter by next week for sure.'

'Aaaaaand the ghosts are already rearing their well-endowed heads,' I said. 'Great.' Paul was the guy who I used to break into the school with to shag after hours.

'Well, he really is a douche, however well-endowed he might be,' said Amy, grabbing my second bag. 'Erica is here, too.'

'Great, great, great!' I clapped, navigating the famous half-mile-long walkway from underground platform to taxi rank alongside my buddies. 'Men I've shagged and the women they shagged after me! Let's start a party!'

Jo held out her arm for a cab. 'That's exactly where we're going,' she said, waving. 'A party.'

I looked puzzled.

'We've got a breakfast meeting in Bongo at ten.'

'Put to work without so much as a shower,' I sighed. 'It's like I never left.'

A car slowed and as Jo directed the driver in fluent Italian, Amy and I loaded my two suitcases – my whole life – into the boot.

'Welcome back to the jungle,' she said.

I limped my way to the hotel after the meeting – a productive one, full of timetables and workshop planning and song sharing. We were all excited, anticipating memories and regret already.

'Y'alright?' Jo asked. 'It's like walking home with a *kindergartener* who is trying not to shit before we reach the bathroom.'

'Urm – well, these are new trainers, and also my trousers are rubbing,' I said. 'I . . . I got a bikini wax yesterday and I think sitting on the train all night has rubbed it up the wrong way a bit. The, like, the sweat or something.'

'Aaaaaand there's the vagina talk we know and love,' Jo said.

'You asked!' I said.

'I was just being polite!'

'You have a vagina, too!'

'I don't want to talk about that one, either!'

Jo and I bicker like we've been married a hundred years. She's a straight-talking, big-hearted, Italian-blooded Brooklynite, with great references on hipster music and breathtaking literature. She doesn't wear make-up, sweats so much in the Italian heat she switches up her shirts three times a day, and is a raging insomniac who gets by on four hours' sleep a night. We're so very different, and yet right from the first time we met she irritated the fuck out of me in a way that made her my sister.

'You've done well to go even two hours without saying vagina, to be fair,' she said, and then, 'Oh, shit.'

'Guys,' a voice intoned from behind us. 'Guys, I just need help with some boxes please.' It was our boss, Roberto, an Italian-Australian with a history of cock-blocking me in the most extraordinary ways. He'd paired me up in a room with Jo for the first week of orientations – I think to test the waters on the I-promise-I-won't-shag-any-of-the-people-I'm-in-charge-of-training pledge everyone was openly so amused by.

'You guys gonna be okay sharing this week? Sorry about it.' He wasn't sorry about it.

'Jo couldn't be more thrilled,' I said, winking at her.

We dumped our stuff beside the elevator and followed him to the van and back as he said, 'Does anyone know where the light switch is for the storeroom?'

We started down the stairs.

'Oh,' I said. 'I remember from last year – it's at the bottom. You have to go down in the dark and do it when you're already there. I'll show you.'

We started down the steps as Roberto said, 'Well, that's just fucking ridiculous. Somebody is going to get hurt. You can't walk down fucking stairs in the fucking dark. Somebody *will* get hurt. Where's the fucking light switch?'

I rolled my eyes. 'Oh!' I said, putting on a high-pitched, stupid voice, 'My name is Roberto and I can't walk down stairs in the dark! I need a light to put one foot in front of the other! Oh! Walking is so hard! Blah, blah—'

And then, of course, 'BLAHHHHHHH!'

I tumbled down nine or ten marble steps, riding down mostly on my ankle, so that as I hit the floor the pain stabbed in my foot, Roberto glaring at me madly as he found the switch for the main lamp.

He stared at me. 'Are you kidding me?' he said. I thought I was going to throw up. 'Come on, start grabbing boxes.'

I pulled myself up and tried to put some weight on my ankle. 'Ouch,' I said.

Roberto stopped shuffling fruit baskets and said, 'Ouch?'

'Ouch.'

By evening it had swollen to the size of a tennis ball, because I continued to walk on the damned thing. Jo had all but laughed, too. Nobody took an injury ascertained in such comedic fashion seriously until I hopped one-legged to the bar, flung my leg up on a stool and said, 'I don't think it's supposed to look like this.' It throbbed, and I hobbled home propped up by Jo on one side and

Amy on the other. 'My support system through it all,' I said, wincing.

And so, the first night back on the Riviera, I was already broken. I lay on bed, my sore, recently-waxed-and-then-friction-burned vagina covered in Nivea, wearing my sexy nightie because it was the only thing I owned that might let my 'down there' *breathe*. I had Band-Aids on my ankles, and my foot was elevated above knee level to help the swelling. The ice pack and bandage felt only mildly dramatic and, since Jo was on the phone, I also had cotton wool in my ears and an eye mask across my face to block out the light.

'There she is,' Jo said, as I bid her goodnight. 'The mess I love so well.'

The tone for the summer was set.

\*

We sort of half-sat, half-lay over each other on the train station floor, alternating between reading aloud chapters of *84 Charing Cross Road*, passing the book along every page or so, and trotting off to buy another espresso or bag of liquorice.

'Your ankle is better, then?' Amy said.

I did a little kick in the air. 'Yes, ma'am! Just needed a day's rest, I think.'

Sundays were like that. The team was responsible for picking up the influx of trainees arriving from all across the English-speaking world, who'd trickle in from 9 a.m. to about 7 p.m. Amy, Jo and I always liked to take the morning shift – me, mostly because I'd need a nap before the welcome drink that evening, and them to get it out of the way so that the welcome drink could get started on sooner. I was in charge of the master copy of names we worked off as trains offloaded our charges, where we issued welcome packs and allocated hotel room keys and walked them to where they'd be staying, all whilst answering questions about Wi-Fi and beaches and smiling, smiling, smiling. It was fun, interactive work, with long stretches to shoot the shit and catch up on what the last year of our lives had done for us. I'd sneak off outside every thirty minutes or so for a roll-up, standing by the sliding glass doors and watching the others laugh and joke and stretch and drink even more espresso.

Kids would arrive with us shell-shocked and unsure what to expect, mostly, and occasionally there'd be somebody a little older or more self-assured who asked *us* about *our* day, and chatted easily about the trip they were off the back of, or how their friend did the programme last year. This would always stagger me – who knew who, and how. The world is so very small. Smaller, once you start exploring.

I'd bark orders from the sheet I held in my hands, and we'd tag-team in and out of walking duty, smiling duty, and I-really-just-need-to-nip-off-for-a-smoke duty. And by nightfall, 150 new tutors later, we'd head on down to the nearest piazza for those drinks, where normally I'd take the opportunity to zone in on the cutest ones. Jo would give me shit every year for 'abandoning' the Red Shirts, as we called ourselves (because, well, we had to wear monstrous red T-shirts) and then she'd watch me from afar as I teased the new recruits, assuring them that if they *needed anything, anything at all,* that they were to only ask. This year, though, I wasn't into that.

'But, you're . . . you're so *present,*' said Fern, as we lined up at the bar for another prosecco.

'I told you!' I said. 'I told you in Rome! The wind beneath my sails is changing. And I like it.'

'I like it, too,' she said, clinking her glass with mine.

'I'm like, becoming a woman or something,' I said.

'Teaching English made me into who I am,' I'd tell everyone on their first morning. We lined up, senior staff and all, ready to introduce ourselves to the sleepy but keen faces before us. 'When I first got here, sitting where you are, I was a chubby British girl with zero experience of summer camps or teaching or life, really. I actually wanted to leave by the third day. I didn't think I could do it – that's why it's so funny that I'm here now, as your trainer. Four years ago, I could've just quit. But I didn't. I didn't quit. I shut up and watched the best and imitated or made up what I didn't know for myself. I forgave myself my mistakes and kept giving the job my one hundred per cent best, day-after-day-after-day, and by the end of my first summer I was a totally different girl getting on the plane home than the one who'd arrived. This job built me into who I am. I wish you that very same luck.'

We were a well-oiled machine. Everyone knew when the break snacks needed laying out as much as whose turn it was to run the next part of the workshop, and what activity came next. Often one of us would turn to say, 'Could somebody just . . .' and a smiling face would shrug and say, 'Already did it.'

The days were long. We'd frequently have to be at the training venue for 8 a.m. and wouldn't leave until long after everyone else had, at 6 or 7 p.m. We'd take our debrief sessions to the bar after work, with about thirty minutes remaining to shower and change before dinner because by 8 p.m. we'd schlep everyone across town to a restaurant big enough to seat all of us. There'd be a 'bonding activity' after that – a trip to another bar. I slept about four and half hours a night, and drank far more in an evening then than I could do a whole month – six months! – any other time, and the line between Red Shirts and orientees blurred with increasing voracity as the week progressed. We did what we loved and loved what we did, and there was never a single moment – even in my sweatiest, most frustrated flashes – when I wanted to be anywhere else.

I loved running teaching workshops. It allowed me to play up to the performer inside me, but in a way that left me feeling genuinely useful. I'd get great feedback from my superiors, and Jo would sit and watch me from the back of the class, because she said it was hilarious how my snaggle-tooth would catch on dry lips as I talked wildly with my hands, and even funnier how I'd hop from one foot to another, energised and animated. I loved getting interactive in my classes, demanding that the group use their bodies to engage their minds, and that all inhibitions were to be left at the door. We'd act out classroom scenarios and discuss ways to plan lessons so that we were as excited as the kids, and I'd make everyone periodically repeat back to me what we'd learned so that I knew it was hammering home.

Teaching is a thrill for me – I find kids easy to manage and get a kick out of harnessing young and wild energy into mental growth and spiritual curiosity. But working with my peers, with people of my own generation, who not only need solid information with a killer delivery, but who also judge me on my shoes and smile and other things kids would never do, was a whole new challenge.

I consistently got feedback that I was honest. And the more I got the feedback, the more transparent it made me want to become. Because, yes, these teachers-in-the-making wanted to know where to find the best resources and improv a rainy afternoon activity with just a single cardboard box and a packet of Skittles. But they also wanted to know that it was okay to be scared. Terrified of fucking up. They needed as much reassurance about themselves, and what they thought and felt and wondered, as they did instruction about the actual job at hand. Understanding that started to open a door for me. In many ways, I was looked up to. Not like a doctor or a rock star or a parent, but definitely as an example of confidence. Of ability. And that was so new to me. I'd never given myself credit for what I knew, for what I could contribute. For the difference I could make.

Without prowling the fruit breaks and evening dinners for my fuck for the week, I found myself in corners with groups of girls complimenting me on something I had done or said that day. My sessions ran over because people had so many questions, and I often wouldn't get a break because folks would loiter afterwards, picking up on a point I'd made or asking me to tell them more about a particular experience I'd had.

I'd run the same workshops in the same way for years, but this was the first summer that it didn't just feel like I was going through the motions, like it was a good way to get laid because everyone wants to fuck their teacher. I had more room in myself to be generous about my time, and my insights, and that was reflected in the way people responded to me.

Teaching felt different. It felt like it had real value and, in turn, that I did too.

# TWENTY

On the first Friday of the summer, at about ten to midnight, I had a roll-up in one hand, a half-drunk beer in the other, and was stood in the middle of a prayer circle.

It had been an emotional week. After the isolation I'd felt in Rome it was like coming 'home'. I cried a lot – about the school visit we did, an argument I had with Jo, focaccia bread, a beautiful description of ricotta cheese in a book I was reading, people being nice, getting my period, getting baby oil on my favourite dress. ('I swear to God I am going to drown you in that baby oil,' Jo threatened.)

Somebody had pulled me aside earlier that evening to explain, 'My grandmother died the week before I flew out here and I didn't want to come. And I did, but when I got here, I didn't want to be here. And then you said, on that first morning, that you'd felt the same, and so I stayed because you said you stayed. And I'm so, so thankful that I did.'

I cried at that, too. I was humbled into stunned silence, and all I could say was, '. . . Thank you.'

The night was crazy – so many people finally working up the courage to tell us about their week, to compliment us or tease us without worry of repercussion. A guy I had hardly spoken to, who I don't quite know how I ended up in the company of, started to tell us about his life. As we slurped down our drinks and ordered the next one, he told us how he had opted out of high school when he was younger as a protest against formalised testing. How he took classes at a local university to make up for it now because he realised he needed that piece of paper. He explained how he did calligraphy and Arabic and travelled and not one word of it was wanky rhetoric designed to impress people – he just really wanted to share his story, because it was those experiences that had brought him to this place. And he was so thankful to be here.

The guy wasn't even twenty years old yet.

He said, as we drank even more beer, that every time he finds life getting hard he thinks of his granddad who emigrated from South to North America, not knowing any English at all, and who worked his way up to master language and living. Knowing that his grandfather had the strength to unapologetically build a life from nothing means now his grandson can come to bars on Italian beaches and hold an audience captive with his honesty about living his best life.

And his words – his deliberate choice of them – made me realise that it was him who had written on the end-of-week feedback form: *Laura is an inspiration for teaching . . . and my life.*

We stood up for a group hug, because he declared he had one more thing to say, and before I knew it eyes were closed and addresses to our heavenly father muttered, and once again I was sobbing, because *me* an inspiration for *his* life? There is not one single thing I could've taught this man, and in five minutes of genuine conversation he taught me more about myself than I ever realised I was looking to learn.

As we pulled apart a tall, floppy-haired blond was standing before me. *Hal.*

It hit me, that he'd been around all night. I'd been so intoxicated by the emotion I felt for our first group of new tutors that
summer – and how they'd made me feel about myself – that the
beer had gone down quickly and easily, and I was in a heady state
of total bliss. The kind where everything sort of . . . *washes over
you*. But, now that I thought about it, I was sure he'd pulled up a
chair at dinner. And then walked in the same group as me to the
bar. And he'd been sitting with us, chatting, listening, for the past
two hours or so. I didn't need to be surprised, then, when I found
myself ambling with him along the beach to our final
destination.

I cannot tell you what we talked about. We were together, is all.
The words blur into a feeling, and that feeling was . . . togetherness.

I remember I was wearing a floor-length blue dress. It had a
lace back and I wore a pink tube top underneath instead of a bra.
It was cold, that night, for June, and so I had gone out with my
leather jacket, too. In the end it was something I simply carried all
night. My hair was pulled to the side in a messy sort of half-pony-
tail-half-bun, and I wore a lot of black eyeliner. I felt pretty when
I was talking to him, and I think that's because I was laughing so
much.

I remembered that we'd seen him jogging through the town one
night, as we sat drinking *spritz* at an after-work meeting. And then I
remembered that earlier that day, I'd asked who he was. All of the
new recruits have to put on a sort-of performance at the end of their
week. They're split into groups and given an age group and a subject,
and have to throw together a short skit to demonstrate teaching
techniques to the rest of us. Hal had done something stupid on stage
– this crazy dance, by himself, when one of his 'cast-mates' had
forgotten their line – and it had me bent over double in hysterics. I

remember leaning over and asking Amy, 'What's that guy's name again?'

He was young. Boyish. Charming. American, of course. The charming ones always are. On that last night, I remember holding my drink and stirring the ice around the glass with the straw. I didn't feel like I had to impress him. We were two people, chatting, shooting the shit and using the witticisms of the other in order to be witty ourselves. It was light, and playful, and at one point he made me laugh so hard that I told him I just needed a minute – I excused myself and went around the corner so I could collect myself. As soon as I circled back around to him and his eye met mine, we both creased into giggles again, and for a good long time we simply stood opposite each other, laughing and laughing and laughing and laughing. That was Hal.

'Ohmygod,' I said to Jo, several days later. She was in the bathroom of the room we had decided to continue sharing. I didn't want my own room. I loved my roommate and was forcing her to love me and my baby oil, too. 'Jo. Hal messaged me.'

'What did he say?' she asked, through the door. She hated when I talked to her as she peed. Can't I have just one second? she'd say, only half-angry.

'Come read this,' I said. 'This is . . . this is really nice.'

**To: Laura Jane Williams**
**From: Hal Hart**
**Date: June 12th**

This is going to be a very strange message – just to provide some warning.

I need to tell you that I've fallen a little bit in love with you . . . but that's a lie. I freaking love you HARDCORE! You mentioned you had a blog where you write some of your stories. I checked it out – it's so good!

I came here this summer because it sure as hell beat working at McDonald's to pay for university, and I've always wanted to travel – but I never expected to be changed, or have everything I knew thrown out like yesterday's trash.

I'm the type of person who thinks everything needs to be planned. That being impulsive is some sort of kiss of death to productivity. I don't know . . . being impulsive has always been a challenge for me, I guess. (Huh. Except for when I'm on stage, oddly enough.)

But you . . . you shook everything up and made anything seem possible. It all makes sense after that first day of teaching with those kids looking at me so eager, smiling, a little boy hugging my leg and a little girl singing. Now all I can think about is your wonderful, partially clothed banana. You made me believe I could do this job.

I'm not really sure why I wrote this awkward message.

Maybe it was to say thank you.

Maybe it was to let you know that you affected me in a really significant way.

Maybe it was just to get all this off my chest.

Anyway, you said to 'live on purpose' and that struck a chord with me. I think I've been building a life around the wrong reasons.

Okay. I, urm, I'm ending this before I get any weirder.

Thank you for everything!

I beamed from ear to ear, and colour filled my cheeks.

'The kid likes you,' Jo said.

'He didn't have to be so kind,' I said, already scanning the note to reread his compliments. He'd said I affected him. Me. My . . . *personality*. Just, me, when I hadn't even realised he'd been paying attention.

'Nice people do nice things – and he's nice. So.'

'We've used the word nice six times in thirty seconds. Is nice a synonym for something?'

'Nice is good,' Jo said. 'Nice is really good.'

'But . . .' I said. 'I don't know what to do with nice.'

Jo sighed and smiled. 'I know you don't, Jane, but it's kinda fun watching you figure it out.'

'Why are you calling me by my middle name?' I said.

'It suits you,' she replied.

And then we did it again. And again. And again. The same week, repeated four times – the same workshops and questions and activities and dinners. And every week it got tighter, more fluid. More interesting, too. My confidence was growing. I liked what was unfolding. I was part of a group of such thoughtful, supportively people that it made me behave more thoughtfully and supportive, too. I liked that side of myself – I liked when I could see that I was making a difference to the days of others. From my workshops and teaching, yes, but also on a one-on-one basis. Small interactions where, when I said, *Hey, how's it going?* I found I was really interested in the response.

I was also throwing up a lot.

It happened whenever I felt a surge of emotion from the people around me. It began so abruptly that had I been having sex, my instinct would've been to take a pregnancy test – but I was a full six months into the celibacy pledge now. It was mostly during the day that it happened. The first time was when somebody said, as we were lying outside one of the lecture halls, reading to each other – *The days are passing by too quickly. I want this to be our lives forever.*

I did, too. Operating on the coast, within the same two-mile radius day in and day out, doing what I loved and was good at, with people who I loved and were good at what they did, too – it was restorative. I didn't know what I was going to do in the next incarnation of my life. And I suppose I was apprehensive about the rest of the summer in the convent, too.

'I don't even think you can wank in a convent,' Kane had said to me. 'I think that kind of shit really pisses God off.'

I laughed. 'Nah, mate – not my God. It's how I pray to him. Right before I cum is the only time I say his name over and over and over again like that.'

Within a minute and a half of saying, *Me too. I don't want this to end either,* bile rose in my throat and I felt light and dizzy and full and upset, all at the same time. I skipped through the corridor and made it to the toilet just in time, where I stayed on my knees, hugging the toilet bowl, confused as to what just happened.

'Jane?' Jo said, lightly knocking on the door. Amy appeared behind her.

'You okay?' she said.

'I don't think my belly likes this talk of saying goodbye,' I said, flushing the loo and blowing my nose. 'That was definitely in direct correlation to the feelings I have about you guys.'

'A little emotion sickness, Jane,' Jo said to me, rubbing my back. 'You've learned how to love again! And your body is in turmoil over it.'

'Shut up,' I said. 'And find me some water.'

# TWENTY-ONE

Three weeks after I'd first received his note, I sat down to write back to Hal. He was out in southern Italy somewhere, on a teaching assignment. I was still in Sanremo.

**To: Hal Hart**
**From: Laura Jane Williams**
**Date: June 25th**

Wow. What an email. I have no words, except those shaped as an apology for taking so long to get back to you. Internet has been scarce here, and I wanted to wait until I had time to write back properly before I told you that your message made my life. Seriously.

I spent a really long time feeling like I was fucking up because nobody ever told me that it was okay not to know what I wanted to do with my life right away. Everything was a blank page for me. And if I can tell that story and make somebody else feel even marginally better about being scared or knowing or not knowing or even just inspire a bit of living-on-purpose-even-if-the-end-isn't-quite-figured-out-yet-ness then, well, that just about makes all my own tears and strife worth it. You know? I hope that doesn't sound too self-important.

Anyway. The very fact that that email came from a guy who all the other tutors knew I couldn't look in the eye because he sent my tummy funny makes it all the better.

I hope you're continuing to have a great summer! Go get 'em tiger. And remember: when in doubt . . . it's a banana in a hat.

LJW xo

He wrote back the next day.

**To: Laura Jane Williams**
**From: Hal Hart**
**Date: June 26th**

Well, after I didn't hear from you I was concerned that you were disturbed by my fangirling, or that you were just tired of receiving messages like that from newbie tutors. So. I'm relieved. Relieved that my message was well received, even though you must get them all the time.

In all seriousness, though, I've really been inspired by your attitude and outlook. Your writing is so entertaining that I find myself surfing your website and learning way more about you than I should – I'm hitting stalker status.

My whole experience this past month alone has been incredible. Already I know that I'd like to return next summer. I'd love to learn how to lead orientation like you guys. Maybe then we could work together! Who knows what could happen.

Thank you again for everything. Thanks for making wherever I'm going that little bit easier.

I voiced opinions I didn't know I had, in those weeks, sticking up for myself and stating needs in a way I'd never done before. It felt okay to say, after a particularly hectic session or quiet low moment, that I needed a hug or a drink or both. If somebody made a joke at my expense – a silly, flyaway comment that we all do, and me most of all – I'd say, 'Hey – *that hurt my feelings.*' Not in a dramatic way, or an accusing way, just as information. I was growing into parts of myself that, before, I'd written off as weak. By letting myself be vulnerable I was actually demonstrating strength. I didn't have to pretend I was the strongest in order to be the strongest. I was the strongest by continuing to be myself.

'Urm, I'm not sure,' I said to a blonde Canadian, in response to a question about school placements. 'I'll have to ask somebody important about that.'

'Oh, sorry,' she said, 'I thought you were, like, in charge of everybody. Who should I ask then?'

Comments like that kept popping up – comments that alluded to my leadership skills and how others looked to me for what to do next. I was laughing them off, because wasn't I just gobby and bolshy? The one who would say what others wouldn't because she didn't care what people thought?

But I did care. I cared, deeply, from my toes to my eyelashes about my team. About the people we were coaching. About the schools, and the projects and preparing everybody well to go on out there to have the summer of their lives.

I cared about telling my story, my journey, in teaching, in as authentic a way as possible so that others felt encouraged to know they could do it too. Because it's a scary thing, heading halfway across the world and learning a new skill that you then have to implement in a foreign setting. And kids are crazy – let alone kids who don't speak your language. Then there are the host families they'd all be paired with, and letting them know how to handle being a guest in an Italian home. So much.

I cared about making people feel good, without it being at the expense of feeling good myself.

I didn't care about being the best or being in charge or bossing people about. But, somehow, because I'd committed to simply being true, those around me deferred to me. That was new and disorientating and weird.

'I don't know,' Jo and Fern said one night. 'It's like . . . it's like you've always had superpowers, but before they were used for bad. Like, seducing boys and manipulating people to get your own way. And now . . . and now you've seen the light and are using your superpowers for good.'

'Its not that you were Darth Vader before,' Jo said. 'It's just that you're definitely showing more of your Luke Skywalker now.'

'Did you guys secretly hate me before?' I said, in genuine shock.

'No!' they choursed.

Fern said, 'You're just making it so much easier for us to like you now. It's hard to resist somebody so flagrantly doing their best.'

We were gathered around a low wooden table, squeezed in, sat on top and up against one another. We'd been drinking in that self-aware, measured way that happens at networking events and funerals: glasses filled conservatively but regularly, lest the truth reveal itself at the bottom. I'd been throwing up almost every day – sort of pre-empting the sadness of goodbye. We'd thrust ourselves into the month and weathered the midway slump, coming out the other side riding on a runner's high, and now, in *Il Cave* we were nestled in continued celebration of being together.

'Play something for us,' somebody said to Jacqui, an actress from New York. We'd been jamming out all night as part of a super-informal 'Open Mic Night' that we held every Thursday for the orientees. We'd all pulled out the crowd-pleasers: Romina had done her 'Stand By Me', the boys, some Disney favourites (they knew that's what the ladies loved), Jo had done some jumping up and down at the back. Kane had played his didgeridoo. I'd rapped 'Gangsta's Paradise', because, obviously. We'd laughed, we'd drunk, we'd cornered and been cornered by the new tutors with enough red wine in them to approach us, earnestly, to stammer, 'I just wanna say . . .'

As we'd ushered out the college kids, citing curfews and the eve of their last big day, promising a big party night once they'd 'graduated' the course and making sure they knew how, exactly, to get home, Jacqui took to the small stage and, instead of laughing and joking and clinking glasses and sneaking outside for cigarettes and secret chats, we sat. We listened.

Jacqui is small – diminutive, women's magazines might say. She has translucent, Cullen-clan-esque skin and a wide, upturned mouth. She perched on a bar stool, solo in the spotlight, and tuned her ukulele. And then she sang. Haunting, folksy melodies and meaning-ful, heartfelt lyrics about love and longing, lust and becoming.

She sang with her eyes closed.

That struck me.

It was exposed. Really, really vulnerable.

With her words, with her body, with her voice, she handed us her soul, because she trusted us, her friends, with it. It seemed to me, as her tones warmed us and we applauded and she sang something else, and then something else, and then something else, that she trusted herself.

She could share the deepest, most raw parts of the stuff that made her because she knew she'd be okay. She wasn't asking us for permission to feel what she felt – in her songs or in that moment. She was, in the most gentle, quiet way, utterly genuine and made no apologies for that.

Slow streams made tracks on my cheeks at first, and then Fern noticed and leant across the table to squeeze my hand – but I couldn't let go. I gripped on to her fingers and stared straight ahead. They flowed. Not hiccupping sadness or wild upset – a leak. My eyes leaked, as if my whole body was filled with emotion – gratitude and understanding and questioning and curiosity – that had nowhere to go except *out*. It was sensory overload. It was fullness.

I watched Jacqui continue to sing, and somebody said, as she paused to choose her next number, 'Oh! Laura!'

Amy reached to rub my back and Jo said, 'Jane!'

I could say nothing – I could only smile. I had no words for the gratitude in my heart, in my bones, for this. For everything that had led me to this, this moment where I was rootless in name and grounded in my bones – tethered, through virtue of love – to the strongest, most caring and giving women I could ever hope to know, who had, without knowing it, brought me back to life through example.

Jacqui finished and the bar started to close. Still I cried. Wept, really. We sat on the steps outside of *Il Cave*, and I hugged my knees to my chest. There was a bottle of Baileys and an ice bucket being passed around and as it reached me, I saw Amy shake her head at Jo. *No.* I got passed over for the next person. I was working myself up into a state.

Finally, Amy said, 'Is this just emotion sickness, wee one? What's going on?'

I stared up into the kind, concerned faces of my friends, mortified by my own drama and totally averse to restricting the flow of my feelings. It was the walls of a dam bursting, running over the streets of my veins and oozing out every last emotion inside of me.

'You . . . you . . . *you fixed me,*' I stuttered. 'You fixed me!'

My words were barely comprehensible through the sobs, but they got it. They always did.

Amy stroked my hair. 'Oh love, we didn't fix you,' she said. 'You fixed yourself. Look at you. You did this.'

I saw David's face, and her face, and the vomit in the toilet bowl after all that vodka. I saw Pete and Jay The DJ and the black guy in bed beside me in Paris. I felt the humiliation of *French girls . . . don't do that.* Big Dick and his rough, beautiful hands around my neck, the way the water of the shower stung my most tender parts the next morning. Chad. Lovely, sweet Chad. I saw faces I didn't have names for, rows of boys and men who I'd taken to my bed and then asked to leave. I saw Detroit and chip shops and Calum and Roman streets and felt the loneliness of so many nights in bed, alone. The emptiness. The nothingness. The hope.

'I let you help me, though,' I said. 'I let you love me.'

'That's what we've been gunning for all along, Jane,' said Jo.

# TWENTY-TWO

Called DREAMERSchool, it was founded by a blisteringly successful entrepreneur who'd made his fortune in the chocolate industry, of all things. White, old and recently widowed, he'd no family to spend his Euros on, choosing, instead, to host an annual competition across Italy to find gifted, willing and talented teenagers demonstrably dedicated to making a difference with their lives. Applicants submitted poems and designs for inventions, or plans for urban development and comic strips – they didn't have to be traditionally smart, but they did have to be committed. Those judged to exhibit exemplary skill or vision were invited to one of four all-expenses-paid, two-week intensive summer camps, housed in the convent. They had visiting speakers from fields as diverse as environmentalism and screenwriting, ran their own projects and films, lived together, ate together, took trips together, and also tried to avoid getting caught when they gave or got the finger in an empty classroom after dark. At the end of the two weeks they were supposed to leave with new skills ready for use in the wider world, to fulfil their potential fully. My job was to teach them English for an hour and a half a day, in whatever way I saw fit, and sit with them at mealtimes to converse with them, too. The tag line for DREAMERschool was *sogni in colorati* – dreams in colour. I liked that. Spectacular, exhausting, inspiring, smart, I've-never-thought-about-it-that-way multicoloured dreams. The kids, then, were referred to simply as *colours*. They were a bright, sparky bunch, and they kicked my ass.

'But, where do you live?' Giulio said, lifting his plate up to signify to the cook's assistant that he'd take seconds. 'In England, where do you live?'

He was getting cross because I kept telling him the same thing.

'Here!' I replied, leaning to one side so I, too, could be served an extra helping of *pasta al burro*. 'Everything I own is in my bedroom upstairs. My home is here.'

Giulio shook his head, frustrated, presuming the language barrier meant I'd misunderstood. He tired of me quickly and slipped back into Italian to talk with the other *colours* about something I couldn't understand. Trilling tongues conducted melodies loudly, passionately, and then with sudden aggressive precision, stopped.

Bill, the chocolate businessman, walked into the room. Chairs scraped back, feet shuffled, *colours* rose to their feet. I scrambled to join them.

Giulio had been telling me about his love for John Lennon. His English was incredible, especially for a thirteen-year-old boy; he was able to express complex ideas at a high enough level that it wasn't a chore to talk with him. He had thick bones and heavy-set shoulders, used his hands to gesticulate wildly, luring listeners into the passion of whatever it was he was advocating. His enthusiasm was contagious. He'd said, earlier, 'The Beatles! My heroes! *There's nowhere you can be that isn't where you're meant to be* . . . It's a sort of poetry and philosophy, no?' I let Bill's Italian words wash over me as the *colours* stared at the food going cold on their plates. Even the kitchen was quiet. *There's nowhere you can be that isn't where you're meant to be.* The universe has a funny sense of humour, I thought. I had no idea what I was doing after this summer, no idea about my future, and yet there I was, indirectly tasked with helping young impressionable minds plot theirs.

I glanced at Megan. She pulled a funny face across the room. Bill was generous with his cash, but hadn't so much as made eye contact with Megan and me since we'd started, meaning he hadn't endeared himself to us. Megan was fun – a fortunate turn of events, since we'd be sharing a room for the next three months. She'd be my co-teacher, roommate, dinner companion and, within days, start up an affair with one of the Italian tech consultants, meaning she, too, would try not to get caught as she got slipped the finger in an empty convent class-room after dark. It was a set-up that worked well: we both got space enough to breathe, but also had a co-conspirator for the unlikely situation of two young lasses in an Italian convent. I adored her, because I have two settings for all my relationships: obsession, or broke. We spoke the same sarcastic language and the luck of it was astounding.

The *colours* unfroze, all moving at once to sit back down, relaunching into frenzied soliloquy with words tumbling out over the top of one another.

'What did he say?' I asked Giulio, not caring he was mid-sentence with an equally geeky young girl. I'd caught odd words but he'd spoken too fast for me to properly understand.

He turned. 'He said that we are very fortunate to be here, and to pay attention for every moment that we are awake. This is a beautiful experience that not many people have the opportunities for.'

I shovelled cold pasta shapes into my mouth as I nodded.

'Oh,' he added. 'He also said if anyone gets caught drinking or smoking they will be told to go home.'

'Ah,' I thought, already gagging for a fag.

Plates got cleared and he tried again, after I asked him to pass the water. 'So really, where do you live? Where do your parents live?' The jug was held mid-air, waiting reward for an answer.

'Derby,' I said, in the end. 'I live in the middle of England. Derby.' He filled my cup.

The thought of it dried the saliva on my tongue. I couldn't return to Derby. Too many ghosts. Not enough opportunity. I was hungry to see more of the world, and was tentatively encouraged by the hand-ful of readers following my blogging adventures. People seemed to react to how I was beginning to write a little more honestly, chron-icling more openly about loneliness and change and fear and long-ing. I'd started to rearrange The Sex Memoir into something more heartfelt, too; more reflective of the emotional journey behind the sexual one – and was slowly beginning to entertain hazy ambitions about seeing it published. I didn't allow myself to believe I would ever get anywhere, of course, because books are written by other people, not people like me. But the half-commitment at least provided some-thing to occupy my mind when brain vultures approached, circling my sensibilities to hiss, *Laura! Laaaaaauraaaaa! When are you going to start taking yourself seriously? When are you going to settle down? You can't keep treading water like this forever, you know* . . . The point of being in the convent, I knew, was not to plan what I would do or where I would go after the convent, but rather to sit with myself no matter how uncomfortable. The small solace of continuing to write was enough to distract me.

Valentino stood to issue announcements about the rest of the day's activities. I took the opportunity to wink at my teenage lunch companions and slip away from the table, catching Megan on my way out of the dining hall.

'I need a smoke,' I whispered. 'Convent life is killing me.' She started to stand before I'd even had chance to add, nodding at her lithe frame, 'Let's get out of here, Legs Eleven.'

The building itself was beautiful, and as grand as you'd imagine. Two storeys seemed like four because of the ceiling height. The first floor was my favourite – all dark wood and dimly lit corridors – and it was impossible to get lost; the design was a hollow square around the sprawling courtyard, with rooms of all sorts off to both sides. And so, if you followed the corridor long enough, eventually you'd end up back where you started. One side of the grid had been set aside with the rooms for the kids, staff and visiting professors, one side held empty spaces that had been converted into makeshift classrooms, and the last two were off-limits: that was where the monks lived.

I longed to know more about them. *Il fratelli* – the brothers. They kept themselves to themselves, frustratingly. On one of my first days at *Chiostro di Sant'Agostino* I accidentally (on purpose) got lost so that I might nose around their living quarters, only mildly concerned that while I could pass off my wanderings as confusion to anyone who asked, God himself – herself – would know that I was obnoxiously curious enough to poke around where I'd been explicitly told I had no business. I only permitted myself to peer into rooms with doors already open – morally that seemed sounder than turning handles – since behind any closed door could be a living quarters, with monks doing monk-like things. I wondered if they masturbated. That's what I'd been doing. Sex was something I thought about a lot (still) (always) because blood beat in my loins as a woman and I'd been reduced by circumstance to unsatisfactory wanks in the shared bathroom that, whilst only used by me and Megan for bathing, was somehow filthy with leftover grime from whoever was in there before. It didn't feel much like 'cleaning oneself' so much as 'hosing oneself down without touching anything but yourself'. I longed to bring up the cleaning issue, but was unsure how to tell a monk to please give it some more elbow grease. What was particularly maddening was that on my exploratory mission I could see that their side of town seemed in tip-top condition. It was fascinating: in the cracks between oak door frames and heavy wooden doors, I spotted a stark contrast to the impressive bare minimalism of the passageways.

It seemed the bedrooms were as sparse as ours, in that there was a metal-framed single bed, chest of drawers and a double wardrobe (though, really, how much clothing could a monk have?) but each room seemed to have its own little indulgence. A coffee maker here, a wad of lush blankets there; a small kitchenette with two types of cereal on the counter, and the odd chocolate bar made by Bill's company. I hadn't even seen a glimpse of any shiny wrappers on our side of the convent and my envy grumbled at their good fortune – even more so because everything really was pristine. The monks clearly applied higher cleaning standards to their quarters than to ours.

It wasn't much like being in a convent, often, but then halfway through a song-and-dance class break – an excuse to sing English lyrics and loosen our bodies to loosen our minds, because that's the kind of English teacher I am – I'd see the waft of brown robes as I came out of a silly shoulder-shimmy, an ever-present reminder not to get too comfortable with my surroundings. Sometimes, one of the brothers would loiter at the entrance to where we worked, watching one of us in a tutu and wonky wig, directing the class through a drama activity to hone the past perfect tense, or forcing one of them to do twenty press-ups because they spoke in their mother tongue when our rule is: in English class, you only speak English. I'd put money on them thinking we were fucking insane, not to mention mildly unprofessional, but any judgements were characters of my own mind and not their reality. Their half-smiles and slow gait acted as a surreal backdrop to an otherwise quite normal summer camp, and generally they seemed to like us. You know. From a safe distance.

The convent made things feel calmer. The main entrance was a whopping great door, twice the height and width of anything I'd ever used before. Coming and going through it felt like there was supposed to be a moat and a drawbridge, it was that imposing. We had a key the length of my forearm that we had to wriggle through an iron hole and as much freedom as we felt when using it to get out, we felt the same level of comfort and safety on leaving the outside world to come back in. Both were a joy. The convent was a comforting joy.

\*

'The kids don't believe I am homeless,' I said to Megan, as we found a spot to roll a smoke. 'Every mealtime they ask me the same thing. I'm sending myself crazy trying to explain that . . . well, that this –' I gestured to the ominous womb of a building behind us, almost knocking the cigarette from Megan's hand, 'IS my life. This is it. This is all I've got.'

'Gurl, I hear you,' Megan said, leaning back against our bench, blowing smoke out of one side of her mouth. She was all endless legs – albeit bruised – and swan-like neck. 'Don't forget I'm in the same boat. I have no idea what I'm going to do when I fly back to the States. Move to New York, maybe?'

'I see you in New York,' I said, having only ever spent the grand total of one night there myself, back with Andrea. 'New York would suit you.'

'Mmmmm.'

'*Where will you live, Laura?*' I said, in an accent mimicking the Italians. '*What job will you get? Aren't you afraid? Does it make you sad to be away from your family? Do you wish you owned a house? Don't you want a boyfriend?*'

Megan pulled her smoke from her mouth and saw it had gone out. Frowning, she scrambled for the lighter as she said, 'They're figuring it all out, too, I guess. They just wanna know it's cool to be afraid. That the answers will come.'

I looked at her. 'That's actually ... yeah. That's a pretty sensible assessment. Very sensible. I'll bet they're surrounded by folks telling them that if they do this subject at school, or this hobby after hours, it will lead to x-y-z success. But that's not true. That is *so* not true.' My own roll-up went out, neglected as it was by my chatting. Sticking it between my lips and reigniting it, I added, 'Good talk, dude. You make sense. I find Italians a very fearful people.'

'Sorry about these crappy cigarettes,' Megan said. 'I don't know what my problem is but they're rolled looser than a gossip's tongue.'

Carlos, the IT technician, emerged in the distance carrying camera equipment and a grin that flipped my stomach. He was so very happy to see his lady, and it made me jealous.

'*Tesoro,*' he said, dropping his stuff and kissing the top of Megan's head from behind us. '*Come va?*' They smiled at each other, soundlessly communicating thoughts and emotions I didn't want to bear witness to. I liked both of them individually, but with them together I felt like a gooseberry.

'I'm gonna go get back to my writing, I think,' I said excusing myself from the public display of affection before it intensified. 'Thanks for the nicotine. Let's get a beer after dinner?'

'Sure,' said Megan. 'We can go to the port. We need to plan tomorrow's lessons.'

Mealtimes became more of a pleasure, after that, when I started to exhale into owning that I didn't know what was going to happen next, but that it was okay.

When the *colours* asked about my tattoos I told them. I said: *This is a banana in a hat, to remind me that as long as I believe in something, that is all that matters – even if I am the only one who understands.* I explained about a more faded one, from my late teenage years: *This one means 'yes', because I believe in saying yes to life, you know?*

I told them, *Sure, I had my heart broken once. But I wouldn't be who I am now if we'd stayed together, so I'm actually kind of pleased. I like who I am now. Having my heart broken was a part of how I learned to grow up.*

Days later, I assumed my usual spot in the courtyard to work on a blog post about the *colours*, my notebooks splayed out to one side. A student who I'd eaten dinner beside the night before, Chiara, came over and flicked through it, and though I bristled at the invasion of my privacy, I softened visibly as she stopped at the blank pages and said, 'Your future.'

Unwritten.

Unwritten but mine to do with what I will.

'My future.' I smiled, meeting her eye and accepting the reassurance – the insight – of the seventeen-year-old. She continued on her way, smiling.

Loano, the small coastal town where the convent resided, was pretty enough, if not a little touristy. The *lungomare* – beachfront – was wide and paved, with section after section of beach customised by the bar it was owned by. Beds and umbrellas and changing cubicles littered, uniformly, as far as you could see, because an Italian knows how to beach: they don't lie on a towel on the sand and get dirty or make do. An Italian 'beaches' properly, arriving in a killer outfit, carefully peeled off in the changing rooms to be swapped for a bathing suit . . . which has matching accessories for a lunch break at exactly 1 p.m. Italians get changed fully before leaving the beach, too. Where I'm from you throw on a dress or even head home wrapped in a towel when you go on vacation, big wet patches on boobs and bum growing. But not in Italy. There were gift shops lining the beachfront, too. And then, set back behind all those winding, bendy streets with exposed brick and hidden piazzas, with restaurants offering cheap, delicious seafood, were glimpses into the lives of people who lived there year-round, TVs blaring from front rooms and laundry hanging between build-ings, casting shadows on sun-bleached brick below.

At about 4 p.m. every day I'd use our heavy key to give myself an hour or so to wander around town, to think about what I was writing that day, lapping from the quiet train station at one end, to the new Mafia-built marina at the other. Sometimes I'd slap on trainers and jog it, other times I'd pull out my camera and task myself with seeking out beauty I hadn't yet spotted, training my amateur eye to find the stories of the city.

'You've got a lot of photographs of doors,' said Megan, flicking through my computer photo library at the bar where we sat drinking beers and smoking roll-ups. I was smoking more and more and more at the convent, like I was nervous about something. Unsettled. I'd come to write and watch the sunset, and she'd sought me out because, 'I need English conversations, gurl. I gotta converse a little quicker than these Italian guys can go.'

'Huh?' I said, noting that she was, of course, right. 'I guess I do have a lot of doors.'

'It's a bit Freudian, no?' The waiter set down a beer before her, ice cold so that beads of water rolled down the glass.

'The doors?'

'The doors.'

I wiped condensation from the rim of my beer, and then my finger on the tablecloth. 'Spell it out for me.'

'It's like, what's behind it? If you open the door, where does it lead? That's basically what every single one of our conversations is about: what comes next.'

'Doors as questions,' I said. 'You have to deliberately push forward to discover the answer.'

'We're so fucking profound.' She leaned back in her chair and looked towards the sea.

'We're so fucking tipsy,' I said. 'Do you think the *colours* will know we're three beers in at dinner?'

'Probably. But I think we're charming enough to pull it off.'

'Your confidence is staggering.'

'Well, dude,' she said, sighing happily, 'if I know one thing, it's that people will think of you how you tell them to think of you.'

'Okay, Deepak. That's enough from you.'

'You can think of me as fearless and willing,' she said. 'Same way I think about you. Now. What do you *want* to be behind the door?'

# TWENTY-THREE

'I'm with Hal!' she said down the phone. 'Hal is here!'

'I miss you!' I'd squealed down the phone to Jo, weaving through Loano's backstreets on my 4 p.m. stroll. 'Where are you? I haven't heard from you in days!' Reaching the gelateria I loitered outside, craning to see if they'd made raspberry chocolate that day.

'OHMYGOD! JANE!' Her voice was raspy and hoarse. 'I miss you, too!' I couldn't see my favourite flavour on the board. *Damn it.* 'In fact, I was just talking about you!'

'Awwww, you love me!' I carried on walking, intending to circle back around to the main road.

That's when she said it: 'I'm with Hal. Hal is here, with Irish Stu!'

My heart leapt into my throat. 'Oh?' I smiled in spite of myself. 'Oh, that's . . . cool?'

Jo laughed. 'I think what you mean to say is, that's *nice.*'

I could hear some fumbling and laughter in the background, and a male voice said my name. 'Laura?' It was Irish Stu, one of the more talkative new tutors whose jokes and easy-going nature had endeared him to the Red Shirts as soon as he got off the train.

'Hi! How are you? What's happening over there?' I was pacing. I wasn't walking anywhere; I was turning on my heel every thirty seconds to meander the same strip of road because *Hal. Hal. Hal.* Hal?

'We're in Baiardo,' he replied, referencing the village up in the hills where our company owned a cluster of houses. When tutors weren't needed at camp they were provided with free accommodation and food until they had to get back on a train to their next destination. Everyone crossed paths with everyone in Baiardo.

Jo came back on the line. 'I wish you were here!'

I wished I was there too. It wasn't even that far away – a few hours, maybe. Hal's boyish smile appeared in my mind's eye. 'How long are you there for? Maybe we can meet up, if you don't mind travelling an hour or so? I could come halfway?'

'I leave in the morning,' she told me. 'But, hold on. The boys don't. You should meet them!' Jo knew exactly what she was doing.

Irish Stu came back on the line. 'Hey, Laura? What are you doing tomorrow?'

We made our plans.

At the convent, I couldn't focus. I had the same spot, same time, every single day. Working on my book, on blog posts, on emails to Calum or to Mary-Kate in Paris and occasionally to Mum and Dad, in edited, not-quite-the-whole-truth form, like we do with our parents when we're trying to make out we're doing better than we are. I occupied my space near *padre's* office as the *colours* continued classes in their part of the convent, two sides of the rectangle away. I played two roles, like I always did, no matter where I ended up: my extrovert and my introvert. I'd stand in lessons, poised and sure. I was a good teacher. A fucking great teacher. The kids and Vale, the lead on the DREAMERschool project, told me so – generously and often. Then, for eight or so hours, I'd watch midday sun turn to low twilight, into night, and inhabit the shadows from my makeshift desk. Poke around in the places that hurt, journalling and reading and reworking my writing. Unpacking my parts, inspecting them. I was starting to think that if I could figure out what I was made up of, it would cease surprising me; that looking the worst parts of who I was dead in the eye would mean feeling braver. Because then nobody could shock me with what they didn't like about me: I'd already know, because I'd spotted it first. I wondered what Hal would find not to like about me. He'd built me up too high in his imagination, I thought. We'd lunch tomorrow and then he'd know. The illusion would be shattered. I closed my eyes and tried to remind myself that the point of it all is to be unsure. That I could be both unsure, and hopeful.

'I'm . . . I feel so stupid,' I said, running straightening irons over my humid, frizzy hair, and adding another coat of mascara. 'Do I look like a drag queen? I look like a drag queen.'

'You look beautiful,' Megan said from her bunk bed. She leaned over the edge and peered down. 'You're tan and healthy-looking, and if you stopped grimacing, you might even look happy.'

'I feel really dumb. I don't even know why I'm nervous. I don't know him. He thinks he knows me, but he doesn't.'

'Just go have fun,' she said, returning to her book. 'And take condoms.'

'I am CELIBATE, Megan.'

'Maybe you were yesterday,' she replied.

'Oh God,' I said. 'Don't. I'm only six months in. I'm not doing this because I want to fuck him. I'm doing this because . . .'

'You're allowed to want to fuck him,' Megan said. 'You're not bound by the laws of this journey of self-discovery to remove all sexual desire from your loins.' She lay back down. 'I've literally never known anyone give themselves as a hard a time as you do.'

I looked back in the mirror. 'I'm just trying to be a good human,' I said.

'You don't need to try so hard,' she replied.

*

On the way out of the convent, the seventeen-year old who'd told me about my blank-page-of-a-future, Chiara, stopped me.

'I'm writing about you,' she'd told me at lunch, teaching over with for the day. We'd done a 'love parade' through the centre of town, even stopping by the mayor's office. We'd written love notes to hand out to strangers and offered free hugs, and sang songs whilst holding up signs that said things like, You complete me, and I see you, and All you need is love. I'd gotten the idea from Giulio, after he gave a presentation in class, and Megan had teased me that I had love on the brain.

'You're writing about me?'

'For the camp website. I hope you'll like it.'

Chiara looked like my mother's best friend. Her confidence and determination was astonishing – but the older I get, the more I think confidence is the privilege of the young. We grow into fear when we comprehend how precious what we have is to lose. Chiara spoke impeccable English but with an American accent because she learned from How I Met Your Mother reruns. She wanted to be a doctor, and tended to take a leadership role naturally both in and out of the classroom.

'I just sent you the link on Facebook. Tell me what you think, please!'

'Oh, Chiara!' I said. 'I'm sure I will love it. I'll read it on the train.'

'Tell me what you think,' she repeated, and I headed on out, loading up Facebook on my laptop so that I could read it offline on the way.

They often say 'there is no way to happiness, happiness is the way', and our teacher Laura has surely found her way.

Usually people get lost when they think of happiness as a destination. Laura thinks of happiness as a mood, and she lives her life intensively saying, 'Yes!' to it every chance she gets.

There was a time when Laura was sad and she thought she would have felt the same way forever. Then she came to Italy and learnt that 'the more positive you are, the more positive things happen to you.'

She teaches us that 'saying yes to life' is a genuine way of life because you always have to be ready for the big opportunities the universe gives you.

She tells us to never stop dreaming because a dream is the greatest strength we have.

*I'm already a good human,* I thought, watching the countryside whizz by from the empty train carriage. *I'm already a fucking good human.* I gave myself a pep talk. *What if I act from a place where I believe I am worthy of this boy?* I wondered. *What would happen then?* I made eye contact with my reflection. *Treat it as a big experiment,* I thought. *Maybe you'll get a story out of that, too. Maybe you'll get a story out of already being a better person than you thought.*

# TWENTY-FOUR

I talked too much. Rambled. Got nervous about the silences that hung and so overstuffed them with anecdotes and unfunny jokes. We met in Sanremo, so some folks from the office joined us for lunch on the marina. Hal barely said a word. He was quiet and it unnerved me. Irish Stu and I mostly drove the conversation, swapping quips and stories, and it wasn't until we headed down to the beach as a three that Hal seemed to step back into himself, as I recalled him. We stood on the rocks and Irish Stu jumped off into the sea, taking a swim to the nearest shore ahead until he was only a wee bobbing head in the distance, leaving us alone together.

There was no sense of one-upmanship to the dynamic. To Hal and me. It wasn't a battle, like with Pete, or a seduction, like Chad. He asked a lot of questions – questions about the convent and the love parades and *padre*, and questions about my tattoo and my blog. He wanted to know me, and I wanted him to know me, too. It was . . . *nice*.

'This is,' I said. 'This is . . . you're good at this. Conversation. You're good at conversation.' Nothing came out right the first time, no matter how much I rehearsed comments to him in my mind. I couldn't practise my thoughts.

We both had sunglasses on, so I couldn't see his eyes. 'I accept the compliment,' he said, smiling. 'Especially because I'm trying so damned hard to impress you.'

'Shut up,' I said, giggling. *GIGGLING*. 'You are not.'

He laughed. 'Am too, ma'am. You're "Laura From Orientation". Do you know the pressure I'm under right now?'

I felt physically small beside him. He must have topped six-foot-something and had broad shoulders and a sturdy chest. So much of our talking was directed directly ahead. We didn't look at each other much. Standing and watching Irish Stu became sitting and watching Irish Stu, and with gazes fixed on the horizon we sat and time passed.

'Can I get personal?' he asked.

An Italian father wearing tight Speedos dove into the ocean beside us, splashing seawater on to our legs.

'Sure you can,' I said, admiring the man's sleek entrance into the water.

'You're celibate.'

'That sounds like a statement.'

He nodded. 'Well, yeah. I guess it is.' Eyes were straight ahead, still. 'You're celibate. I read it, on your blog. I'd sound disingenuous if I made out I hadn't read that.'

I'd written some posts from the convent about my decision to abstain from sex for the year. It helped me to clarify, to myself most of all, why I was doing it. I didn't feel deprived by my choice, or badly done by. It wasn't, if you'll pardon the pun, *hard*. Not having sex simply meant that instead of looking to people – to men – to recognise me as a desirable sex object, I was learning how to engage them as people, because I was asking to be treated as human, too. How to be respectful and kind, so that I got respect and kindness. That had a knock-on effect with my female relationships: other women weren't the competition, and there was so much more to talk about than just boys. Blogging about this was helping to inform new ideas about myself, especially after my time in Sanremo, and how incredible those weeks were. I had an outlet to put thoughts into coherent words about the thrill of being good at my work, of wanting to share my stories. It all added up to make me feel like more than one big massive clitoris: I had, it turned out, things to say.

'Okay, yeah. I'm celibate. Just for this year.'

'So, you're not . . . dating?'

'Urm. No. No, technically I'm not dating.' I wanted to add that I'd make an exception, for the right one, but I didn't know if that were true. I didn't know if he'd think I meant him. I didn't know if I *did* mean him. I didn't want to scare him off. I was scaring myself.

'That's really cool of you.'

'Thank you. I'm doing my best.' I felt super-awkward drawing attention to my sex life.

'There's a lot of pressure around sex. It can be a relief when that is off the table, you know? Like, it must leave room for a bunch of other stuff. Talking, and friendship, and – and do I sound really lame right now?'

'No!' I laughed, relieved he didn't think me totally ridiculous. 'Not at all. I agree,' I said. 'I would've before – thought it lame, I mean – but six months in and I don't. I agree. When sex comes back into my life it will be a bonus, but for now I don't miss it.' I thought of hat-wearing bananas and my girls in Sanremo.

He said, directly, 'Did he hurt you?'

'Who?' I said. 'My ex?' I didn't want to give him a name.

'You don't say online, really, why you're taking time off . . . men. But I figured—' He was getting frustrated with himself, unable to say what he really wanted to.

'Yeah, he hurt me,' I said, brushing invisible marks off my arms. The sun beat violently. 'But, I'm learning that we've all been hurt. That's the deal with trying, isn't it?'

The shape of the rock was digging into my bum and I was uncomfortable.

'You don't seem like you'd hurt easily.'

Irish Stu started to reappear, first as a blotch and then as waving arms.

'Because I'm no wallflower?'

'Because you're no wallflower.'

'I don't think he did it lightly,' I said, another piece falling into place. 'I don't think he did it lightly at all.'

'No,' said Hal. 'I'd imagine not.' Then he said, 'So, if you could be any mythological creature, what would you be?'

It was easy. Really easy. Fluid. I laughed a lot, but not from the belly, like I'd done as we danced in the piazza. I chuckled, amused by every other sentence, light and curious. He circled the conversation around to our emails, about how he'd read the archives of the blog and how seeing my perceived evolution had made him feel braver.

'It's nice to figure out you're the same in person as you are online, and that the person online was the same as the one who I met at orientation.'

I didn't know how to respond to that. The person online was a version of me. The cleverest version. The rehearsed one. I was writing more truthfully lately, but it didn't come easily. 'The online honesty thing is quite new, actually. I'm still learning how not to make everything into a funny anecdote.'

'Explain.'

'Just ... It wasn't always this way. I'm trying to like ... own my flaws.' I said it in a funny voice, embarrassed, and then added seriously: 'Will you laugh at me if I say I'm on a journey?' Irish Stu circled around the rocks where we lay.

'No,' said Hal. 'I think that's lovely.'

Irish Stu sensed, I think almost immediately, that he was interrupting something, although it was also interrupting nothing, and declared, hoisting himself out of the water, that he was going to buy an ice cream.

'I need to cool off,' I said, standing to assess the best way to clamber down into the sea. 'I've decided: I'm going in.'

'I'll come too,' Hal said. We padded to the flattest part of the rocks, where they lowered into the deep blue of the sea. 'Here,' he offered, 'take my hand.' I laced my fingers between his, and we jumped.

By the time I saw them get on to the bus back to Baiardo, Hal had relaxed enough to twerk through the glass as the bus pulled away. 'This was a day of magic,' he'd said, hugging me goodbye. 'You're magic.'

I squeezed him tight. 'You're more magical than you realise,' I said. 'And you have sand on your chin.'

He grinned and wiped it away.

'See – always making me better.'

'See you,' I said, smiling.

'See you soon,' he said, smiling too. 'I hope.'

*

'Shit!' I said to Calum, one week after my date with Hal. I'd hugged him for a full five minutes at the station. 'I don't know what to tell you. He made me feel all mushy inside.'

I picked up his bag and threaded my arm though his. He was passing through Sanremo for exactly twenty-four hours, en route to Switzerland, and I'd have a slice of the afternoon with him because then I had to get back to work at the convent. We had a schedule of conversation topics to cover and went straight to business. Time was of the absolute essence. 'Do you want *aperitivo*? Can I take you to my favourite *aperitivo* place?'

'Is that the thing with the snacks? I want the thing with the snacks.'

'It's the thing with the snacks,' I said.

We traversed the corner and stood at the road crossing. I'd missed my BFF – I hadn't seen him since leaving Derby almost a year ago. He'd never quite made it out to Rome to visit.

'Urgh, you disgust me,' Calum spat. 'Can you not put your arm so close to mine until I'm tanned too? It's humiliating.' He'd lost weight and had a new outfit I'd never seen before. He looked as handsome as ever.

'Oooooh, somebody doesn't like it when they're not the cute one,' I teased, heading over to the other side of the street.

'Give me two days and a bottle of olive oil,' Calum said, 'and the ranks will even out once again.'

I leant over and pulled his arm to let an aggressive *nonna* pass by behind us. 'Oooooff, the old ladies move fast here!' he said, leaving her plenty of room. We took a seat outside a favourite Red Shirts haunt and he stared pointedly at my tobacco as I flung it on the table.

'I know,' I said. 'Just this one last pack and then I'm done.'

'Two words,' he replied. 'Oral. Fixation.'

I ignored him. 'And one last thing about Hal.'

'Let's not start our reunion with lies, Laura.'

'Okay, this so won't be the one last thing about Hal, but just for now, I talked to him about David.'

A waiter came and I ordered for us in Italian, prompting Cal to say, *Show-off.*

'You talked to your crush about your ex-boyfriend? Well, your flirtation devices need work, you twat.' The waiter reappeared with a tray of snacks – mini pizza and mozzarella with oiled baby tomatoes. We dug in.

'No – it was nice.' I sliced into the *frittata.* 'He asked about him.'

'Pete used to ask about him.'

'Well, you said Pete was a good one.'

He took the other half of the omelette. 'He was. You missed a trick there, sweetheart.'

'Well. There's Hal, now. I mean. I barely know him, and he lives in America, and I'm celibate, and he leaves in, like, two weeks, but . . .'

'Laura. Enough. We're not playing this game, this time. He sounds like a good man. He sounds incredibly worthy of you.'

'Yeah,' I said, picking up tobacco to roll a smoke. 'He does, doesn't he?'

'So it's time,' he said, throwing candied almonds into his mouth.

'Time for what?'

'Come on, baby girl. You know.'

# TWENTY-FIVE

**To: Hallam Hart**
**From: Laura Jane Williams**
**Date: July 27th**

So, I'm in Sanremo with my Best Friend in the Whole Wide World, and we went paddling at the place you and I went with Irish Stu last week, and I told my Best Friend in the Whole Wide World all about the Day of Magic and you, and it made me sad that there's no date for further Days of Magic . . .

I wondered how I am supposed to know when you might be around because technologically speaking, you're off the map.

Let me know? xo

**To: Laura Jane Williams**
**From: Hallam Hart**
**Date: July 30th**

Hey! After I wrap up teaching here on Friday, I have two weeks to travel before my flight home. I have no experience in being a nomad, so I will need your expertise in order to make the most of my adventure. Help!

Please note that I may not have much access to technology in this part of Italy, but I **am** still an active member of the

smoke signal network, and pride myself on knowing the ways
of the carrier pigeon.

**To: Hallam Hart**
**From: Laura Jane Williams**
**Date: July 30th**

Here's the deal: I have a bunch of plans, and you don't have
any. So, hey! Make mine your own! Choice is yours . . .

– I'm still teaching the weekend after you finish. You could
  come to Loano for lunch? (Or forever?)
– Jo is coming to Loano next week – we'll be around til
  Thursday if you want to join us!
– On Friday I'm going to Geneva, til Monday, to visit my friend
  Emma. Come!
– After that I'm going to Baiardo for a week, to chill out before
  another round of teaching at the convent.

**To: Laura Jane Williams**
**From: Hallam Hart**
**Date: August 1st**

Yeah, okay – Geneva sounds good. What flight are you on?

**To: Hallam Hart**
**From: Laura Jane Williams**
**Date: August 1st**

I'm on the easyJet flight from Nice to Geneva at 13:50 on
Friday 10th, and return 20:10 on Monday 13th . . .

**To: Laura Jane Williams**
**From: Hallam Hart**
**Date: August 2nd**

This might be crazy but . . . I just booked it. See you on the train to the airport? Ventimiglia to Nice, right?

# TWENTY-SIX

I was going to Switzerland to cycle around a lake, with a boy I barely even knew, who agreed to do so on the exchange of fewer than five emails.

'I need to go shopping,' I said to Megan, showing her the email thread. 'I don't know what this is, but I want to be ready for it.'

'I'll tell you what this is.'

I frowned.

'It's your genesis. Not because of a boy, not because you're excited, but this happiness, this giddiness, this . . . *willingness*. You're unfolding, gurl. Don't you see it? Do you know what I'm talking about?'

I caught my reflection in the glass of the convent window, all wide, bright eyes and shiny hair and smiling face. I looked strong. Capable. Together. I was looking at my friend. I wasn't surviving anymore, I knew – I was thriving.

'I'm going to fall for him, aren't I?'

'Doesn't matter,' Megan said. 'Whatever happens, you're golden. You got this. Look at you.'

The last few days of camp dragged like a motherfucker. Megan and I passed the time observing the unfolding romances of the kids around us – six weeks of DREAMERSchool and we were ready for the break.

We'd introduced a game called *Secret Love*, where everyone at camp had pulled a name out of a hat, and was tasked with stealthily making that person feel special as all hell. It wasn't only in operation during class time, but throughout the whole of camp. All gestures had to be delivered in English, because when language is made fun you don't mind learning, and the point was, yes, to learn, but also to appreciate how to pay other people attention (teenagers are self-obsessed little shits, sometimes).

None of the kids wanted to play, really, when we first introduced it. They were shy and self-conscious. But then they started to take baby steps, until it snowballed into something thrilling. I first knew the tide had turned when, on the way to lunch, there were posters that said *Ilaria, You are amazing!* strewn across the light fixtures. After lunch, instead of the usual student presentation for the website, somebody asked for a montage video to be played. Giulio's secret love had collated footage of him goofing around and set it to music. He burned purple from across the room, but bounced out of the room later six feet tall.

Megan walked into her class to find a presentation board with a list of the reasons she was the 'Best teacher in the world', and instructions to hit play on the school laptop across the room. It was a video of kittens playing with bubbles, and even she said, 'I actually really do feel special.'

One of the girls found her bedroom door taped over with the lyrics to Bruno Mars's 'Just The Way You Are', and I got a handbag full of love notes, too. It was lovely. Love was lovely.

Some of the love even fostered genuine love. From the second or third day we'd noticed the dynamic between Valeria and Matteo. They always seemed to be sat next to each other, no matter what the activity. No big deal, just a quiet magnetism that meant they were so often in the same space at the same time. During drama games she'd look to him from the audience as he took to the floor, and a smile from her sent his performance into comedic overdrive, as if the only pleasure for the rest of all eternity was to hear her laugh. He'd return to his seat looking at her, and she at him, and nobody else existed.

'Matteo?!' squealed Valeria, at lunch. 'No, no! DREAMERSchool is only for two weeks, and then I must return to Milan and he to Rome.'

'So?' I said.

'I'm not that kind of girl,' she said.

At dinner one evening I said to him, 'Well? What are you going to do?'

'Oh nothing,' he said. 'She hates it when boys pretend to be her friend and then want to be her boyfriend. She told me.'

'That's interesting,' I said. 'Shall I tell you what I think?'

The eighteen-year-old said, 'You will anyway, I think.'

I laughed. 'I think she might be a little more afraid than you realise.'

Days passed and emotion visibly grew. There was a big final show put on for the public, and in their parts they were to play a couple getting married. I choreographed a sort of 1950s moment where she hooked her arm around his neck, and he could gently tip her back. Somehow, when we weren't looking, that had evolved into a kiss – she'd put her hand over her mouth, and they'd do a 'stage snog' that made us all giddy to see, even if it was only pretend. (And even though it was just pretend, I swear brown robes seemed to meander by at the exact moment, every time we practised. Every single time.)

On the day before the show we did a full run-through, including a rousing rendition of David Bowie's 'Heroes' to introduce the concept of Superheroes and Villains. As their scene approached there was laughter and sadness and giggling and seriousness, and then came The Dip. Only, instead of placing her hand over her mouth, Ilaria let her hand fall. Matteo bent down to her, in his arms, and in front of everybody they kissed, and we cheered.

'So that's romance, huh?' I said to Megan.

'That's romance,' she said.

I caught the train from Loano station, to head right up to Ventimiglia, where Hal would be waiting and then we'd hop on the train across the Italian–French border to Nice. I was wearing a blue dress that was a mix of cotton and a sort of heavy Lycra-type material, so it clung to my bum but was casual enough for daywear, and I'd dressed it down with brown flat boots that made me feel like G.I. Jane. My hair was in long, loose waves and I'd worn minimal make-up because I'd reasoned that lipstick on my teeth and chin was far more mortifying than looking a little plain. We were about to cycle around a lake, anyway, so he'd probably see me a lot worse.

'Hiiiii!' I said, waving slowly at him from one end of the train platform to the other. He waved back and smiled. He seemed . . . taller? We held eye contact as he stood where he was, still waving, and I tried to look nonchalant as I headed towards him. Everything moved in slow motion. The walk was endless. He stared and he stared and he stared. When I reached him, I went in for an Italian-style cheek kiss, and he went in for the American-style hug, and it meant I got caught up in his arms and we banged heads and he stepped back in surprise, but then forwards in concern that he'd hurt me, and as he did so he stepped on my toe – wrapped up in my fortified new boot, fortunately – and we leapt apart, stunned at such a violent greeting.

'Is that going to set the tone for our whole relationship?' he said, laughing, and I laughed, and then must've looked shocked because he corrected himself, 'Our whole trip. I meant to say, is this the tone being set for the whole trip? And our relationship. Because we are friends, and that is a relationship. And now I am being very weird.'

'Let's find the train,' I said, walking one way as he made for the other, and then we switched, and laughed, and I felt more stupid then I ever have. *Our whole relationship.*

We rode to the airport – twenty minutes or so – in vague silence, only murmuring formless pleasantries or apologising when our knees accidentally knocked or shoulders brushed. He kept his fingers tapping against the armrest, like he was preoccupied, and I pulled my phone out of my bag to check the time every thirty seconds or so.

'Gosh, I'm so tired,' I said, in lieu of anything else to say.

'Yeah,' he replied, bored. 'Me, too.'

It was a relief to see the airport come into view.

The thing about having learned to be alone, is that I became very good at it. Maybe I always was. I couldn't remember the last time I'd flown with somebody, and the luxury of it was heady. Hal watched my bag when I went to pee, and passed me the entertainment part of his international newspaper. Conversation was awkward and stilted, but the process of checking in, getting to the gate and then finally boarding the plane ensured we navigated our discomfort with silent gestures and so, by the time we landed in Geneva, I felt like part of a team. A very quiet team, but a team. A team of two.

We hopped on the airport shuttle into town, noting Switzerland's cleanliness and efficiency – the way everyone spoke English meant we didn't even have to ask 'Information' for help, and everything was so well signposted.

'I didn't even ask you how you know her,' Hal said, as we dumped our traveller backpacks in the luggage hold and found a seat for two in the middle of the bus, so that we could see everything going on.

'Emma? I met her maybe two years ago – through teaching. I was her teacher trainer a couple of summers back, and she knew one of the other Red Shirts from her hometown. I HATED her when we first met.'

'But you like everybody!'

'It's my job to seem like I do,' I explained. It was easier to chat as the scenery outside the windows changed. 'But, no. She was a bit over-the-top, like everyone at orientation is when they're trying to make an impression, me included, and determined to sort of . . . I don't know. We're both alphas, basically.'

'Have you had boyfriends at the company? Like, do you date the people you work with?'

He was only making conversation, driving us forward, and yet I faltered, 'I, urm . . .' In my imagination, I scolded myself for not answering his questions directly, like the grown-up I knew myself to be. But I couldn't get my tongue around words that told the truth, when my truth was complicated and fraught with stories I was embarrassed for this nice boy to know.

'Sorry, that was a bit personal. Don't answer it. Tell me about Emma.'

I swallowed and let myself talk quickly so that the subject wouldn't circle back around. 'I didn't see her again until the summer after we'd first met. We were placed at three or four weeks of camp in a row together. There were only five of us at the first camp and the other two girls there were both deadweights, so we sort of had no choice but to get to know each other otherwise camp wouldn't have run at all.' I smiled at the memory. 'She had an Italian boyfriend near Milan who she lived with when I lived in Rome, and we met up a few times, and now she's working at the U.N. here in Geneva.'

'Wow,' Hal said. 'You . . . you have a very . . . interesting life.' He stared out of the window as sunlight streamed across mid-level office blocks and fancy statues. 'You know very interesting people.'

I shrugged. 'Isn't everyone interesting?'

'Not everyone has friendships built across a million nationalities and several different countries,' Hal said. 'For some of us, this is our first time out of America.' He made me sound like more of an exotic creature than I was.

'Were you scared?'

It was his turn to shrug. 'Not scared. I was ready. I . . . I guess I knew there was more than just going crazy studying in New York, you know? It's an island of ambitious, cut-throat geniuses. I was kinda scared to leave my mom behind, though.'

'Have you got brothers and sisters?' I wanted to know what he looked like as a toddler and when he kicked his first football and who he took to prom and when he learned to drive. I wanted to know how he'd become who he was, because he was kind and gentle and good.

Hal imitated my accent, 'Harve-ewe-gawt-brothe-ers-aaaand-sisssters?'

I smacked his arm. 'Well, now you sound like a dumb yank,' I said. 'Because if you knew anything about anything you'd know I'm not posh. I'm common as they come.'

He leaned towards me. 'Is common like, lower class?'

'Common is lower class, yes. I'm clever and I travel but my accent is . . . regional, is the polite way to say it.'

'Like a redneck? We have rednecks. Chewing tobacco and having sex with their cousins?'

'I'm, like, halfway between that and the Queen.'

'Well. You seem like a classy broad to me.'

The way he said it made me blush. I couldn't be smart with him. I could only be myself.

'So, brothers and sisters?'

'Oh, do I have siblings? No. Well. I have a half-sister, from my dad's second marriage. But it's just been me and my mom most of my life, after Dad left.'

'You like her?'

'Like my mom? Sure! She's my mom. She's my bestie. I love her.'

'That's good,' I said. 'A man who appreciates his mother.'

'You'll like her, too,' he said, nudging my shoulder with his own. 'You'll get along.'

'If she raised you, sir, I'm sure we will.' My skin was tingling at the contact. I wanted to be pure for this boy. Untouched, untainted. Clean and without a history. I wanted to be the girl he would take home to Mother.

We hopped off the bus at the stop I had scribbled down on a scrap of paper, and took in the view. The sky was flawless and bright, the streets wide and lightly paved. It felt like room to breathe. There were few skyscrapers or high buildings, and trees lined every which way. The piazza we'd reached was right by the U.N., and we walked through water sprinklers coming up through the ground in pretty patterns, under a giant 'broken' chair that made for a great photograph, to pose in front of the flags of the world.

*Nations Unies*, the sign said. United Nations.

'Your friend must be hella smart,' Hal said.

'Almost as smart as me.' I shrugged. 'I hope you can keep up.'

He laughed, posing for another photograph as I snapped him, all turquoise T-shirt and snug jeans, boyish floppy hair waving about as he tipped his head back, gangster style, to pose.

'It's almost time to meet her,' I said. 'We should go wait at the spot she said.'

'Yes, ma'am,' Hal said to me, reaching out to put a hand on the back of my neck to guide me back to the bus stop. I wondered if we looked like boyfriend and girlfriend to other passing tourists.

We sat side-by-side on the wall beside the stop, watching everybody walk by. I didn't know what to say. How to keep talking. I went to take a breath, to comment on the weather, to say Emma had long dark hair, something – anything – and as I went to speak, finally, Hal said, 'It's really—' but I was already saying, 'She's got—' and the words tripped up over each other and we both stopped abruptly, catching eyes and then laughing, nervously. Shyly.

Silence lingered.

I watched an orange dress and near-black hair round the corner and said, 'There she is! There's Emma Rada!'

Em approached from the other side of the road, waving as she saw me, grown up as all hell and exactly like you want your U.N. interns to look.

'Hiiiii!' she said, coming in for a hug. 'So good to see you!' We squeezed one another before she stepped back and sized up Hal. 'Hey,' she said, extending a hand. 'I'm Emma.'

Hal met her hand. 'Oh, you're American! Laura didn't say you were American too.' He continued to shake her hand.

Still holding on to him, Emma said, 'Well, Laura hasn't said much about you at all – so we'll start from zero together.' I think she was trying to intimidate him, like all good girlfriends should do with the boys they meet.

A bus pulled up alongside us. 'Oh,' Emma said, releasing his hand and missing not one beat. 'We can get this one. Your airport tickets are still valid, if you're ready to go now?'

'Yes!' I said. 'I need to shower so bad. Let's go.' It was so typical of her to be efficient. Military. *Go go go.*

Hal helped me adjust my backpack on to my shoulders and I passed him the last pages of his newspaper, pages he'd been determined to bring off the plane with him, even though that seemed more a bother than anything else.

'You're right, I shouldn't have tried to bring this,' he said, and I laughed.

'D'uh.' He wrestled with the oversized pages, trying to fold them, and we followed Emma to get a seat. 'I'm always right.'

We shuffled down the aisle, letting Emma lead after holding up our tickets to the driver. Hal dropped his bag in the luggage hold and spun me around to help take off mine. He placed it gently on top of his, and as the bus began to move I grabbed hold of his T-shirt to steady myself. He headed for where Emma had already snaffled four seats that faced each other.

Emma's eyes whipped back and forth between us. 'So, you guys are dating?' she said. 'This is romantic?'

Hal looked at me, and then to Emma, and then to the floor. 'No!' he said, a little too enthusiastically, forcing my hand so that I echoed, 'NO!' with him, too. I was looking at Emma, pleading with her not to say things like that, feeling Hal's gaze on my neck but too heartbroken at his ready agreement to turn and meet his stare.

'No,' I said. 'I'm not dating, remember? Not for this whole year. Hal and me, we're mates, aren't we, Hal?'

He didn't answer. I commented on the lovely weather.

# TWENTY-SEVEN

We went to an outdoor showing of *The Princess Bride* by the lake that night, lying out on blankets and leaning on each other and picking at a quinoa salad we'd thrown into a big Tupperware, forks hitting each other as we dived in to feed. He kept whispering things to me, leaning in to point out another person who'd arrived in costume, or couples obviously on a date, nestled into each other like jigsaw pieces.

'They look so in love, look at them,' he said, his breath in my ear and my vision blurred because he was so charming, so inquisitive with Emma, so gracious to her friends, so gentlemanly to me. In the dark of the Swiss evening I knew: I had been waiting for Hal all this time.

Before we went to bed, Emma grabbed me in the kitchen and said, 'You like him, don't you? And he likes you? Did you bring your *boyfriend* to cycle this lake?'

'No,' I said. 'I don't know.' I kissed her cheek goodnight.

'I've literally never seen another guy so obsessed. He hangs on to your every last word.'

'He makes me want to be better,' I said. 'He's one of the good ones, don't you think?'

'I do think.'

'I'm still, sort of, learning what to do with the good ones.'

Emma said, 'I'm pretty sure you don't have to worry.'

\*

I set up the timer on my camera and made them pose with me.

'You literally have lived this past twenty-four hours through that camera lens,' complained Emma, holding on to Hal's NYU-T-shirt-clad back and staring right ahead at the impending flash. I put my hand on my hip and through smiling, gritted teeth said, 'I just want to remember, is all.' The camera clicked.

Hal ruffled his hair so it almost stood upright. He looked like a toddler not long woken up. 'You look like a toddler not long woken up,' I said.

'I'm not much of a morning person,' he grumbled.

'I am!' I cried. 'You're about to have so much FUN!'

'I hate you,' he said.

I got on the bike, and then fell off the bike.

'Okay there, England?' said Hal, 'You ever ridden a bike before?'

'Shut up,' I said. 'Of course I have. Just . . . well, this feels different.'

'It's a road bike,' said Emma. 'That's why. The tyres are way thinner. See? But you'll be okay. We'll walk to the edge of town instead of cycling through the traffic, and then it's wide open road for miles, and that's where you'll get the hang of it.'

Emma looked like a fitness model, tight and toned in her spanx and vest top, skin glowing from the reflection of her bright green sunglasses, hair all long and swishy in a ponytail behind her. Hal had the boyish jock look about him, all long limbs curving into low-slung basketball shorts. We all looked ridiculous in our helmets, but that was small solace for the lumbering and ineffectual idiot I felt struggling to ride the goddamn bike.

Emma's friend Reid joined us, a blonde fellow U.N. worker from North Carolina, another effortlessly sporty American who made me curse my country's lack of obsession with high school athletics.

'It's mostly flat,' said Reid. 'At least for today.'

And for the first two hours, it was. I figured out how to stay upright on the thin frame of my bike, understanding how to alter the gears to be a little higher than I needed because the resistance made it easier to pedal overall. I hadn't even looked up on a map where, exactly, we were going: I just knew we were cycling around a big body of water, and that it would take two days. Halfway there was a youth hostel we'd booked beds in for the night – another experience I'd never had before, but one that Emma assured me would be good for me.

It was about thirty degrees, the sky cloudless. We biked along a country road for miles and miles, with slow-driving cars giving us a generous wide berth. Either side of the road were swathes of green, lush trees, and to the right I caught glimpses of sun bouncing off water, glistening in invitation.

I had to keep up the rear. Reid took the lead, since she knew the way, Emma followed her, and Hal lingered, looking over his wide, muscular shoulder to wave and point at anything he thought was cool – which was a lot. Hal thought seagulls were cool. The donkey in the field. Rabbits.

'We're free!' he cried, freewheeling down a small hill. 'FREEEEEE!'

His enthusiasm excited me by proxy.

'Wow,' said Reid, as we dropped our bikes on a grassy verge to drink water and pee. 'We . . . we haven't come very far at all. This should have taken us about forty minutes, not nearly two hours.'

They didn't mean it nastily, but everyone looked at me. 'I can go faster,' I said, wandering off to find a loo. *I can't go faster*, I thought to myself. *This is as fast as I go.*

We went faster. And now, three, four, five hours into our cycle, there were hills. Big ones. Big ones that were HARD. It was embarrassing, mostly. Everyone would tootle on off ahead, and I'd rock up twenty minutes later, panting my way, purple, to where they'd pulled off the road to eat trail mix and take a break. Their break would be done when mine was just starting but, sensing everyone's eagerness to arrive at the hostel before darkness fell, I'd insist I didn't need any more time and hop right back on, forcing a smile and jazz hands so that Hal didn't think me a total Debbie Downer. If I had only been with Emma I'd have told her to have a great trip and hitchhiked back to Geneva to stay the night in her bed.

He dropped back as we arrived in Lausanne, matching my more leisurely pace to cycle side-by-side.

'This is incredible,' he said. 'Never in my wildest dreams did I think I'd end up cycling through Switzerland in my life – let alone this summer.'

'It's pretty cool, huh?'

'The coolest.'

We talked about the view and our family, the uncomfortableness of the saddles and what we wanted to achieve at work.

'You're gonna be some great big name one day,' he said to me. 'Your writing is . . . You're going places, kid.' I liked that he was proud of me.

'And you're going to China? Really, really?'

'Yup. Next year, to intern. I'll be there about six months.'

'I've never been to China,' I said.

'Come visit.'

'Is this the bit where I book a ticket based on five email exchanges?'

He looked at me, almost causing me to fall off the bike. 'I'm just following your example,' he said. 'Taking life by the balls.' In his boyish grin I saw a future. I saw a tiny Chinese apartment where we could roast vegetables and play Scrabble and host dinner parties. I saw him in my parents' living room, and at Calum's birthday party, and in Paris to visit Mary-Kate for the weekend. I saw him at my book launch, talking to my editor about the time we went to Switzerland together and he first heard about this story I was penning, and everyone in the literary world would think him a darling.

Not long after that he started to sing the chorus of Barbara Streisand's 'Don't Rain On My Parade', and we pulled into the car park of the hostel in rousing harmonies as we continued to work our way through show tunes of the ages. That's how it was with him: gratitude and song and silliness and answers to each other's questions. I couldn't help but make plans.

# TWENTY-EIGHT

The hostel was quiet and clean: unsurprising, given what I'd already learned about Switzerland. Emma yelled at the man at the desk over our reservation, which caused me and Hal to laugh hysterically and have to excuse ourselves, but she had somehow secured a private room for four: a set of bunk beds and two single beds side-by-side.

'Shotgun top bunk!' I yelled as we entered with our bikes, throwing it against the wall and climbing the ladder as Hal said, 'SHOTGUN BOTTOM BUNK!'

Reid shook her head. 'You two are literally the same person,' she said. 'Literally the same, childish, bonkers person.'

I was still in my cycling gear, getting my clean Swiss sheets filthy, but lying down felt so very good. I starfished as widely as I could and closed my eyes.

'Whatchu doin' up there?' Hal asked from below.

'Starfishing as wide as I can. Watchu doin' down there?'

'Starfishing as wide as I can.'

'I'm going to go shower,' said Emma.

'Me too,' said Reid.

I fell asleep, waking up to Hal shaking my arm. 'We have to get dinner,' he said, quietly, and I rolled over to face the wall. 'I'll buy you a Coke . . .' he said. 'Get upppppp . . .'

He pulled my shoulder, forcing me to roll back so that when I opened my eyes, he was centimetres away from my face.

It was seconds. Maybe even just one second. One single second of startled eyes meeting close, intimate, over the border, and the electricity of it was enough to make me sit bolt upright, narrowly missing hitting my head on the ceiling.

Hal used rudimentary high school French to order us dinner, including the Coke he'd promised. It was adorable, watching him struggle for the words, stuttering, trying to impress his table of ladies.

'So, Matt should arrive tonight, and we'll meet him for breakfast at eight a.m.' explained Reid. 'He has already cycled around the lake once today.'

'Your friend Matt has already cycled the whole way around a lake that is taking us two days to cycle?' I asked, failing to sound cool.

'Urm, well, technically once and then half again, since he'll carry on until the hostel.'

'Wow,' said Hal.

'Wow,' I said.

'Wow,' even Emma said.

Matt was beyond hardcore. Tall, agile and long-haired, he was exactly how you'd imagine a cyclist to look. He had all the right clothes, studded shoes and attitude: 'We *could* just go the road way,' he explained over granola and yoghurt and bread rolls and juice the next morning. 'But the vineyards are totally beautiful and worth the hills to get up there.'

'Well,' said Reid, 'how does that sound to everyone?'

All eyes fell on the weakest link in the chain. 'Lovely,' I said, wishing I felt less need to impress Hal with how 'up for it' I was about my life. Couldn't we skip to watching black and white movies in bed, already? 'You might have to be patient with me, but I'll get there in the end.'

Hal squeezed my shoulder. 'That's why we love you,' he said with a wink, and I didn't so much cycle the hills after that as float up them.

It was two days later when he told me properly. With the weekend gone Emma was back to work, and so Hal and I went off to explore Geneva's wide, paved streets and open cafés and the campus of the U.N. We ended up at a small 'beach' by the side of the lake and, since we had luggage with us, decided to shimmy into our bathing suits to paddle in the water. It was like being on the Sanremo shore all over again. I went left, he strayed left. He swam off right, I swam off right. We paddled and lay out and swam and ate overpriced doughnuts from the beachside stand.

We were in the water. We'd swum out a little, to the roped-off area, and were half holding on, half kicking our legs to stay afloat. My eyes were closed as we lazily chatted, soaking up the sun and his conversation, both. I couldn't tell you what we'd been discussing but then he said, 'I guess I feel bad, because there is kinda somebody back in New York?'

I thought I'd misheard him, because what he was saying made no sense. I opened my eyes and, blinking, waited for my penny to drop, to get it, but all I could comprehend was the way his intonation had risen at the end of his sentence, like a question. Like he wasn't sure of what he was telling me.

Slowly, I said, 'You have a girlfriend back in New York.' Mine wasn't a question. I looked just left of his shoulder, beyond him. Acted only half-interested. I knew any sudden movement would betray me and I wasn't sure how I would react if I didn't control myself. Had I hallucinated this whole trip? Could I truly have misunderstood so extensively that I'd made up his fondness for me? Was it because it had been so long since I'd been with a man? What the fuck?

'Not a girlfriend. I mean, I guess she kind of was?' Another question. 'But then with me travelling for three months, and we were only ever really dating, it wasn't . . .' The spaces between his words were loud.

'Why aren't you finishing any of your sentences?'

'Because I don't know how.' For the first time in our trip he levelled his gaze to me and didn't waver. He wasn't being shy anymore. He was searching my face for something, and I was impassive and cool and disappointingly unreadable because I wanted to scream in humiliation.

'You've never mentioned her before now,' I said, holding eye contact, brow relaxed, mouth in a straight line. A challenge. The old Laura.

'I know,' he said. He seemed sad, but I didn't want to know any more. I had a million half-formed thoughts muddying my mind, not least of which was how I was competing with the unknown once-a-fucking-gain. AGAIN!

'Do you think we've drunk enough water today?'

He crinkled his forehead, confused at the change of topic. 'Urm, no, probably not?' His uncertainty about everything – her, me, our fucking hydration – was maddening.

'I'll go buy us a bottle. It's not good to be out in the sun without keeping on top of fluids.'

*Of course he has a girlfriend,* I thought, swimming away from him. *I'm so fucking STUPID.* I was furious. He should've fucking told me. I had deserved to know this. I had deserved to be met by him as earnestly and honestly as I'd presented myself because isn't that what this had all been for? To fix myself enough that I might fall in love with somebody new, and be loveable in return? I got the water and by the time he came out of the lake I was back-to-business with my poker face on. We didn't talk about the non-girlfriend again. I think he was too scared to bring it up, given my frostiness, and I sure as hell wasn't going to.

'Did something happen?' Emma whispered, side-eying Hal ordering three beers at the bar. 'You've not smoked this whole trip, and now you're asking strangers for a spare Marlboro.'

I shook my head. 'I just fancied a smoke, is all,' I said. 'I'm tired of being a good girl. You know what I'm like.' Emma raised her eyebrow. 'And, I'll only have one. I just need a fix.'

I'd made a decision, and that decision was to totally ignore what Hal had told me. Forget it. Pretend it had never even been said, really, for the basic fact that it would spoil our fun and it didn't have to because all of this felt too good to deny. My insides were in turmoil. I felt woozy and confused and: I'd fallen in love. In the exact moment he told me there was somebody else I knew. He was telling me too late, because I had already made the leap. I couldn't care that he 'sort of' had somebody in New York. He had me, here, now. And I knew he felt the same. His actions spoke one hundred million times louder than his words. It was his actions I trusted.

*Fuck him,* I thought, scanning the crowd for a smoker I could bum off. *Fuck him to hell.*

'We've got exactly twenty-three minutes before we have to go catch our bus,' he said, as he reappeared clutching three 1664s.

'Well then,' said Emma, raising her glass in toast. 'Here's to reunions all over the world, and making new friends, too.'

'Here, here,' I said, downing my glass in two big gulps. Hal slipped his arm around me. I let him.

The plan was to catch a late-night flight back to Nice, and then walk around the city for the night until the first trains across the border and back into Italy started up, so that we could head up to Baiardo where we'd get free accommodation and food in one of the company's houses. We showered at the airport, changed clothes so we were a little warmer, and set off to find bread, cheese, and a cosy spot to take turns napping.

'They're on a date,' Hal said, pointing at a couple a little closer to the shore, sharing a blanket just like we were, drinking beer – just like we were. 'They look happy.'

'What isn't there to be happy about?' I said, shovelling blue cheese dip and crusty baguette into my mouth. 'This is a certain kind of heaven.'

Hal smiled, reaching for a cherry tomato off the vine. 'Food, candlelight, and good company? Mine too,' he said. 'This is my heaven too.'

It dropped really cold, really quickly, and it didn't feel safe snoozing on Nice's rocky beach, exposed to the elements and the unsavoury night crawlers who were appearing in droves. We walked around, watching some skateboarders and listening to street musicians – Hal grabbed my wrist and we twirled around, bags strapped to our backs, beer cans in hand, following the lead of the other to dance slow circles around our moon-cast shadows.

We sat on a bench on the promenade as the clock went from midnight to 1 a.m., 1 a.m. to 2 a.m. My head was on his shoulder, his arm over my back. A club nearby must've let out, because a throng of drunken French people stumbled out past us in a flurry, and the noise of it, the interruption to our silence, was enough to make us break towards a private part of the beach to hide behind the lifeguard tower, where there was less wind and sunbeds that we could move to lie out flat. Bags stashed underneath our heads, we looked up at the stars.

'I'm sorry about before,' he said, finally. I didn't say anything. 'The thing I'm most afraid to tell you, even more than that, is that . . .' I could hear him mentally coaxing himself to just say the damned thing. 'Well. The thing is: I'm a virgin.'

His voice came from the darkness, as we lay side-by-side on a double lounger, barely touching but breathing each other's air.

'You are?' I said, turning to face him.

He turned to face me too. 'Yeah.'

The waves lapped cautiously against the stony shore, cast in centre spotlight by an almost full moon. I said, 'On purpose?'

He was so handsome. So chiselled and demonstrative with his emotions. So friendly and welcoming and inviting. 'I just . . . never found the one I wanted to lose it to, I guess, and then all this time passed . . .'

I knew whatever I said next was important. This was a watershed moment. I had his trust; I knew this wasn't something he was telling me easily. He didn't seem ashamed, embarrassed – not that he needed to be either of those things – but he searched for clues in my face self-consciously. 'Is that why, you know – is that why you asked about me being celibate?'

'Yes.'

'Because then you knew I wasn't expecting to sleep with you?'

'Yes.'

'Because you . . .' I was dying inside as I said it. 'Because you didn't want to sleep with me?'

'You make it sound bad,' he said. 'But I don't know a bigger compliment to give you.' His nose was almost touching my own. 'It feels safe. With you,' he said.

'Because you're a virgin, and I'm celibate?' I whispered.

He smiled, and I melted. 'I don't know what I'm trying to say.'

I closed my eyes, rolling on to my back.

'Thank you for telling me,' I said.

'Thank you for understanding,' he said.

We fell asleep, shrouded in our new intimacy, little fingers wrapped around each other. I don't know how much time passed, but a security guard came later, at some point, and told us to move along to the unfenced section of the beach. The morning light failed to take our secrets with it, and I looked at him differently in the day, with what I knew now. I looked at *us* differently – the celibate old maid and the young, untouched virgin.

Having been a teacher there, arriving in Baiardo I was like a celebrity, with my new full name becoming 'Laura From Orientation'. I overheard two twenty-year-old Canadians say through an open window, 'Yeah, Laura From Orientation is here with Hal, that cute NYU guy.'

'Ohmygod, he's *so* cute,' the other said.

'Did you hear that she used to be really slutty, though? Like, everyone thinks she's this amazing, lovely girl, but if you ask anyone from before this year about her they all say the same: big, company, ho.'

I suppose that would've hurt my feelings had I not spent all that time telling myself worse.

Being a little senior on staff meant I was able to sweet-talk my way into a room in one of the empty houses down the hill, but Hal was put up in the biggest house at the top, where there were six or seven other tutors. Because most camps were suspended over *Ferragosto*, the Italian bank holiday in the middle of August, there were about thirty of us – including friends of Irish Stu, who ended up bedding down in the same house as me, though I stood my ground on keeping a room for myself. It was the first time in months I hadn't been forced by circumstance to share the space where I slept. I looked forward to masturbating.

Hal and I attracted a wee posse – the Irish guys and us, plus a Canadian girl who'd had her first lesbian fling at camp. We took walks together and sat around the dining table playing Bananagrams, making sure to break at exactly 3.30 p.m., when the local shop was open for exactly ninety minutes and we'd stock up on cheap wine and warm beer. I had a list of movies I should watch, given to me by Giulio back at the convent, so we'd nap together like puppies and push beds together to watch old black and white films, like I one day hoped we would.

'Oh? You're not shagging him?' said one of the Irish lads one night, as Hal bid me goodnight and made to walk up the hill with some of the others.

'Dude!' said Hal. 'That's not cool.'

'I really thought you two were,' he whispered, quieter this time. 'Does that mean you're single?"

'That's not cool either, bro!' Hal said, over his shoulder, and I liked him laying claim to me. I liked that he'd forgotten about whoever was back in New York. It made me think this didn't have to end badly.

# TWENTY-NINE

For a small town, Baiardo knew how to celebrate. A stage went up in the tiny town square and as night fell there was a pop-up bar selling plastic cups of what can only be described as 'alcohol' for one Euro fifty. After a group dinner of pasta and pesto, plus a few bottles of that cheap wine we'd stocked up on, we got wind of the event, and scrambled to the marketplace to see what was what.

'OHMYGOD THERE IS DANCING!' I squealed, excitedly, and within seconds was peeling off the jeans I'd put on under my dress, because Baiardo could get cold when all you were doing was sitting in old buildings looking at the moon.

We joined the locals in the dimly lit arena, and for the first time in a long time I felt young and untethered. I took everything so seriously – myself most of all. It was a relief to dance and turn and laugh as Hal sashayed with a woman old enough to be his great-grandmother, and the others all did dirty bump'n'grind club dancing to the cheesy hits being played in a language hardly anyone understood.

There are photographs of that night. I found them the next morning on my camera. They progress from staged shots out on the balcony as I yelled at everyone to pose nicely, to us all sat around the table at dinner, and then playing cards and finishing off bottles afterwards. We'd all thrown our belongings on a table as we'd danced, including my camera – everything being safe, of course, in a town of barely 300 people. There were pictures of parts of faces not my own – selfies gone wrong of drunken English tutors eager to use whatever was to hand to document their own hilarity. Slices of ears and tops of heads. I vaguely remember somebody telling Hal and me to smile, outside somewhere, maybe on the balcony, and there was one snap of us, his cheek pushed up against mine, both of us tanned and glowing from Swiss air, limbs wrapped around each other, bright-eyed and smiling, waiting to be framed on a mantelpiece.

Then came the dancing shots. A stream of five photographs of Hal and me on the dance floor. In the first one there was a toddler, maybe three or four, watching us from a distance as Hal dips me back in his arms, ballroom-style. Neither of us is looking at the other. In the second one, though, I've been pulled back up, and am in close. I'm looking up at him, his hand on the small of my back, firm and guiding, and he is looking down at me. He is looking down at me like I am the only woman in the world, and nobody else exists, just me, and him – a world in itself where the camera doesn't lie. That look doesn't break for the rest of the dance.

As a new group of tutors arrived at the houses, pushing our number up to almost fifty, it was easy to be distracted from whatever it was we were doing together. Not that Hal and me left each other's side, of course: the films and the leaning and the walks and the talking didn't stop, it's just – I didn't analyse it. The days were lazy and blurred into each other comfortably, until it was our final night before I had to go back to the convent, and he to America.

I wanted to get him alone. To somehow cement the time we'd had together. To conclude this properly. By the time it got to midnight at the final dinner out on the terrace, I knew I had to make a move. It was all I could do to pull on his shirtsleeve from where he was telling an overly animated story to a gay man, and say, 'I'm leaving now.' The gay guy looked at me, gleefully, winking bitchily that he was grateful for my departure.

I made the rounds, saying goodbyes to old and new friends, and as I went to leave he said, 'Wait. Let me walk you home.' The gay guy's face fell. I saw the two Canadian girls exchange glances.

'You – you don't have to do that,' I said, and he interrupted me to say, 'Come on.'

We walked in silence to the path leading to my house. The old ruins of the church were lit up from the underside, casting shadows on our faces and hiding the emotions in our hearts.

The words stuck in my throat.

I didn't know what to say. How to start. How to suggest that, maybe, this was a something, and I was leaving, and he was leaving, and perhaps that didn't have to mean the end of whatever this was. That I hadn't meant to fall in love – that it was an error, a misjudgement. I thought it would be different. That we could just have some fun. I didn't mean for it to get so filled with gravity. I didn't mean to have never kissed him, to have not told him.

'You've changed my life,' he said, pulling me to face him, putting his hands on my shoulders. 'Do you know that? Do you know that by being you, I've been the most me I ever have?'

I stared at the ground.

'You're the most remarkable woman I have ever met. I don't know whether to be intimidated by you, or more like you, or marry you. This has been the summer of my life. Of my dreams. And it's because of you.'

I scuffed at the dirt with the toe of my shoe.

'I love you,' he said, pulling my chin up with his hand.

I looked at him. It was all I had wanted to hear. All I'd needed to hear. I loved him too. I loved him too, so lightly and honestly and truthfully and real, and yet . . . The words. I couldn't. I was terrified. I was at the final hurdle, the bit where it all feels so good. And he had somebody in New York, was the reality. How could he want two of us? I couldn't do it. I couldn't be the second choice, the other one. I'd come too far, respected myself, now, far too much to let him play me for a fool.

And so I said, 'See you,' hitting his shoulder playfully with my fist, turning to walk home alone. 'Get home safe.'

# THIRTY

An inbox of ghosts waited for me back at the convent. Two weeks' worth of correspondence equalled ten per cent junk mail, twenty per cent work-related missives and overwhelmingly almost two-thirds men I had shagged or had wanted to shag at some point in my past.

As I got older I was beginning to learn that that a hefty amount of my history relies on me staying reassuringly single. News of professional success can make its way to the eyes and ears of people I know, from school friends to university peers, to other writers, blog followers and folks online, and often I get a wave of support that sees old flames, if we can call them that, skip the chance to congratulate me. They just don't bother. But when those same old flames – apparently, we are calling them that – get a whiff of my relationship status altering to one that might put me off the market, they're the first ones to reach out. They don't want to be with me, but it seems there is comfort to be had from knowing that I'm not with anybody else. That's how it feels, at least. The fact that photos had sneaked up on-line while I was away, uploaded by folks not me, and now I had a bulging inbox before me, suggested the theory was, in fact, not without merit. Everyone wanted to know who Hal was.

The first note was from Pete, a face I hadn't thought of in weeks. It said, simply, *I'm buying that tan a beer when you're next around.* I got an immediate reply to my question, *Do you still have a girlfriend?* He said, *Yes.* I told him to leave me alone.

The only 'proper' friend I ever crossed the sex line with emailed to say he'd be in Sanremo soon. He was sorry, he said, for not being in touch before. *Even my dad complains that I need to email more*, he said. I replied: *Yes, but you didn't have sex with your dad the last time you saw him, did you?* I was, it seemed, ready to start staking a claim on my boundaries.

There was a note from an electronic penpal, a guy I'd worked a camp with years before and with whom I exchanged sporadic emails about love and philosophy and favourite TV shows, but – I barely processed it. I barely processed it because I saw Elizabeth's name. The same Elizabeth who'd told me David and Gwen had become a couple. There was no subject heading, but I knew what she was going to tell me before I opened it. That's why I left it until last.

'Hey beautiful,' Megan said, arriving back at work after her own vacation. She had a small overnight bag with her and nothing else. Dropping it to the ground, she said, 'You already all up in your routine?'

She hoisted herself up on to the low wall opposite me, folding her legs into herself.

'Megan?' I said.

'Oh God – did Switzerland not work out like we hoped? I saw the photos on Facebook and, fuck, you guys were just the cutest. I presumed . . .'

I couldn't look at her. 'Megan, I'm about to know something I do not want to know, and I'm going to need you to be very gentle with me afterwards. Okay? I think I am two hundred per cent about to lose my shit.'

'Okay,' she said, her tone reflecting my own. 'I will just sit right here, with you, and do whatever you tell me to.'

'Thank you,' I said. 'I'm probably going to do that emotion-sickness thing I do, and then need beer. Lots of beer.'

I hit the email tab and took a long, deep breath.

Hey it read. *I saw on Facebook that you've been travelling all over. You look really happy – who is that cutie in the photos?*

*I just wanted to let you know that they have a date: they get married a week on Saturday. I thought you'd want to know. I'd want to know.*

*Love you, and I'm here if you need me.*

*Ibby x*

'Megan?' I said, looking at the sky above her head.

'It's happening, isn't it?'

I rubbed my temples, and scrunched up my eyes against what I'd just seen.

'It's happening. They really are getting married.'

Earlier in the summer I'd caught a *color* crying in the bathroom at DREAMERSchool.

'What happened?' I said.

'I'm sad,' she replied.

'Why?'

'Because everything is changing and I'm scared that the things that are important can't come with me.'

In my voice, with words that came from somewhere other, I replied, no hesitation: 'It's funny. The things that are truly important have a way of sticking around. And the things that don't make it? Not so important.'

Her disbelieving face came to me as I snapped shut my computer.

\*

When we were sixteen he bought me a Frank Sinatra album and filled the lyric booklet with rose petals. At seventeen he wrote me a poem, a poem he'd performed as a drama piece for our Theatre Studies exam, written about me, for me, from him. It came in a frame and was written in his own hand. At eighteen, it was a small wooden box, designed as a place to keep our memories and engraved with my name. In it I stashed ticket stubs and the pressed petals, notes left on pillows and photographs of trips to France and India, on the back of elephants in Thailand and in front of temples in Cambodia. When we were nineteen, he'd gone skiing with his family for a week. I told him not to call because I'd miss him too much – I hated to be apart. When he didn't call for eight days, I was devastated and incensed. *He's forgotten me,* I thought. The day he arrived home so did nine letters, all at once, postmarked from *Val d'Isere*. He'd written me a love letter every day of his trip, and missed me as much as I missed him. He slipped me books we'd read about in the culture section of the paper, bought tickets to Joss Stone gigs and the Buena Vista Social Club when both were cool. He never asked me *where* I wanted to go out to eat, he'd ask *what* I wanted to eat, and then he'd call our favourite places to see if they had it on the menu that night. David had, since before I understood it, worshipped me. Loved me better than any first love could've, and it set the bar so very high. I wasn't mad at him for moving on, for loving somebody new. I'd loved him harder than anyone else in my life, and I wanted him to be happy. He was. He was getting married. He had a whole new adventure to pour his love into, and I was left behind, my hands full of adoration and love and long-ing, and totally terrified of where to put it.

I sat with my eyes closed and leaned against Megan's arm. We'd been there for a good half hour, smoking and rolling another, smoking that and rolling another. From outside the convent walls we watched three grimy-looking southern Italians knock on the oversized door. They carried gifts: for one, a small box that looked as though it carried cakes, for another a simple flower. Just one. The third, a woman, stooped low with a shawl covering her back, neck and head, could barely support herself on the walking stick she dragged along the ground. Nobody came to answer their knocks and, as my smoke burned down so that I could feel the heat on my fingertips, I jumped up and walked across to them.

'*Poi auitare?*' I said. *Can I help?*

I struggled to understand them. They spoke in a lot of dialect, but their eyes were fluent in discontent. I understood. '*Va bene,*' I said, '*Va bene. Veni con mi.*' I opened the door with my stupidly large key and motioned for them to come through.

'Are you coming back?' said Megan, as I went to get help.

'Just give me a minute,' I said, grateful for the distraction.

I was furious with myself. Furious that I had run away from Hal like a mute teenager, and furious for not finding the courage to say, *A girlfriend? Really?* I was everybody's second choice – or, at the very least, never a strong enough contender to be somebody's first.

'I just wanna ask,' she said, as we lay on the cold tiles in our shared room – Lucifer, the heatwave, causing sweat to pool in my bra, 'are you mad about the wedding, or about Hal?'

I rolled an unopened can of ice-cold Coke across my stomach, and then my forehead. It felt like my blood was on the boil. Lucifer was getting stronger and stronger, hotter and hotter.

'Fuck if I know,' I said, letting the condensation roll down my skin to the ground. 'I'm mad at all of it.'

'What happened in Switzerland?'

'I fell for him.'

'And then?'

'And then I was scared.'

'And then?'

'And then I carried on falling, even after he said there is somebody – not a girlfriend, exactly, but a girl – back in New York.'

'And then?'

'And then he said he loved me when we said goodbye, and I didn't say it back.'

'You're full of all this love to give, but you didn't want to give it to him?'

'It's the fact that I was so bloody petrified to give it to him that made me realise how desperately I wanted to. But. I couldn't. I just couldn't.'

'Oh honey,' said Megan. 'Oh, honey, honey, honey.'

'I don't know what I'm trying to achieve,' I said, sitting up to pull the ringer on the Coke to take a long slug. 'The shagging around, the not shagging around, the up and the down – surely it isn't supposed to be this fucking complicated?'

I finally got back to my penfriend. He'd emailed me to say, *What are your views on love?* It was timely, and a bigger question than I could tackle.

I sat down to write my riposte. I stood up and went for a walk to get ice cream instead. I put off returning to the convent by letting the barriers fall in front of my face at the train tracks, instead of breaking into a jog to cross before the carriages blasted by. I was grateful for the delay – so grateful, I let it happen twice.

Hands sticky from Nutella *gelato* drips, an hour after I first left I returned, marvelling at the new route I had discovered as I deliberately drew out my return. I took a deep breath and wrote my ending before my beginning, because that seemed like the best place to start.

> *This is why I needed to walk before I sat down to write. My reticence in penning any of this has roots in my changeability. I so long to be the girl who understands who and what she is, what she stands for, is reliable and constant. But that is absolutely not me. To borrow from Zadie Smith: Ideological inconsistency is practically my doctrine – a discourse on what I once believed, what I understand now, and how I hope to unpack the mental boxes still unknown means I'm forever unfinished business. Isn't that exhausting?*

I was exhausted. Exhausted that even now, after all this time, I thought about getting dumped and feeling humiliated and struggling to move on. Three years is a long time. I let the different parts of my personality battle it out.

*Nobody wants to listen to this self-pitying bull.*

*He doesn't even remember who you are anymore.*

*People break up all the time. Why do you think your broken heart is so special?*

And then, inexplicably, the kind voice in my mind spoke louder than all the rest. *There's no set way to get over anything,* I whispered to myself. *Write to see what you say. It's okay. Go on. You've got this.*

I did as I'd instructed myself.

*I see hope at the end of my rainbow,* I wrote slowly. Deliberately. *I can't ever promise anybody that I will love them forever, but goddamn it I'll promise them I'll try, every day. I'm ready to experiment with myself and see how it feels to give 100 per cent. They tell me it's quite the experience. It's been so long I don't think I remember. I'd like to be reminded.*

I was looking forward. I liked hearing myself be generous. Allowing room for hope. Never mind three years being a long time – for the lightness I suddenly felt, that feeling of achievement, I would've waited three years more. I could've run marathons with the energy that burst through my soul.

I might've missed my chance to tell Hal how I felt in Baiardo, but that didn't alter the fact that I loved him, too. I'd worried for so long that nobody would want me again that when they did, when it sneaked up on me in the middle of a year-long vow of celibacy, when I wasn't supposed to be dating at all, it panicked me.

*What to do?* I wondered. What to do.

# THIRTY-ONE

I woke up before my alarm. Sunlight crept through the gap in the wooden shutters to the balcony, and I rolled over to see Megan lying mummified in her bed sheet on her side. It was worse with my eyes closed than with them open: my imagination was darker than the off-colour ceiling. *She'll be waking up, too,* I thought to myself. *I'll bet her dress is hanging in the bathroom, and her sisters will bring her breakfast in bed.* It was as if I was there, sat with them: the only blonde in a row of black-haired beauties in matching silk dressing gowns, sat breaking bread at the table of her family home. She'd get ready there, I knew, same as I knew her sisters would indeed be the brides-maids – and his sister, too. I forgot about Holly. Holly, who would've been *my* bridesmaid if the story had been different. Holly, his younger sister by less than a year who I taught how to shape her eyebrows and pedicure her toes without getting polish in the cuticles. Holly, who I'd stayed up with on quiet nights at the family house in France, chatting about the boy she was head-over-heels for, and how it was okay that she didn't know what she wanted to do with the rest of her life. She was a sister to me, too. I'd fought for that relationship: we didn't get on for years. Not really. And then, suddenly, we did, because it seemed obvious we'd be sat around dinner tables and spending Christmas together for the rest of our lives. His family had been mine: I hadn't just lost him, but his mum and dad, his brother and his sister.

I wondered if she was relieved that, in the end, she got a different sister-in-law. One who didn't worry about things like eyebrows and toenails.

I closed my eyes, breathed heavily, and made a decision as old as time: to, in the face of adversity, paint on my brightest smile, and treat myself. I'd slip out for breakfast before class started. Saturday didn't mean much at DREAMERSchool, so it was business as usual in the convent. Megan would be in bed for another hour, and so I crept around the room slipping on trousers and a shirt, running a brush through my hair and a mascara wand across my lashes.

It was stupid to check my emails before leaving. I don't know what I expected to find. And yet, I knew it would be there. A reminder. The last tether. I needed that. I needed somebody who knew us both to reach out on this day to say, *You haven't been forgotten.* I hadn't realised that's what I'd been hungry for: acknowledgement. How many of our friends would be stood clapping and cheering and throwing confetti for the happy couple, my face never once crossing anybody's mind? I'd been so committed to building my new self that I hadn't heard the echoes in my mind suggesting that in David and Gwen's new life, I didn't exist. I was nobody. To be never considered at all is far more hurtful than to be considered badly.

It was an email from Carol that did it. I'd worked for Carol in restaurants across the North Yorkshire area, where I'd grown up and gone to high school, since I was sixteen years old – since I legally could. She was ten years older than me, and represented everything I thought womanhood should be: independence, class, glamour. She liked me, because I was good at my job and took on all the extra shifts she offered me. When I was saving up for a trip to Sri Lanka at eighteen, and then for further travels with David, she let me work like a dog, disappear for months, and then come back to pick up right where we'd left off. She'd seen me fall in love with David, and he'd worked for her for a while, too. She knew Gwen, who'd worked Saturday shifts throughout sixth form. Most importantly, Carol had been in a relationship with our boss, who then went on to marry another restaurateur in the area. Carol knew what it was to watch a man you had loved make another his bride. I'd thought her weak at the time. A little pathetic. When a man doesn't want you, you head on out to find one who does, I thought. Little did I know.

*I just want to say*, she wrote, *that you're being thought of today. You haven't been forgotten. Everything you feel is totally valid – totally okay. This may not be where you thought you'd end up, where you'd be or with the one you imagine it all with, but try to find thanks for that. Get yourself good girlfriends, and a bottle of prosecco, and raise your glass to this adventure. To this wild, wild ride. And know that I'm sending so very much love to you today. Every day. Even if it doesn't feel like it this morning, I promise you: you'll be fine.*

I didn't start crying until I'd ordered my cappuccino and croissant. I sat outside in the piazza, only 8 a.m., the heat already creeping into the day with force, Lucifer angry and proud, and a loud, clear thought crossed my mind: it all really happened. I really did love that well, and was loved that well, and it didn't work out. *He really is marrying somebody else.*

I burst into heavy sobs that I tried to swallow down with my coffee. I saw an entire life that would not be mine. Not now. I saw the marquee I thought we'd have in the garden at the house in France. My uncles dancing with his aunts. His cousin – she'd never be my flower girl, and I'd never now be the daughter-in-law to hold his mother's hand when we helped Holly try on her wedding gown one day, too. I wondered if his mother still used the bags, earrings, skirts I'd bought her for Christmas, for birthdays, to say thank you. I wondered about his dad.

There was always an unspoken fear about his mortality because David's granddad had died in his fifties, and his great-granddad too. It was a fear I held as if he were my own blood. My own dad. His baby brother, no longer a baby – he'd come to me and show off about his lasagna from cookery class every week, impressing his brother by impressing his brother's girlfriend. I'd watched Tom grow up. Watched him enter high school and then leave high school, too.

I don't know if the pain came more from him leaving me for her, or from the knowledge that they would have a marriage far better for him than I would've provided. Part of the pain came from knowing, despite every protestation I'd made, that this was exactly right. That it had unfolded exactly as it should've done. This wedding had never been mine to have.

'Oh, HONEY,' said Megan, as I walked back into our shared room. 'Why didn't you wake me?'

'I didn't know it would feel like this,' I said, biting at my bottom lip, face damp. 'I thought I'd be okay. I didn't know.'

We went to teach our three hours, and then I crawled back into bed, where I slept for the rest of the day, the curtains pulled shut and the heat rising.

It was hot in the darkened room, even though it must've been 6 p.m. already. I hadn't woken up once. As soon as my head hit the pillow I'd collapsed into dreamless, empty slumber. I didn't know what else to do. I was exhausted from crying, and the only way I knew to forget was either to get blind drunk, or nap. All monks considered, I took the nap. I took the oblivion of sleep.

'They're married, now,' I said to Megan, who lay behind me, spooning me tight. 'He gave her his name.' I closed my eyes. 'They're husband and wife,' I said. 'Mr and Mrs.'

Megan didn't say anything. That's an admirable trait in a person: knowing when to stay quiet. Knowing when to let the other person talk. 'Married,' I repeated.

Megan rubbed the top of my arm, and I leaned into the sympathy of it. Air hung greedily to our skin: it was humid, and sticky. I didn't want to inhabit my own body.

'Have you got any tobacco?' I said, eventually. 'I need a smoke. I always need a smoke.'

We plodded to the balcony of our room – a balcony that opened up on to the flat roof above the kitchen. We rolled cigarettes and sat back against the window. The sky was overcast, grey; the heat oppressive. Cloud kept in the temperature, and it was suffocating. The weather felt like my mind, overbearing and heavy.

'I didn't know I had been waiting for this day, all this time. I half-expected it not to happen. Half wanted it not to happen. I'm haunted by them both and it's mortifying because they'll never, ever think of me.'

'I know,' said Megan. 'This must hurt so, so bad.'

'I cannot feel this way anymore,' I said. 'This is it: it's done. They are married. Married. If any part of me thought that, maybe, this was all a hoax, or that he'd change his mind and come back to me, that's done, now.

'I think that's why I did it – why I trod water in my own life for all this time. I was holding my breath for him to save me. But he's not coming back to me. He's eating steak and having his first dance. He doesn't remember me. I have to forget him, too. Not just pretend to, but actually do it. Move on. Stop running from place to place to place reinventing myself and buying time before we could be back together. I need to choose a plan. Choose myself. Go to London and try to sell this book and the next time I fall in love with a boy I am going to tell them. I'm not going to hold back in case David decides he wants me after all. I'm not keeping free, open . . .

'God,' I said. 'I'm so much more than somebody's ex-fucking-girlfriend.'

In seconds clouds had rolled in off the hill and sank low above us in the sky.

'This,' said Megan, 'is it. This is your moment, Laura. This is your declaration.'

'You've been so patient with me,' I said. 'Thank you.'

'What are friends for?' She smiled.

We rolled another smoke.

'Gah!' I howled, upwards, to the hidden moon. 'I'M DONE! I AM DONE BEING THE GIRL WHO GOT DUMPED!'

The last word had hardly left my smiling mouth when the first raindrop hit my forehead. I stood up, breathing deeply. Inhaling new life.

'I'M FREEEEEEEEEEEEEE!'

Megan followed me into the centre of the roof, face upturned to the sky, too, where rain came quicker and quicker now, and with our arms spread, faces thanking a god, a universe, the drops covered our bodies, heavier and heavier until we were wet though to our skin, and we spun and we spun and we spun, wetter and wetter until we were dizzy and laughing and fell to the ground holding hands. It was over, now.

# THIRTY-TWO

Autumn threatened with a gentle smile, like a favourite babysitter who knows you won't go to bed willingly, but is tasked with putting you down regardless. *Come on now,* she says, *you've had your fun.* The weather in Derbyshire was sunny, but cool. Dramatic, bright white clouds filled determinedly blue skies, their shadows playing tag on worn-down cobbles imprinted with stories and old chewing gum. The slow pace of pensioners and children alike, idle, nowhere to be, not particularly quickly, anyway, gave Wirksworth, a hilly small market town on the edge of the Peak District, a perpetual Sunday afternoon quality.

I sat on the porch of my aunt's tiny semi-detached cottage, wedged into a back lane with views both up to the grassy banks surrounding the area, and down, into the town where shops met pubs met veterinarian clinics and woodworkers and antique outlets. Tea cooled in a mug that warmed my hands, and I lifted my closed eyes to the sky so that sunlight could bathe my face. It was nice to be back.

I thought of him, Hal, often – he hovered over much of what I did. There was more space for him now, in the aftermath of the wedding. I was house-sitting whilst my aunt was away, and relished the solitude afforded me by the location of her house in order to brood most effectively. I was trying to write, to craft the story of my summer into a narrative that would conveniently shoehorn into an anecdote I was more capable of processing. Snippets of it all fluttered in my imagination like wild butterflies, and I was eager to capture them, to pin them down before they went wild forever.

It felt like a comma in my own story, a hovering punctuation mark that allowed me to take a breath before not only leaving one chapter, but entering the next – only he was with me through the scene change. Writing about him meant he was still sat with me. I'd be opening a can of beans for breakfast and remember the kitchen in Geneva where we'd bent over double about Emma's suggestion that we sprinkle bee pollen on our breakfast. The radio would play a show tune and he'd be there in the bathroom with me, all American teeth and jazz hands and smiles. I wondered what he'd make of the man who ran the newsagents and sold me my chocolate, or who he'd end up chatting to sat at the marketplace. I scolded myself for missing him and then gave in to it willingly.

*I will forget him*, I told myself. *He won't always play on my mind this way. It's okay. The ache will ease.*

Needless to say, scant writing was actually done. I couldn't put a beginning, middle and end to a story I longed to still see finished.

'What's his name?' Mama said to me, as we sat in her garden with yet more tea.

'His name?' I said.

'The summer romance.' She smiled. 'The one you're having a conversation with in your imagination, instead of here, now, with me.'

I shrugged. 'Mama, I haven't even so much as held hands with a boy this year.'

'Not a single summer kiss?'

'Not a single summer kiss.'

I was lying propped up by a thousand pillows on the bed with even better views of the village than the porch, snuggled down under the duvet and idly responding to emails and messages, tentatively making plans for my impending move to London. That was what came next: bright lights, big city, attempted book deal for the story of my broken heart.

My Facebook was open on a tab that I ignored in favour of a scintillating piece of celebrity gossip on the MailOnline, and I didn't see the waiting message. I padded downstairs to refill my mug – so much tea to be drunk in England! I'd forgotten – and by the time I clicked back through to Facebook it had been waiting almost ten minutes.

**Hallam Hart**          September 5th 20:35
*how is it being back in england?*

I squealed, and typed as fast as I could.

**Laura Jane Williams**         September 5th 20:44
*hey! are you online?*

I waited to see an indication that he was typing a response. One minute passed, and then another. I stared at the screen of my computer, hugging my knees to my chest, chewing absentmindedly on another Hobnob. It was getting dark outside.

Finally:

**Hallam Hart**          September 5th 20:47
*i am! i'm just waiting for a call from my mother*
*i saw on your wall that you're having an enjoyable time*
*y'know*
*at home*
*i'm glad about that*
*i was worried*

He'd been on my Facebook wall! Reading about my life! Wondering about me! Thinking about me! WORRYING!

**Laura Jane Williams**                    September 5th 20:49
*bless your heart*
*i'm in Wirksworth, in derbyshire, staying at my aunt's place*
*whilst she's away.*

I attached a photo I'd snapped earlier that day.

**Hallam Hart**                    September 5th 20:51
*DAMN EUROPE! stop being so beautiful!*

*I wish you were here with me, I thought. That's all I've been thinking over here.*

**Laura Jane Williams**                    September 5th 20:51
*i know, right?*
*it's distractingly beautiful*
*even today, i made a cup of tea and went to sit on the bench*
*to read my book, and an hour later i was still just staring*
*BUT ENOUGH ABOUT ME*
*tell me all the things about you!*

**Hallam Hart**                    September 5th 20:53
*all the things . . .*

I decided to just say it, get it over with:

**Laura Jane Williams**                    September 5th 20:53
*am I allowed to miss you? i think i miss you*

I needed him to miss me too. I needed to not be going crazy over our memories alone. Was I crazy? Why hadn't he just KISSED ME, for fuck's sake? I hated him.

**Hallam Hart**                    September 5th 20:53
*well classes started yesterday and i can already tell*
*(I MISS YOU TOOOOOO)*
*it's gonna kick my ass*

He missed me TOO! *Fuck it,* I thought.

**Laura Jane Williams**                    September 5th 20:53
*there are many things that happen to me/that i think*
*and i often muse on how much i'd like to tell you*
*ass kicking is good. keeps you on your toes*

We could be together for the rest of all time, I thought, and I could be the one kicking your ass, making you better, forcing you to grow . . .

**Hallam Hart**                    September 5th 20:54
*i have mentioned you on multiple occasions*
*to multiple people*
*since i've been here*
*but they just don't understand*

My heart sang a million love songs.

**Laura Jane Williams**          September 5th 20:55

*well, they didn't cycle 100 kilometres around a swiss lake*
*so they wouldn't ;)*
*when can you be in my life again?*

Now. Until the end of time. I want you, too. Say it.

**Hallam Hart**          September 5th 20:55

*true that!*
*cycling bonds people for life!*
*i want to be in your life always and forever*
*we shall try to work something out when i am in china*

I'll come to China!

**Laura Jane Williams**          September 5th 20:57

*you should totally get a flight that routes through europe*
*THAT'S WHAT YOU SHOULD DO*

I saw flights across the world because he lived in New York and worked in China, and I'd be a writer in London and go on book tours to the places he needed to oversee business in. *We can be together. We can! We can.*

**Hallam Hart**          September 5th 20:57

*oh that's a really good idea. i shall look into that forthwith*

I love you.

**Laura Jane Williams**          September 5th 20:58

*forthwith? Is this a forster novel?*

*JUST KIDDING*
*I LOVE THAT YOU SAID FORTHWITH*

Tell me you love me, I willed.

**Hallam Hart**                                September 5th 20:58
*I LOVE THAT YOU LOVE THAT I SAY FORTHWITH*

**Laura Jane Williams**                     September 5th 20:58
*I LOVE THAT YOU LOVE THAT I LOVE THAT . . . oh.*
*nevermind.*
*you get the idea*
*so classes are going to kick your ass*
*anything else to report?*

Ask me and I'll say yes . . .

**Hallam Hart**                                September 5th 21:00
*it's been great to be back in NYC*
*but i miss the feeling of this summer.*
*the craziness and the underlying wonderment and*
*adventure.*
*i feel different being here and i miss the person i felt like i was*
*becoming in italy*
*it's a strange feeling*
*i've gotten back into a comfort zone mentality*

**Laura Jane Williams**                     September 5th 21:01
*'you get a strange feeling when you're about to leave a place,*
*like you'll not only miss the people you love but you'll miss the*

*person you are now at this time and place because you'll never*
*be this way ever again'*
*hold on to the person you were in italy*
*he was a good one*
*make every day an italian adventure*
*(only with different food . . . i know how you get)*

**Hallam Hart**                                    September 5th 21:02
*i do love my culinary variety*

**Laura Jane Williams**                    September 5th 21:03
*whereas the first thing i made on british soil was . . . italian*
*food*

**Hallam Hart**                                    September 5th 21:03
*Why do you always send me the best quotes or know how to*
*perfectly surmise my emotions in beautiful words?*

Because I understand you.

**Laura Jane Williams**                    September 5th 21:04
*because I'm part of the team, that's why*
*it was one of the entrance criteria*

**Hallam Hart**                                    September 5th 21:04
*forever and ever.*

I swallowed and looked around the room for clues as to what to say
next. I wanted permission to let him know the words of my heart, the
thoughts in my veins. *Nothing will be the same.*

**Laura Jane Williams**        September 5th 21:05

*you know you ruined me, don't you?*

And then he went offline.

*Shit*, I thought. *Shit, shit, shit.*

Then:

**Hallam Hart**        September 5th 21:06

*i really do miss talking to you and having you in my life*

*our wonderful weeks together spoiled me*

*OMG I WAS JUST TYPING THAT BUT MY INTERNET CUT*

*OUT AND YOU BEAT ME TO IT*

HE LOVES ME TOO! HE DOES! HE DOES!

**Laura Jane Williams**        September 5th 21:07

*LIES!*

*GET OUT OF MY HEAD!*

TELL ME AGAIN THAT NOTHING COMPARES!

**Hallam Hart**        September 5th 21:07

*i agree. i am ruined because i will now hold all relationships to*

*the bond we forged in a few short days*

**Laura Jane Williams**        September 5th 21:07

*urm. i was HONESTLY just typing that*

*like*

*really, really, really*

*no fella compares to the Mr Hart i got to know*

*every Whitney song. every dance with old italian men.*

Gone again. *What the hell? WHAT THE HELL!*

**Hallam Hart**                    September 5th 21:14
*Sorry my wifi keeps dying*

FFS.

**Laura Jane Williams**            September 5th 21:15
*that's okay, i'm just handing out my soul here*
*GO ON AHEAD, HALLAM'S WIFI. DIE. SEE IF I CARE.*

Of course I care. Hallam, I miss you. Be with me. I need you. I want you. I'm sorry for everything that has gone unsaid.

**Laura Jane Williams**            September 5th 22:00
*urm . . . hello?*

Nothing.

*Titty-fuck-bollocksing-shit.*

I finished off the Hobnobs.

I didn't sleep much that night. Why hadn't I been braver? I felt impotent, held hostage by the type of fear that undid everything I knew to be real. I doubted myself. And I was frustrated, too – at him. His Wi-Fi died, he eventually said. Right as we could've finally said it. Said everything that seemed to stick in our throats, words that strangled our tongues because the truth is difficult. And demanding and adamant and that's why it is beautiful and terrifying and the purity of it all is like a mirror that reflects every painful part of our circumstance. I wanted to scream. His excuse was suspicious, but I wanted to believe it so I did. I wanted to believe in the romance of our meeting. I wanted to be back on that mountainside, where instead of looking to the ground and kicking at stones I could've held his shoulders, looked him deep in the eye and told him, *My darling. You changed everything. I love you too.* I wanted to be *in* love.

Instead we were a separated by an ocean, and all I had to wrap around my cold body as I tossed and turned in a bed that didn't belong to me were memories that danced in my imagination, double-quick time, speeding up so that I knew eventually – either tomorrow or next week, over months or by next year – I'd forget what it was like to love him as they blurred into a general feeling of *it could've been a something.*

The taste of regret churned in my mouth and I played over my favourite moments with him, working out alternative endings or different courses, a sort of *pick your own adventure* for our story together.

I awoke with a cloud of resignation that hung over me in a bad mood all day. I reasoned that I'd done as much as I could, that if we were meant to have happened, we'd have . . . happened. Men are, by and large, hunter-gatherers. For as equal as all the sexes are, there is, I believe, such a thing as divine 'feminine' energy, and divine 'masculine' energy, and it's that traditionally masculine energy that drives blokes to take what they want. I guess he didn't want me, then. In my journal I wrote him a letter, a letter he'd never see, and penned him a final email. Final for now, at least. I was sending myself crazy.

**To: Hallam Hart**
**From: Laura Jane Williams**
**Date: September 6th**

Hey, you.

So, it's probably the most serendipitous of things that you disappeared. Had technology not failed us, possibly I would've quickly become far too revelatory in my discourse. Thank heavens for faulty wifi and computers with battery life shorter than my nostalgia, that's what I say.

I'll reiterate that much happened to me that I wish I could share with you, because you did ruin me. I'd quite convinced myself you'd most likely forgotten all about me now that you are back in NYC, so any suggestion otherwise brightened up my evening.

You are wonderful.

Stay in touch and fill me in on how class is kicking your ass, and what you're eating for dinner. Book a flight that routes through Europe when you go to China. Know that even if you feel like 'Italian Hallam' is disappearing fast he is still there if you seek him out, and . . . just. You're my favourite.

L x

# THIRTY-THREE

Soon enough it was moving day: I was headed to London to try and sell a book about a boy who left, and the girl (eventually) better off without him. I piled Dad's car with lamps and rugs, canvas paintings and folders of my oldest writing notes. Years of life, accrued accidentally, boxed away in dog-eared cardboard and cracked plastic, demanded, finally, after so much time, that I pay them some attention.

When it had all gone into storage, almost eighteen months ago, before I moved to Rome, I was sure I needed all of it – but, actually, so much had been trashed over the past few days that I was left with only the most special parts of my life with which to build on in a new city.

*Balls to the motherfucking wall*, I told myself. *Life from scratch*. As we sped down the M1, an easy, problem-free journey that took us just under three and a half hours, I spent most of my time watching trees whizz by, companionable silence between Dad and me. I inhaled and exhaled into the idea of my new beginning. My real new beginning. I'd be there to sell my book, to become a writer, to make myself proud. I turned up the music. Everything blurred into itself.

My brother lived in an achingly hipster area of East London, in an achingly hip ex-council high-rise. It was filthy and grimy, and full of the kind of dubious characters that apparently make the gentrification of the surrounding areas okay, because at least we live side-by-side with real locals – despite the fact that, collectively, this influx of twenty-somethings with jobs in *London Meed-ya* will happily fork out over a fiver for a pint and pay two hundred quid for jeans designed to look like they're ready for the bin.

I felt like I didn't fit in, and it gave me a complex.

I had a tiny room at the back of the split-level flat, and from the eleventh floor had skyline views of nearby Liverpool Street. The Gherkin twinkled as late autumn sun turned the sky dusky pink, and on my first night I was forced to gasp at the sprawling metropolis from my darkened room, scarcely believing that this was my life now. I lived in London.

On my first morning I woke up to my brother playing African drumming music and making porridge on the stove, throwing in cinnamon and chopped dates and the tiniest bit of salt. The flat had a clothes horse with a coloured wash hanging to dry in the corner, there were Sunday papers strewn on the sofa, and from where I plopped myself to open my laptop, I could watch Jack cook and craft, his bony spine rippling through the thin T-shirt he slept in.

Jack and I didn't have the easiest of relationships growing up. I have two years on him, yet with the way he is – considered and deliberate, thoughtful and prone to worry – most presume I'm many years his junior. Jack has the spirit of an eighty-five-year-old troublemaker in the handsome body of a twenty-something, and is the person whose opinion I fear most: he takes no prisoners with me, noting that so few people challenge me as he does.

I think, in many ways, I'm an enormously irritating older sister to have. I'm all-singing, all-dancing. I play 'star of the show' and take it upon myself in almost every social situation to make a fool of myself as a social lubricant. I talk and I talk and I talk, laughing and punning, asking intrusive questions and shouting about my opinions, and then, eventually, when I go to take a breath, there Jack is, speaking between my lines in a way so powerful and self-assured that jaws drop and mouths smile – then I shut up. He is almost always everyone's favourite because of this, and I am almost always in subconscious competition for his approval because, when somebody doesn't take shit like Jack doesn't take shit, you want him to like you. Need him to. I'm lucky as all goddamn hell, then, that he has my back.

I had a Facebook message, and this is the part where you're to forgive me for not mentioning Ryan sooner. In my defence, he wasn't relevant. And now he is.

I'd known of him since before I'd left for Rome. He'd been on my university campus many moons ago, as an associate lecturer, and had read me in the student magazine where I had a column that was a bit like my blog, called *Life Unhinged*. It was sex stories and poop, my usual kind of ribald stuff. There was a link to my website after every column, and Ryan started to follow to my work. Directed by the social media buttons on the site, eventually he 'added' me on Facebook, and from there, over the however many years since, we developed a very modern *stranger-to-friends-to-maybe-more* status: he clicked "like", I clicked "share"; comments were tentatively made, and eventually private messages exchanged.

Ryan had been based in Derby, but the day I'd left Rome he had moved to London. He'd been there a few months, now. We'd chatted online recently, my own London life imminent, and I'd kept up the correspondence because I was happy to know somebody else in the big city everyone had warned me could swallow even the most confident girl whole. He made me feel a bit safer.

*Where will you be living?* he'd said.

*East London,* I'd replied.

*No way – that's where I am,* he'd said.

*I'll be right by Hoxton station,* I'd replied.

Turns out, he was four minutes from my house, door to door, and his message that morning invited me to the Barbican, to an art show he and his best friend were going to. Jack had promised me a walking tour of the area, raining though it was, and so I made my excuses with Ryan because family comes first – Jack comes first. But also: I think I liked the *idea* of my first London friend, but also I was aware that his messages were approaching flirty and, though he seemed thoroughly decent – lovely, even – he probably wasn't just looking for a buddy. And I knew a few things to be true:

1. I still had three or so more months of my celibacy pledge and, between my summer of friendship love and Hal's virginity, hadn't been much tempted to stray from my path and didn't want to jeopardise myself now.
2. I shouldn't heal my Hallam-obsessed heart by seeking out affection in another, anyway.

'You won't stay celibate in London for very long,' Jack had warned me. 'Everyone shags everyone here.' I wondered if that were true. I was quite enjoying not having to worry about my bikini line.

I spent my first days in London wandering around the local area, trying to orientate myself in my new city without spending any money. I was in a dispute with the company who'd sent me to the convent – I was down a few thousand pounds, and that was crippling my desired social life because I was broke until I found a job with which to pay next month's rent. Jack was out a lot, leaving at 8 a.m. for work, and often not getting home until 10 or 11 p.m., so in between not actually having any friends in the first place, no money to go out with them even if I did, and a house that was largely empty, eventually my curiosity with Ryan got the better of me. After three other invitations to meet, that I also passed up, I finally agreed.

*Shall I show you the local?* he said.

*I've got time for a quick one,* I said (wankily).

You'd think I could've managed to be a bit friendlier after years of correspondence and the offer of a free drink, but I was scared. In the back of my mind, the bit that I had so successfully spent the rest of the year learning how to crack open wide enough to get the sunshine of goddamn common sense in there, it occurred to me: *I'll be a disappointment to him.* He knew more about me than I did of him – I'd chronicled my life online in painful detail since my early twenties. It would be entirely natural – acceptable, even – for him to have a fully formed version of Laura Jane Williams in his mind, not realising that, like every other human being on the planet, I can exist as twelve different versions of myself, depending on company and mood, dress and time of day.

'Laura,' Jack said to me through frothy, toothpaste-covered teeth, 'don't be ridiculous. Everyone loves you, and he'll be no exception. If he's read about the time you farted in your pilates instructor's face and he still wants to meet with you, I think you're probably kindred spirits.'

'But who wants to meet a guy who spends his spare time reading stories about poop?' I asked, genuinely flummoxed.

'Who'd spend their spare time *writing* stories about poop?' Jack replied.

'Aye-up,' he said, from across the street.

'Hi.' I waved. I watched him navigate the zebra crossing and we hugged. 'It's so nice to finally meet you.' I arranged my face into what I hoped was a contortion of friendliness.

I'd dressed casually, and already warned him that my brother was cooking dinner for me that night – a lie, but a convenient escape should he turn out to be, well, *weird*. The only way I'd been able to feel confident as I'd gotten ready and left the house was to say, in my imagination, over and over again, *Just one drink. Just one drink. Just one drink.* I eyed him up in my peripheral vision as he used the cash-point by our meeting spot, and noted his height, his long, tapered fingers, his jeans and his jacket and his stubble and his little tuft of grey hair at the front of his head, like a lightning bolt to the rest of his ashy blond. *Just one drink.*

He didn't take me to the local; we went to a nicer place near where they do the flower market. I was flattered that he'd thought a location through – I'd come to learn that Ryan thought everything through. He told me about the area as we walked, and it was lovely to amble through backstreets I hadn't yet been down with a man so obviously at ease with himself. There was little that was complicated about him, and I could tell that from the off. He was a graphic designer, had wanted a bigger life challenge than Derby could've offered him, and so had moved to London to join the rest of his mates from university. He was, I could tell by his stories, incredibly close to them, with no hang-ups about pecking order or worries about the future. Just a normal bloke, getting his kicks where he could, with people he enjoyed being around. For somebody as tied up in her own dizzying, often-imagined world, it was like being part of an anthropology experiment. *So this is what uncomplicated is like,* I thought.

I had half a Guinness. He made me laugh. Didn't hide how proud he was to have done so. He asked questions about specific stories I'd documented online – he wasn't shy about letting me know that he enjoyed some of what I wrote and was utterly baffled by other things, but he was obviously engaged with some of my stuff and if there's one thing I like to talk about, it's myself, so I wound conversation around his idea of me, gently making sure he understood my truth.

When he asked if I wanted another, I reiterated that I really did have to go. I could've stayed if I wanted to, but I'd been prepared to find him odd, strange, deformed, *just not for me.* It was discombobulating to find that he was totally the opposite: that wasn't part of the plan. I was supposed to satiate my curiosity and then never see him again. *That* was the plan. I didn't come to London to meet boys – and especially not in the first goddamn weeks. Having previously lost myself in his conversation I was suddenly jolted out of it, a 180-spin as I declared that, actually, I had to leave right now.

'Oh,' he said, as I stood up to leave. 'Short and sweet, eh?' He didn't seem mad or disappointed, didn't guilt trip me for leaving less than an hour after I'd arrived. Rolled with it. Self-assured enough to know it wasn't him, but me. Didn't over-analyse.

*God he's refreshing,* I reflected.

'Yeah – sorry it's been a snatched drink. That I've drank and dashed so to speak.'

'Nah, don't worry,' he said, leaning in to give me a peck on both cheeks. 'I'm just happy I finally got to meet you. It's scary meeting strangers off the Internet, innit?'

I smiled. 'I thought the exact same thing.'

We made for the exit of the pub together.

'Well, it's really cool that you're, like, just how I thought you'd be.'

'I am?'

'Yeah, course,' he said. 'And it's cool that you're just round the corner, too. We London newbies have got to stick together, you know?'

'Yes,' I told him. 'I agree. And it's been really nice meeting you, too. I errrr – yeah. Thanks for the drink.'

He texted me right after I left, telling me how nice it was to put a face and a voice to what he already knew of the online version of me, and that we had to do it again soon sometime – though maybe over a few more drinks (winky emoticon face).

I kept thinking how nobody ever says, *I just want a fella who like, reads something I wrote somewhere, and tracks me down to tell me they want to take my brain out for a drink,* and then ACTUALLY HAS A MAN TRACK HER DOWN THROUGH SOMETHING SHE WROTE AND ASK TO TAKE HER OUT FOR A DRINK.

He wasn't actually supposed to be normal.

'How'd it go?" asked Jack, as my key turned in the lock to my new front door. He was at the kitchen table eating a lamb kebab from his favourite place on the corner, using a proper knife and fork but still keeping his food in the Styrofoam container. It stank.

'No idea,' I replied, running the tap for some water and then pulling up a chair opposite him. 'Upsettingly, I think it went better than I expected.'

My brother laughed. 'You're a twat,' he said. 'What does that even mean?'

I threw the tea towel from the arm of the chair at him. 'Shut up,' I said. 'And tell me about your day.'

I hardly listened to a word he said.

# THIRTY-FOUR

I knew I was interested in him because the next time he suggested we meet up I did my eyeliner a bit flicky, and I only ever do that when I want to make my eyes look bigger because I'm silently asking to be kissed. I'd had no further communication from Hallam since I'd emailed him from my aunt's house, a hint I didn't want to take, and, despite occasional bouts of Facebook stalking, I was doing quite well at beginning to build a new life for myself out of his shadow. I'd had some job interviews and set up a website for my book, which had enough interest from publishers to add a little spring to my step. My budget was managing to stretch a tiny bit further than I had planned for, too, as Jack taught me how to cook from scratch with minimal, fresh ingredients – a skill I didn't know he possessed until I moved in. He was a great wee chef, Jack, and my favourite thing was to drink a glass of wine as he chopped and sliced, slow-roasted and fried, making sense of flavours and smells and understanding that what they say is true: you can taste the love that has gone into every meal.

We met at the same pub as before, me and Ryan, and I excitedly told him of a casual coffee meeting I had coming up with a publisher, the whole reason I'd moved to London in the first place, I said. He was thrilled for me, and we talked about his design company and he told me about his best friend. I asked about his mum, who he talked about so very fondly, and we finished up our glasses, and then had another. 'I'm glad you don't have to run away this time,' he said.

'Me too,' I replied, happily.

We decided to head to the next pub, where the talking didn't really stop, again, and maybe a little more drink was had, and eventually we ended up at a bar, knees touching, fingertips lightly brushing, conversation going in that nonsensical direction it does when finishing the bottom of the glass becomes an exercise in speeding up the inevitable. When he asked if he could take me to dinner later that week and I said yes, we held eye contact longer than strictly necessary. There was so much to be said for his straightforward, simple attitude: *Hey*, he all but suggested, *I like you and would like to spend more time with you. That okay?* I achieved more sense of circumstance in the combined total of four hours with Ryan than I had done in four *months* with Hal. He was oxygen; he let me breathe. Ryan made it easy: his happiness was obviously a choice, and I wanted to emulate that choice. When we left to find it raining outside, he held the umbrella and I held his hand.

He stopped walking, for some reason; I think to look at some Banksy grafitti on Rivington Street, where we'd ambled, dipping in and out of bars all night. I made an awkward joke, about what I don't remember. Something silly. Taking the piss out of him, probably. He playfully shoved me out into the rain. I pretended to be outraged. He pulled me back into the sanctuary of the brolly, closer than before. Then it fell away, and he put his face to mine as we both got wet.

*So this is London.* I smiled to myself.

But then he invited me to his house for coffee.

Coffee.

It was an exercise in self-restraint, in a manner that I hadn't ever had to execute before. I wanted to go home with him. If I were going to break my celibacy vow before the full twelve months was up, it would be with somebody like Ryan. He'd call. He'd romance me. He'd fall in love with me, I knew – and perhaps I'd fall in love with him, too. Leaning into him on the stormy walk home, stopping in shop doorways and under bus shelters to steal long, lingering kisses, it all was almost enough to seduce me into saying yes. But I knew if I did that I wouldn't have learned anything, however potentially perfect this could be. Nine months into a vow of celibacy that had changed the course of my entire life – saved me from myself, in so very many special ways – I knew in every molecule of my beating heart that I would be sleeping with Ryan to forget about Hallam. To achieve something with this one that I didn't with the last. That night I put myself to bed.

But then.

I thought about Ryan when I woke up. And I thought about him all the next day, and a little bit on the day after that, too. And by the day after that I knew I couldn't ever see him again, not because I wasn't strong enough to say no again, but we both deserved more than what that meant because *goodness*. He was such a good one. An upstanding, honourable, thoroughly decent bloke, and I didn't trust myself not to treat him like shit. Now, with the conclusion of the story already established, I'm not sure how much I did really like Hal – nor how much he liked me. Maybe we were only built for the summer, as a reminder of what could be. Ryan would've been such a wonderful boyfriend, back in the real world. But, I was fixated on him. On Hal. On us. I felt like our story owed me a happy ending, so I was going to get it – even if I had to invent it so doggedly that I believed, eventually, with my all, that we were meant to be.

I told Ryan, *I should've said this before, but I've no intention of dating anybody . . . I've come this far (no pun intended) and so I'll stop this before it starts.* I thought he'd be mad, that he'd think I'd deliberately wasted his time. I didn't think he'd respond. He did. It was kind. It made me wonder if I'd made a mistake – until I saw a note from Hal, blinking red in my inbox, as if he knew he'd been on my mind so heavily.

**To: Laura Jane Williams**
**From: Hallam Hart**
**Date: October 21st**

I've been meaning to write to you.

I've been drinking red wine with my roommate, and I started talking about Italy. Then I remembered that I love you.

Then I remembered that you are one of the most amazing women I have ever met, and I wanted to tell you that.

Then I felt awful for not responding to you because life has been crazy and messy.

I miss you.

I love you and miss you.

I paced around the flat, picking things up and putting them down, as if the answer I was looking for was hidden under a paperback copy of *The Alchemist* or the money bank I was given at my christening. I didn't want to give up on Hal – on me and Hal. On the idea of us.

I didn't have much to lose. Not really.

I found the letter I had written to him in my journal, the night after we had IM-ed and he'd suddenly disappeared offline. I still meant every word. It was important to me to tell him what occupied the space between us. The story arc felt too perfect not to be real: I had healed enough to fall in love again, and I needed my conclusion. I'd earned it.

I opened a blog template and furiously, desperately, earnestly typed out the note. I hit 'publish', and I think I did that because somehow making my profession of adoration into 'art' made it more palatable to my ego than out-and-out sending it to him. I closed my computer and went for a walk. My heart beat only for him.

### A Lust Letter – Because I'm a Coward

*Since we met, I've fallen in love with somebody new about once a week. It started with you.*

*You, the guy who travelled through three countries in an afternoon to be with me. You, the guy who sang in supermarket checkout lines and didn't care who turned to stare. You, the guy who twirled me around, teaching me to dance like they do in the black and white movies, never chastising when I messed up the steps (again), just tittering and making a show of yourself to distract from my embarrassment. You, the guy who made the talk meaningful, giggles easy, trust simple.*

*I fell in love with you hard, and fast. Willingly. I was ready to love. I chose you.*

*And I continued to fall, even after you told me that you were seeing somebody – kinda. Maybe. You didn't know how to describe it. Of course, I didn't let you know I'd already fallen too deep to care about the details. Just nodded, changed the subject. Pretended I'd never heard it in the first place. Carried on falling in love because it felt too good not to: it didn't matter that you didn't feel the same. Or that you did, and you just couldn't do anything about it. Wouldn't.*

*Since then falling in love has been a lot easier.*

*I've fallen in love with the guy on Twitter who posts photos of passages from his favourite books. I've fallen in love with the idea of a friend I slept with when I shouldn't have, one night long ago, right before he moved away. I saw him, by accident, when he was in town, at a place neither of us should have been. When our eyes met, his cheeks flushed in a way that made him so handsome. I fell for him, too, and I didn't say goodbye when I left. I wondered what you were doing, and who you were doing it with.*

*I've fallen in love with the guy I used to work with. And the guy I see sometimes at the coffee shop where I go to write. And the guy I've never met, but somehow became a friend on Facebook and who leaves well-timed comedic comments on whatever I post. I fall in love with him as I spend minutes typing and re-typing a suitably witty response, and then I click on to go check your profile.*

*It's always going to be you, even when I'm busy pretending to love somebody else.*

*When we said goodbye, I didn't look you in the eye. I let you tell me that you thought I was incredible. You loved my mind, the way I thought, everything, you said. And I said nothing.*

*I looked to the right of your shoes, at the floor, and folded my arms.*

*I had to concentrate really, really, hard.*

*I knew that if I forgot myself for a second, a single moment of spontaneously emotion-fuelled madness, I'd tell you that before you there was nobody else, not really, not compared to this, and that everybody after you will be measured by your effortless laughter on adventures that gave us bruises on our legs, and the 4 a.m. stories you told on foreign beaches.*

*They will be sized up by how quickly they can ascertain that I'm not being rude or sarcastic, I'm trying to figure out some-thing true, because that's just what I do, and their knowledge of musical theatre will be compared to yours, their willingness to talk about what scares them contrasted to you.*

*All of it will come back to falling in love with you.*

*I'll look for guys with parts of your whole, systematically collect-ing their bits to assemble in the guilty secret of my mind. I'll wish they were you.*

*They won't be. I'll settle for pieces.*

*The one with the poetry has the same reverence for romance you gifted me. The one with the blushing cheeks gets nervous with the same naivety as you. The one at the coffee shop doesn't stand up straight, either. You control how I feel about everybody else, the One in amongst all the other ones.*

*But we never happened. And that's okay.*

*It has to be, doesn't it?*

When I got home I sent him the link to the post. And then I laughed, out loud, alone, as I was so often, in the living room of that flat, because I'd done it. I'd shown my hand.

# THIRTY-FIVE

**To: Laura Jane Williams**
**From: Hallam Hart**
**Date: October 25th**

*Thank you. Thank you, thank you.*
   *I am blown away. After I read those words . . . I couldn't*
*catch my breath. I couldn't really think straight. I tried to think*
*of a way to respond there's so much respect that I hold for you*
*that it's important that I just . . . lay my emotions all out, I*
*guess. Be honest back.*

'OHMYGOD,' squealed Calum, from my London sofa. 'I can't take this. I honest-to-God think my stomach is going to explode. Aren't you nervous?' he said. 'I'm *so* nervous. This is like a movie, or something.' I'd called him as soon as I'd read Hal's response to my feelings, voice shaking, making tracks as I went back and forth in the living room in my pajamas excitedly. He lived in London now, too, and it was heaven to be able to spend so much time with him once again.

'What's up?' he'd said. 'You never voice call.' I'd demanded he come over.

We had tarts and quiche from Broadway Market arranged on a

wooden cheeseboard, and washed them down with lemon-and-mint-infused water Jack had left 'percolating' in the fridge. I sat on the floor, my back against the door, laptop wedged against my thighs, and continued reading, not even really needing to see the screen: I'd read the email over and over again in the hour it'd taken Calum to roll out of bed and get to my flat. I knew what it said well enough.

'I was sitting in a conference about sustainability and urban ecosystem planning with one of the worst public speakers I have ever heard. His sounds drowned out as I got your email.' Calum clucked, appreciatively. I looked up and nodded. 'I've never experienced such a heartfelt and meaningful expression of feelings. I could never even think of articulating my emotions in such an eloquent manner.' Calum sat up to refill his glass, and I remained seated as I lifted my own, forcing him to get up from his position to replenish me. He filled the glass and then sat down beside me to read over my shoulder, legs pushed up against me. 'You were the freestyle, expressive, wonderful and impulsive woman that everyone fell – falls – instantly in love with. I viewed myself as just another one of your fan boys who you had, for some reason, chosen to indulge. I revered you and your magical way of approaching the world. I looked to you for guidance and help.'

'Can I just say, though?' Calum said, interrupting me before the next sentence.

I sighed. 'Go on . . .'

Calum looked at me. 'He was just another one of your fan boys who you had, for some reason, chosen to indulge.' He waited for me to respond, unapologetic.

'That's not fair,' I said, narrowing my eyes.

Calum gave a hollow laugh. 'My job isn't to be fair, sugartits, my job is to level with you on your bollocks,' he said.

I was open-mouthed. 'I wasn't indulging him . . .' I sounded high-pitched and squeaky. Defensive. Offended.

'You were indulging *yourself*,' he supplied, too quickly.

I think he meant that I chose to fancy him, Hal, because Calum had advised me, back in Sanremo when he came to visit, that I had to enjoy a little love affair with *somebody*. That it was *time*. 'You told me to!' I said.

'I told you to go and finally get laid!'

'I only ever think about sex when I'm with you, you know.' I shook my head, getting cross that my celebratory mood was being damp-ened by a hearty dash of bitchiness.

'Laura, we've been through this. You're wonderful, but I really do love penis.'

I rolled my eyes. 'I *mean,* you're the only one fixated on me having sex. I know it sounds dramatic, calling it a celibacy pledge and all that, but it's not the big deal you constantly remind me it is. It was a month in before I even mentioned it to you properly.' We'd never really addressed the ins-and-outs of my libido; whether I had the horn, or missed riding the D. 'Just so you know, it hasn't been some agonising, awful restraint. I do not feel deprived. What I've done – quietly closed my legs – isn't big and revolutionary. I know a ton of people not having sex.'

'Like Hal The Virgin.' He said it simply. Obviously. I knew what he was getting at, and I didn't like the judgement of it.

I slammed my shoulder into his. 'I knew you were waiting for an opportunity to bring that up!' Calum was teasing me, pushing the limits to my humour, but I was sensitive to it. This was special, for me. Different. So much had happened as I travelled, as I lived in Rome and Sanremo and Loano. It felt disloyal that he wasn't honouring that.

'I was waiting for *you* to acknowledge that it's all a bit opportune. Out of all the boys you could have chosen,' he said, crossing and uncrossing his legs, 'you picked the only twenty-something virgin either of us has ever come across.' God, he made me mad. 'Also, you said cutie-patootie-Rivington-Street-kissing-guy made you exercise restraint. So. That sounds like deprivation to me.' We weren't sat closely with limbs wrapped around each other now. I looked down to see space between us; we'd both edged away as the discussion got louder.

'Yes. Because I knew going home with him would be only to forget about Hal, even if I do fancy him. And I'm not that girl anymore, Calum.' He could tell I was about to seriously lose my temper – that we were approaching the line all friendships have where what is unsaid says all that needs to be brought up. He changed the subject.

'When can you have sex again?'

My tempo altered as quickly as his had. 'Mid-December, if I want. Less than two months away.'

He said: 'Are you going to watch the clock count down til midnight and then go choke on the nearest dick?' He was trying to make me laugh at myself. I didn't find any of this funny.

'Only if I'm not hurting anyone by it.'

'Oh!' It wasn't the answer he'd expected. 'So you'll still, like, casually hook up with men if you want to?'

Softening to his genuine intrigue I explained, 'Well, yeah. Maybe. If I want to. But I will do it kindly, and respectfully. To myself and to them, you know? You do understand, don't you, that I don't think all sex is bad?' I didn't want us to fight.

'I'm still struggling, to be honest, to be fully on board with this year. But, like, you seem happier and that. So. Yay! Go team Laura!

Whatever makes you happy! Chase the fairytale!' He didn't want to fight, either.

'What makes me happy is believing in this particular fairytale,' I said.

'Go on then,' he replied. 'Finish reading me his email.' He leaned his head on my shoulder and stared out of the window. I bristled at his choice of word: *fairytale*. He meant it badly. I hadn't. I wanted a fairytale.

*'I knew we shared a special bond,'* I read, . . . *'but I never knew you felt so strongly. You make me seem like this suave and dashing gentleman, when in reality I'm a confused bumbling idiot and got pulled into your magnificent aura. You made me better and brought out a part of me that I have always wanted to be. Since I have been back here, in New York, my days to chaos. I've lost the identity I found over the summer with you.*

*Thank you. I said that already, but it bears repeating. Thank you for everything. Everything that you are, and everything that you have done. I honestly don't know how else to say what I am feeling, because there are no words for it.*

*I realise this response cannot compare to the eloquence of your declaration of feelings, but this is the best I can manage.*

*Thank you. For being in my life. Just . . . thank you.*

*I love you, too.'*

Calum didn't move. 'And now you're going to fly to New York so you can finally snog him?' he said, still watching the sky get brighter with early winter sun.

'Yes. I want you to hold me as I book a ticket.'

He laced his hand around my mine, our fingers a vine. 'This is very theatrical,' he said.

'I want my ending, Calum. I want to be happy.'

He stood up, stretching his arms and creaking his neck. 'Why can't you just chose the lovely, geographically convenient boy?' He went back to the settee. 'Why Hal?' He wasn't being mean in his challenge, now. His voice had softened.

'I can't explain it.' I stood up too, holding my open laptop carefully and walking to the other couch. 'I just . . . I set out to be the girl who doesn't hide from her feelings anymore. Not through sex, not through emotional distance. All that stuff. And at the last minute I got scared with Hal, and I just feel like if I don't go and look him in the eye, tell him what I should've in the summer, I'm not rewriting my character like I deserve. I deserve to be brave enough to do this.'

'To fly to New York?'

'YOLO, right?'

Calum was totally and utterly unconvinced. 'One last controversial question: has this got anything to do with making your book more interesting?'

I smarted, but the deal with Calum is that no question is off the table. He was only asking because he cared. 'I think you'll find my book is already incredibly interesting, actually. So interesting that I have an actual meeting with an actual book editor, remember?' It was an evasive answer.

'Well, yes, obviously, it's amazing etcetera, etcetera. But . . . this would be a mighty fine conclusion to a story about healing yourself out of a broken heart. You know. Flying to New York to live happily ever after.'

'It would be a mighty fine conclusion to my *life*,' I corrected him. 'It was you who said this was like a film, not me.'

'I'm only asking,' he said, holding his hands up in surrender. 'Don't get your knickers in a twist. Now. What about this ticket, Hollywood?'

# THIRTY-SIX

'And what's the purpose of your visit to the United States today, ma'am?'

I looked up at the broad shoulders of the Brooklyn-accented uniformed guard, my passport in his hand, and I said, 'I've come to tell a boy that I love him.'

He looked up from my photograph page. 'I'm sorry, ma'am?' Eyes traced over my hair and to my shoulders, across my chest and down to my legs.

'I've come to tell a boy that I love him,' I said, louder.

The guard smiled with one side of his mouth. I cleared my throat, blushing at my declaration but determined to own my moment. The guard met my eyes and said, 'You're British.'

'Yes.' I stood my ground.

'This boy, he's American?' The guard, he was handsome. The sort of uniformed state worker you see in films. He wasn't teasing me.

'Yes. I met him this summer when we were teaching in Italy.'

'Parla Italiano?' he said, in a perfect accent. *Do you speak Italian?* I nodded. 'Si, un po.' *A little.*

The guard looked me up and down again. An assessment. He was impressed. '*Lui é molto fortunato,*' he concluded. He handed my passport back to me and I adjusted the leather holdall I'd borrowed from my brother on my shoulder.

'Yeah, he *is* lucky, isn't he?'

'Yes, ma'am,' he nodded.

'*Grazie*,' I thanked him. '*Buona serata*.'

I passed through customs and exited the airport.

*Be courageous,* I urged myself. *You've come this far, sweet child.*

The train for the city slowed to a stop on the platform and I hopped aboard. Hal would be waiting for me at the other end of my journey.

I sat on the steps of Times Square. I'd asked him for somewhere central, easy-to-find, a beacon in the sprawling metropolis I'd only ever spent twenty-four hours in before. It wasn't so much the centre of the universe – that landmark, in that important city – as it *was* the universe, in those minutes. With my luggage at my feet and the temperature so cold that I could see my breath, seeing him traverse the corner and look out over the heads of tourists and theatre workers alike, I waved.

'Hi,' he mouthed, half-smiling.

The funny thing about meeting people 'on the road' is how different they seem back in their own, true worlds. When I was backpacking in India as a twenty-year-old, I made a group of friends on a Goan beach, all flimsy, off-the-shoulder cotton tops to best show off bronzed skin and baggy harem pants picked up through barter at the market. When we took a group trip into the tea plantations in the hills one weekend, the temperature dropped and, unplanned, we all emerged from our rooms dressed in the warmer, more practical clothes we'd worn on the plane ride over: jeans and jumpers and long-sleeved T-shirts and trainers. That is to say, we all dressed conventionally, and suddenly what I knew about each individual personality no longer matched their aesthetic. People are just people, but meeting a fish out of water, and then back in the pond, revealed two sides of the same coin. That is to further say: Hal was not the man I remembered.

He was as demonstrably flustered as I secretly felt, and announced how much he hated 'the tourist bullshit' after hugging me briefly, and how we needed to head somewhere 'authentic' before 'he got really fucking mad'. He practically led by a sprint as we steered past people and potholes, making vague attempts at conversation – 'How was your flight?', 'Did you find your way okay?', 'Wow, you've hardly packed anything at all!' – but mostly focused on the destination ahead. By the time we sat down in a Mexican restaurant in Hell's Kitchen I was breathless from the light-jog-of-a-walk and could feel my shirt sticking to the upper part of my back.

'So . . .' I said, after I let him order for us, because Mexican food I know not.

'So . . .' he repeated.

He looked tired. The Hal in my mind was golden and stubbled, bright-eyed as he took in every last sight, sound, taste, smell. My Hal was an adventurer. He loved life, and living, and thought everything was the coolest thing he'd seen or tasted or thought or heard since the last coolest thing he'd seen or tasted or thought or heard. My Hal didn't have circles under his eyes, short hair off the back of his collar, an attitude.

'Is it weird?' I said, finally.

He sipped at his Diet Coke. 'This?'

'This,' I said.

'Why would it be weird?'

I could've answered a million different ways. It was weird because the last time I saw him he'd told me he loved me. The last time we'd spoken I'd said I loved him. It could be weird because I'd flown across the Atlantic to say words I should've said in the summer, months ago, when the English girl met the American boy in Italy and vacationed with him in Switzerland. It could be weird because it was too much, or not enough, or because I was playing the movie version of my life in my head, and struggling to understand why the reality wasn't quite matching up.

Instead, I said, 'No reason.'

We ate, and made plans for the next day. He walked me back to Times Square not two hours after we'd first met, and I waited for Megan to come pick me up because it was with her I'd be staying, not him. An ominous heavy lump sat deep in my stomach.

'He was so utterly self-conscious that it unnerved me,' I said to Megan. She'd moved to New York after the convent and had simply sent a string of exclamation points when I'd emailed her asking to sleep on her couch, because there was a boy I needed to come see. That was her way of saying, *Hop aboard, baby!*

She handed me a spare blanket and pillow as I made up a bed for myself in her living room. 'You know, maybe he was just feeling the pressure. Like, not from you, but from himself. A lot happened this summer, and he probably thought his chance was over, and had gotten used to that. And now, here you are, on his doorstep, changing up the rules of how this was to go – in his mind, at least.'

I'd been in New York less than six hours, and I already knew the truth. I felt it. I would never admit to having known it all along. I could tell Megan knew, too, but that it wasn't her job to say. It was her job to make me feel like I wasn't a total loser. Like I wasn't shoehorning a nothing into a something. 'I really, really hope I haven't come all this way to embarrass myself,' I said.

Megan said, 'Gurl, that you're doing this at all makes you a goddamn superhero.' She fluffed up my pillow. 'And, you know, you got to come to New York. That's so cool! It might be selfish of me, but

I don't care what brought you here – we get to smoke rollies and eat pizza together, right?'

It was wonderful to wake-up to my old Riviera roommate, to see her life and tell her about mine. Convent years were like dog years: three months in a convent with a girl equates to a five-year friendship in the 'real world'. I explained about London and the up-coming meeting at the publishing house and the lovely, beautiful dates with Ryan that suggested a good time could be had by all.

'We're really doing it, huh?' she said, over Nutella and bananas on toast. 'We're really doing what we said we'd do.'

'It's crazy how we can doubt so much when we talk about what we want, but how much is possible if you just sort of . . . do it.' I licked my knife clean.

'Seriously,' she said, pushing her plate away from her 'and this publisher meeting? *They* emailed *you*?'

'Yup! A blog reader saw the website I'd set up about the book, and because she works at a publisher she passed it to her boss. It's just coffee, but it's coffee AT. A. PUBLISHERS!' We high-fived, and got ready for the day.

We toured the city, stopping off hourly for food or coffee or later a cocktail, with plans to meet up with Hal and his friends for a theatre performance by some of his buddies. The loose plan was to get dinner after, but when we met it quickly became apparent that Hal had made plans elsewhere, which was hard to understand in amongst a bunch of people I'd only just met.

'Oh, you're not . . . I just thought . . .' I stammered.

'Yeah, sorry about that,' he said, as the lights went down and we spent ninety minutes in silence, watching his friends and my strangers on a stage that rattled loudly every time somebody took a step.

'Tomorrow?' I said, as we said goodbye, the seconds slipping by too quickly, too unnoted, not like I had wished them to.

'I'll text you,' he said.

If I'd needed yet another clue, this was it. Watching him walk away on some street corner near NYU's theatre building, I got it. Megan put her hand to my back and rubbed lightly, the pity in her touch palpable. I couldn't put the square peg in the round hole.

# THIRTY-SEVEN

Somebody had left a couch on the street, and it felt incredibly *New York*. I'd come out of the bar for a cigarette, 'borrowed' off the barman, and Jo – Sanremo Jo – plonked herself down beside me saying, 'We're probably going to get infested with bedbugs, you know.' She lived in New York too, and I was so thankful to see her.

Three days had passed without a word. Hal and been incommunicado and everybody knew it. Megan, her roommates, Jo, Emma Rada and her boyfriend, who had come down from Boston for the weekend specifically to see me. Mortified isn't a strong enough word for it.

'I do not understand, Jo,' I slurred, legs akimbo in front of me and head slumped against the un-cushioned back. 'I do. Not. Understand.' It was about 10 p.m., and we'd been drinking since late afternoon. It crossed my mind to cut back on the booze for the new year. I'd be over a year without sex by then, and thought I could maybe do with a year without tequila.

Jo reached out and patted my head, like a dog.

'I am humiliated.' I was hammered – black-out-if-I-had-another, hammered. Mascara-down-my-cheeks, hammered.

'No,' she said, not knowing where else to take the sentence. 'No, Laura. This . . . this isn't the way we're going to think about this. It is not. I won't have him do this to you.'

I guffawed. 'He didn't do anything to me, Jo. I did this to myself.' What hurt my pride was that Calum had been right – I'd willed a fairy-tale too hard. 'How did I end up here?' I said.

'On the couch?'

'On the couch, this couch, in New York fucking City, drunk over a boy who I flew all this way for, but who is avoiding me. Avoiding me so much so that I can't even see him for five minutes to ask why he is avoiding me.' I had a thought. 'Am I a stalker? Am I that crazy? Have I come across the Atlantic because I am actually, truly, deluded? Do you think I am deluded? I'm deluded.'

'No!' said Jo, sitting up to come over as matronly and authorita-tive. 'Come on. He wanted you here! This is what you both do! Fly places on whims! And whether or not he thinks this is dumb, or crazy, or he is totally flattered and simply doesn't know how to handle it . . . he's a fucking jackass for leaving you hanging this way.' Jo was angrier than anyone about Hal's attitude. I think she felt, on some level, a bit betrayed, too – she'd been rooting for him. She prides herself on her judgment of character. 'I don't give two shits how much work he has on or what came up, you make the fucking effort for your friends and you two are friends. I came all the way from Staten Island to see you!'

'I know,' I said, stubbing out the stump of my fag. 'And I am so, so grateful. You're my favourite.'

'Anything for my Jane,' she said, rising to a stand and offering me a hand. 'Even infestation.'

'Sorry about that,' I said. 'Call it a lasting memento of this psycho fucking trip.'

'Nope!' she said, pulling out her phone. 'Let's get a selfie, and call that the memento of how we caught rabies.' I blinked when the flash went off.

*

Inside, tequila was lined up. Emma Rada was whispering into the ear of her 43-year-old Spanish boyfriend who she'd met in Geneva, and who had come to America to visit her. Jo was sourcing a salt pot, and Megan was laughing with a friend-of-a-friend. Another girl I'd met during my Italian teaching days was on her way, and so, grabbing a shot glass, I said, 'To those who make the effort,' downing my glass in one and feeling the liquid gold at the back of my throat. Everybody cheered and grabbed a glass, too. Emma's boyfriend leaned over to whisper in my ear, lispy and European: 'He's an idiot. A man wouldn't do this to you. He's a boy, and you deserve more than a boy.' I couldn't tell if his observation made my embarrassment worse or better.

'Order some more shots,' I said. 'I'll understand all this better after another shot.'

'Whatever the lady wants,' he said, waving to the barman.

He texted that night. I couldn't remember what I'd said first, but I know Jo had confiscated my phone when I'd told her. I got it back the next morning, and that's when I read it:

*It all feels so different, he said. I'm not the man you think I am. I'm not the same here in New York. I've gone back to my old life. I don't know how to keep hold of both.*

My head throbbed. I stumbled through to the bathroom where I peed radioactive amber, and then rinsed a dirty glass in the kitchen to fill with water. I drank in heavy gulps, refilled it, and then plodded back to the sofa. I picked up my phone.

*You at least need to tell me this to my face,* I wrote back. *You need to look me in the eye and make me understand, because . . . because I feel a fool.*

*You're so far from a fool I don't even have words for it*, he typed back, immediately.

It was my last evening in New York: five days had passed in a whirlwind. I sat in Washington Square, people-watching. The purple and gold of NYU students flickered by, and it was hard not to notice the staged confidence, the unease, of teenagers out in the world for the first time. I was late to meet him – had gotten lost on the way. I thought I knew where I was going, and, when I got confused, was too stubborn to ask for help. My phone didn't work without Wi-Fi so I had no way to call him. I half expected him to have gone. I half expected him not to show in the first place. He was late too, though, and so I waited.

'What I should've said,' I explained once he arrived, my voice barely more than a whisper, 'what I should've said, in Switzerland, or on the beach in Nice, or in Baiardo, is that getting to know you has been one of the most transformative experiences of my life.' I'd had a speech prepared. I spoke calmly and measuredly, but I didn't feel it. 'I don't know why I couldn't. I was . . . scared. But. You were scared too, and still said those words, so . . . I wanted to say them as well. Here. To your face. Here, halfway across the world because, because I figured we deserved that. That you deserved to hear them, and I deserved to say them.'

He stared out at a group of kids playing hacky sack.

'Are you listening to me?'

'Of course I'm listening,' he said, softly, continuing to stare.

I wasn't here to ask him to love me back. I wasn't waiting for a declaration. I wasn't in the business of persuading anybody to feel anything other than what they did. I pressed on: 'I don't need you to say anything, I guess, because I see that maybe I had it wrong. I thought . . . I thought when you kept emailing me, kept saying those things . . . I thought you felt what I did. But. I think it was maybe a different version of what I did. A different language.' I got that, now. I'd spent a lot of money to get it, but thousands of miles from home there it was. My lesson.

He shifted to look at his shoes. *Is this how I seemed that night in Baiardo?* I wondered. *When he was so full of words and I didn't have the capacity to hear them?*

'Can you say something?' I pressed.

He finally looked at me. 'What do you want me to say?' I couldn't put words in his mouth. We sat that way, side-by-side, watching the hacky-sack players, both.

Eventually, he said, 'You live there. And I live here. And, and I'm about to move to China. And you . . . you have the whole world at your feet. You're meeting with publishers, Laura; your whole dream is coming true. Don't wait for me. Don't wait for the other shoe to drop.' He started to say something else, but stopped himself.

'Go on . . .'

'I just,' he said, 'I'm just not the guy to be at your side for this.'

The breeze picked up and I realised it was dark, now. We'd waited out the day and the sun had set on us. It was time to leave, if it hadn't already been.

'I had a really great summer,' I said.

'Me too,' he said. 'You changed my life.'

'But not enough to still be in it.'

'I carry you with me every second of every day, Laura.'

We sat. 'The kind thing to do would be to kiss me,' I said.

He scooted over, smiling, and held my face between his palms. He lowered his head so his lips met mine, and pressed his mouth to me. He had tears in his eyes.

'See you in another crazy location, somewhere in the world, one day soon?' he said.

I nodded, agreeing to the lie.

I was on my third pint and second shot of tequila when Jacob, Megan's roommate, sat down beside me. I didn't look up, not even when I heard him say, 'Same please, bartender.'

I picked at the chips in the basket in front of me. I don't know how long I had been sitting there for, but it had been a while.

'I just don't understand how I have done all of this work, fixed myself with so much commitment, and still I don't get the guy,' I said, apropos of nothing. Jacob had been there the night we'd all drunk tequila on Emma Rada's boyfriend's tab, and checked in with me every time paths crossed in his apartment. He was a singer-songwriter with a deal with Sony Music, and an absolute romantic. He made me feel like less of an idiot.

'Honey,' Jacob replied, 'I've known you five days and even I know the answer to this one. You didn't fix yourself for a guy – you did that work for you. To be whole without a man. To know you never needed to be fixed in the first place – just honest.

'You spoke up. You made it happen so that you didn't have to wonder. Every person you'll meet for the rest of your life will say the same thing when they hear this story. They'll say: *I wish I had the courage to do something like that.*'

I eyed him suspiciously. I like how this all sounded in his mouth. The way he saw it.

'You found your courage and reaped your reward. You got your answer. So many of us don't, but you did. You got your answer. That's the win. That's what makes you a champ. It doesn't matter what the answer is, as long as you ask the question.'

I *really* liked his take.

Megan appeared in the bar doorway, looked at the glasses in front of me and said, 'That bad?'

I fondled my glass. 'That good, actually. I'm just gonna go throw up, then I'm gonna tell you all about how Jacob here just spoke more sense in one minute than I have done all year. Excuse me.'

\*

The flight home was a delicate one. I felt like I'd been at the gym; that I'd pushed myself, torn some muscles, and was tender because they were being built into something stronger. I got back to the flat just after my brother had left for work, and he'd left me a note telling me he'd missed me, that he couldn't wait to see me later. *You don't have to have a romance to have a romantic life,* I thought. I'd been missed, and that felt like a coup – and that I'd missed him, too. I threw my laundry in the machine, took a fat nap, and by the time afternoon rolled around I realised one important thing: I'd told a boy I loved him, and it hadn't consumed me. It hadn't worked out as I had dared hope for, but that I had hoped at all was special. That I loved myself enough to hope, and survive, and thrive, was a fucking marvel. Jacob had been right: I was superwoman.

# THIRTY-EIGHT

I didn't get a book deal. Not with my first meeting, anyway.

The offices were set back from the Strand, and I marvelled at how I must've walked past the block dozens of times on all my childhood trips to the city, never knowing that behind this set of glass doors lay one of the world's biggest publishing houses. It was raining heavily, the day I went for coffee there, and I took respite in the alcove separating the street from the courtyard in front of the sliding doors towards what I hoped was a future. My future. Pulling a compact mirror from my bag, I ran my fingers through my hair and dug about for some lipstick. I swiped and blotted, rubbed a finger across the tooth I'd also, somehow, hit, and willed my butterflies away. I had a meeting with the commissioning editor of non-fiction, who'd emailed to ask to see some pages. I'd sent him what I had – chapters about the break-up and feeling sad – depressed, now I look back on it; about going to Paris and Jay The DJ and Chad. He'd read about teaching in Sanremo and the convent, and about Hal and my inability to say *I love you too* on that Italian hillside.

*Is the book finished?* he'd emailed. To which I'd had to admit that it wasn't – but that maybe, by the time we met, I'd have my ending. It irritated me that Calum had been right – I had been looking to Hal to tie up my story of healing a broken heart nicely. Romantically. Calum saw that before I did.

I took a breath and headed inside the multicoloured offices, prouder of myself than I ever had been. 'Laura Jane Williams,' I announced at reception, taking a seat until he was ready for me.

'Laura?' a voice said. 'Great to meet you.' He extended his hand and shook mine virgorously. We rode the elevator up to his floor, and a hundred sets of eyes watched us walk down the corridor from the lobby to the kitchen, where he – the commissioning editor – made us tea, and then continued to watch as we meandered across carpet to a communal meeting area with brightly lit booths. He was disarmingly handsome. Maybe thirty-five. Spoke with a silver spoon in his mouth, but not so much that you'd hold it against him. I could see who the eyes were for, and it wasn't me.

'Well, you can obviously write,' he said, getting comfortable, as if I must've heard the compliment a thousand times. It wasn't obvious, not to me, and I hadn't. I made a mental note to myself: FUCKING REMEMBER WHAT HE SAID, LAURA. REMEMBER THAT FOREVER. YOU'LL NEED THAT.

'Thank you,' I said.

'And you've obviously been working very hard on building an audience and honing your craft and living an exciting life, so as to write about an exciting life.'

I beamed from ear to ear. 'Thank you,' I repeated.

'I'm not the editor for the book. I'll tell you that now. I do not want to buy your book.' The way he said it was blunt and to-the-point, but I trusted his pragmatism. 'But let me tell you,' he added, 'I believe in the story. I believe in the story and I think I know some agents who will, too, because ultimately, this is a story for a lot of people who know heartbreak. Which is . . . everyone, really.' He said some things about target demographic and mentioned other authors' names, some of whom I had heard of and others who I hadn't. 'You can use my name when you email them. The agents. I'm happy for you to do that.'

I understood him. He was professional and kind and said if I needed a pep talk, anytime, he was happy to give me one. That was huge, to me – that a professional believed in me. 'Keep working on it,' he said, encouragingly. 'You've got what it takes.'

Forty-five minutes later and I was back on the street where I'd started. *You can obviously write*, I replayed in my mind, heading home to keep working on the story that had landed me the meeting in the first place. *You can obviously write.*

# THIRTY-NINE

Something clicked. I'd been badass enough to own my feelings, and then badass enough to meet with a publisher. I didn't have the guy, but I had something better than that – I had *me*. I had all the things that made me. *You can obviously write.* I threw myself into it – honing dialogue and restructuring and reading as much as I could, noting the ways my favourite authors captured time and place, mood and setting. That was my work – the writing. I'd wake up an hour earlier than I needed to in order to edit the manuscript I had, and I'd sneak in extra writing time when I could at my job. I had to have a job, too. I was one of the only women at a Shoreditch-based tech company, and doing it almost purely for the money. If anyone asked me what I did, I told them about the book. That was what gave me purpose, what excited me. How I paid my rent was irrelevant, to my mind. I got up in the mornings because I loved to tell stories.

Search Engine Optimisation – the way you make stuff show up in Google – conferences are a male-dominated event. Technology, as a field, often is. I found it tough not to be cynical at conferences that bled into the evening (and they always bled into the evening) because one could never be sure if you were chatting to a potential client or business lead, or if you were being sized up for a shag. I tended to seek out the other women at events like this, since there is strength in numbers, and whilst I was officially in attendance as an employee for somebody else's business, I really only attended to see what I could learn to set myself up as a business; to strengthen where my own website showed up in Google. And for the open bar.

The bit I'm about to get into is the bit about how I had sex again, after eleven-and-a-bit months of categorically not having sex. I cannot fully articulate why I decided I was ready, but a combination of my New York bravery and the encouragement about my book meant I felt confident and sure of myself. Not in a cocky, mean way, like before, but as a woman of the world. Things were going well – I had an income and a lofty dream that recently became an achievable goal. I was writing and blogging and living in one of the best cities in the world. I was making friends, and was increasingly comfortable with myself. The world was my oyster.

He locked eyes with me across a group of smokers outside, the free bar evident in the rambling, loud conversation that was part discussion about the future of user-generated content, and part pissing contest to demonstrate who had the biggest dick.

Playing ball in the boys' sandpit makes me spikier. On my guard. Sassy. I don't subscribe to the necessity of having to 'act like a man' to get ahead in business, but I definitely held back my softer side for the ladies' room. Out in the networking world I was all raised eyebrows and short sentences and deliberately made sure to avoid a higher-pitched tone in my voice. I worked hard to take up space, to not shrink myself to make the men around me comfortable with how a woman 'should' be. I hadn't set out to have sex that night, so I wasn't trying to impress anybody but myself, for what it's worth. I suppose that's when it happens, though, isn't it? That's what they say.

'So, what do you do, then?' an older guy asked me, leaning into his jacket, liquorice-papered roll-up in hand and flame of a match wavering in the wind of a particularly chilly night. He lit mine, and then his own.

'I'm a copywriter by day,' I said, 'and a writer-writer by night.'

'Writing? Difficult market.'

'I'm still young enough to be a romantic.'

The other guy, the one across the circle, kept demanding eye contact. The Peacock. He mouthed something to me, something that looked like, *I fancy you*. Just like that. Hi. We haven't met. I fancy you.

At my side of the group, Mr Cigarette was busy trying to bum me out. He was attractive, but old. World-weathered. Sad-seeming. Forty-seven isn't ancient if you still believe, but this guy carried cynicism around like an old friend and it added decades.

The Peacock winked at me. I was, in spite of myself, somewhat amused. He was the one cracking jokes and putting other fellas in their place with one-liners – I could tell even from my distance. He had acne across his forehead, but instead of letting that define him, he seemed to have built a personality centred around there being so much more to him than what he looked like. Confidence of that magnitude is enthralling and powerful. It's kryptonite. He had my attention.

It took the length of my smoke to figure out the guy bemoaning the state of the world had died at thirty-three and had been waiting to be buried ever since. Disenchanted doesn't come into it – he was miserable. Miserable people are determined to make everyone else feel the same. The Peacock wasn't miserable. The Peacock was *fun*. I held my own and made folks laugh, too. Talked digital marketing strategy and did impressions of my boss, both. I'd caught The Peacock's attention because I was as comfortable with myself as he was, and it gave a feeling of not having anywhere to hide – and no need to, either. We had our vibration set to the same level.

'We're going with the boss man to his members' club,' he intoned in my ear, after crossing the crowd. He pulled on my elbow. 'Go and get your coat.' I liked his certainty, and I liked the way he smiled when he said it. It hadn't been a question, but it was definitely an invitation.

He waited for me outside, escorting me to his waiting taxi. There were five of us squeezed into the back seat, and I sat opposite him. Clambering out into a deserted square, I'm-not-quite-sure-where, I followed the group into a velvet-upholstered, dark-wooded, stuffed-and-mounted-animal-head den, reminiscent of a very upmarket country pub. Champagne was waiting in flutes, fifty or so people about to arrive, I guessed, and polite conversation was being made. I gave the waitstaff my coat and busied myself chatting to other conference-goers, not giving away that I had no idea who was host-ing the party, nor where we were. I was on an adventure, and having a mighty fine time with it, too. The Peacock and I didn't stick side by side. It wasn't suddenly a date. He did his thing, and I did mine, and it wasn't claustrophobic or needy or with expectation, but as he passed and lightly touched my shoulder or lower back, it was very clear we were there for each other.

In the loo, I caught my own eye at the sink as I washed my hands, and I looked . . . healthy. Happy. Alive. I wasn't drunk, particularly. I mean, I'd had quite a lot over the course of the evening but the even-ing had been seven hours long. I was nicely woozy. Fuzzy. As I caught sight of the girl in the reflection I actually uttered the exclamation, 'Oh!' because I wasn't a girl. I looked womanly. Self-possessed. I saw flushed cheeks and a new fringe skimming arched eyebrows that had attitude. The corners of my mouth were upturned, the collar of my shirt jutted up *just so*. I looked so very sure of myself. Ready for anything. Everything. That woman was me. I looked like a beautiful woman on the verge of everything she ever wanted. Possibly, I already had it.

I came out of the bathroom stall downstairs, and he was next in line, waiting alone. It was like a loo in somebody's home, a big old corner of the carpeted downstairs, near the kitchen entrance, and I smirked at him as I lingered in the doorway. He rested against the striped wallpaper, dimly lit by antique shades. Time paused.

Oh, to be kissed. He pulled me towards him from where I stood, opposite, and pushed his face millimetres from mine, causing a lurch in my stomach and gratitude that his hands on my waist took weight I don't think I could've otherwise supported myself. I melted into him. The space between my legs throbbed. I was hungry to take off my clothes. To lie with him and feel his manliness on top of me. I knew in that moment that eleven months, two weeks and three days after I'd given up sex, that I was ready to go back into the bedroom. With him. Tonight. I laced my hands behind his neck, in his hair, and we didn't kiss. It wasn't a kiss. We didn't make out, like teenagers. It was a snog. We snogged.

'You're a cocky fucker,' I said, in the back of a cab racing through pre-dawn streets to my flat.

'I literally am,' he said. 'I literally have a really big cock, so yes, I'm a cocky fucker.' He pulled me into him and we snogged again, blood pulsing in ways I'd forgotten it could. It felt fun. Without gravitas. I was in that cab because I really fancied the man, and knew I was about to have Samantha Jones sex – the rare kind, where nobody expects anything of anyone else except a really good orgasm.

Eleven months, two weeks and three days doesn't seem like a long time to go without sex when you're not having sex, but being pushed up against my front door, a bulge stood to attention against my thigh and hands in my hair, a mouth on my neck – the promise of it was like diving full-bodied into the deep end of a swimming pool after baking in the sun. I was all-consumed. Heady. Alive.

It was the best sex of my life, in that I came. From sex. I came from penetration alone, on top of him, a feat achieved only once in a decade and a half of sexually active years. The Peacock was indeed as cocky as he suggested, but it wasn't that. It was the focus of it. That I was the focus. I didn't understand until I had writhed with little semblance of control on top of him, flushed and sweaty and as though a wave was pulling me, pulling me, pulling me, under, under, under: it was sex that put my pleasure first. The Peacock was, staggeringly, the first bloke I'd taken to bed who didn't want me to perform, in one way or another; to bend and talk dirty and act like his personal porn star. More than that: something had shifted with me, too. I felt no need to validate just how desirable I was by bending, and talking dirty, and acting like a personal porn star. I didn't take any 'shoulds' to bed with me. I didn't feel the need to impress him. I had the best sex of my life because I wasn't hiding. I had the best sex of my life because more than anything, I wanted to be seen. I was vulnerable. It was sex as expression. As an act for two.

I'd had no idea what I'd been missing out on, and so we did it again, and then again, and then once more in the morning, too. I came and I came, and it was bloody lovely.

# FORTY

'But,' he says, early-morning light peeking through the blinds. 'You know I could never date you seriously, don't you?'

I lifted my head from his bare chest. '*Really?*' I arched an eyebrow, attempting playfulness. Call me stupid, but I thought, dick still wet from me as it was, that he was kidding.

'You're fun and all, but . . .'

We'd been dating, in the loosest sense of the word, for about three weeks. After our first night together we'd crossed paths at another SEO event, and inevitably gone home together then, too. There'd been cocktail hour, after that, an evening where I got dressed up with him in mind – flicky eyeliner and all – and he opened doors and paid the tab and steered my lower back with his hand as we walked through Liverpool Street station and to my house. I took each encounter as it came. No forward planning. No imagining Sunday mornings in bed, reading the papers, or wondering what my cousin Paul would make of him at a family wedding. I didn't want his babies, his last name. I didn't want his validation. All I wanted was to enjoy not knowing, and enjoy that I knew how to do that – to not know, and that be the point.

I sat upright, slowly, pulling my thighs to my naked chest. Protection. More naked than my nakedness, suddenly. 'You're not kidding, are you?' I pulled at my hair to cover my shoulders, understanding that he absolutely was not. I knew exactly what he meant when he said, *I could never date you seriously . . .*

The Peacock tickled the small of my back with his fingertips gently, betraying the mortifying sentiment of what he was saying. 'Well,' he said, slowly. 'You're not exactly the type I could introduce to my mum. You're trying to sell a sex memoir.'

'A sex and celibacy memoir,' I corrected, stopping myself, abruptly, from saying any more. When you've just woken up with a man it's about as humiliating a thing you could ever want to not hear. I was being told, in no uncertain terms, that because of my perceived sexual history, I was not worth this man's time outside of the bedroom.

It had only come up the last time I'd seen him, a few nights ago. *So, I've been Googling you . . .* he said, which didn't surprise me or alarm me, because what does Google exist for if not to corroborate the facts of a love interest's history? I'd Googled him, too; mostly only finding a LinkedIn page that showed an impressively quick ascent to a directorial role in his company, which was hot to me. I dig ambition.

'I saw the website about your book,' he'd said.

We were in his flat, a sparse bachelor pad of a place on the Central Line. I'd come over late, after going for dinner with a friend. 'Yeah, I told you I was writing a book.' I'd climbed into his lap on the sofa, snuggling into his chest.

He played with my hair. 'It's very . . . graphic.'

I was tired. 'Graphic?'

'You talk about some pretty private stuff.'

The conversation hadn't continued much from there. I didn't feel like it needed to. It didn't seem so much like he wanted a conversation about what he'd read so much as to acknowledge out loud that he'd seen it at all. I'd misread that, it seemed, because he was pressing the issue now.

I felt so degraded I couldn't speak. My head spun with dizzying thoughts, most of which were to berate myself for being so fucking *stupid.*

*You are a dirty slut,* I told myself. *Look at you – barely a month home from confessing your love to a man halfway around the world, and you're waking up with a man you almost fucked in the loo at a work event. You're disgusting. You're pathetic, and worthless, and are still, after all this time, using sex as a weapon. He's right – nobody will ever love you because, how could they? You're nothing and he knows it and he's laughing at you and so is everyone else. Even Hal. Hal is laughing at you too.*

When I started writing down my story, I felt sick rereading the chapters where I first detailed how I coped with a broken heart. It took seeing my story from a distance that way, in black and white, on the page, to say stop. To see how I didn't want to be that person any more. I closed my legs and I did the work and I learned how to be a little more okay with my imperfections. With my dark bits, as well as my lighter bits. Isn't that everyone's story? That we're all learning how to accept who we are?

I'd finally fallen in love – with Hal, yes, but more obviously, with myself. And that sounds hackneyed and clichéd and all the other *post-female-memoir* truisms we love to poke fun at, but it's the adventure of a lifetime, liking yourself. Finding ways to carry on, brave as can be; figuring out how to love and be loved, all whilst being your own loudest cheerleader. Own biggest fan. Own hero.

I waited for so long for somebody else to come save me, and there I was, being insulted by a naked man with an overly large cock who had absolutely no concept of what I'd done to bring myself to a point in my life where I had enough self-respect to say: 'I'm sorry that we've misunderstood each other. This has been fun, but I have to go now.'

We'd hung out. I'd gone home with him that first night, but I'd also told him: *I don't want a booty call. I don't care how unfashionable it is to say that, but take me out.* I'd been proud to have learned about myself enough to say: *Be a man and treat me like a lady. This is what I need.*

It had been fun. The drinking in dim bars, the hands on knees, the texts throughout the day, the falling. I'd broken my celibacy vow because it felt silly not to do what felt natural. I wasn't fucking him to validate myself, or hurt anybody – I was dating him.

Waking up that morning, though, to be told that essentially my past means no future with a chap I quite fancied, until he was so grossly misogynistic, at least, made me question everything I thought I'd learned about myself. I walked to the tube knowing, intrinsically, with every iota of my being, that I was more than what I'd just been reduced to, but I couldn't figure out *how*. It was easier to concede that, yes, he was absolutely right. I'd shagged myself into useless-ness. A man with a chequered past who settles down is a champion, a woman who does the same has reduced her worth, and has to settle for less than the virginal one with more self-respect. A tale as old as time: one rule for them, another for us.

It's funny how easily you can concede defeat.

But then, the more I beat myself up over it, the more it woke me up when it hit me. I was an idiot. I was an idiot because I *had* changed.

My story is one about sex and the body – and it's one about feel-ings and the heart. Nobody else gets to decide what my history is. I got hurt, like a bagillion other people have been, and I had to figure out my shit, like a bagillion other people have. That's not sickening and unworthy. That's human.

I'd do it all again, unapologetically. And I will continue to date again, in hope. Unapologetically. I will meet a million different men at a million different events, and with some of them I will think: *Okay, let's see if there is something here.* I will go out with them and drink with them and laugh with them and wonder about them. Sometimes, I'll go home with them too. If it feels right. The only kind of slut that makes me is the emotional kind. I'm an emotional slut, playing fast and easy with my feelings because the alternative – shutting off my feelings entirely, as I had done – is just too damned depressing. It's par for the course that some men won't understand that. That some won't understand that I'm proud of what I did to become who I am. Not that I shagged around, but that I got down in the trenches with every last damned hang-up I have, and shone a light on the fuckers until I wasn't scared any more.

I did the work.

I did the work, and I will never not reveal what that work looked like. I'm still learning, but I have learned enough to understand that you have to own what you're ashamed of or else it owns you. My one won't be deterred by the dirt under my fingernails. My one will thank me for it. My one will understand. The blokes that don't understand, who don't get what it took, they aren't my one. The ones that don't understand are another lesson learned, all in the name of what will be.

# FORTY-ONE

**Some months later**

'That's . . . that's him,' I said, words catching in my throat. Gasping. Tears threatening. 'The one I literally just told you about. My ex. *The ex.*' My friend looked how I felt: like she'd been slapped. 'It's been four years, and he is there, at the bar, with his dad. He's wearing his wedding ring.'

I shouldn't have been there, outside a shitty Cranbourn Street boozer. I seldom went out drinking in central London: a combination of the price, and the crowds. I'd even emailed my old school friend, a girl I hadn't seen since I was thirteen and was wearing braces, to say, *I'm so sorry to have to ask, but I'm coming from Oxford Street – can we meet in the West End? I know it'll be crazy busy.* It's like I'd known it was a bad idea right from the off.

I'd been talking about him, oddly enough, only that afternoon at work. I'd told the girls at work – I worked at a PR firm now, specialising in health and beauty; a job that required zero brainpower and left swathes of time for my writing – that when he left me, I truly thought I would never recover. I told them how I'd dreamed of him almost every night, and then after I found out they were engaged, I dreamed about her, too. I told them about the Christmas I went home after I'd been dumped, lying on my bed with my mother, sobbing, frustrated, muttering over and over again: 'I think about him every minute of every day, and then dream about him every minute of every night. Why won't this end? I don't love him any more but this memory, it won't leave me. Why won't it leave me?' I was telling them how I finally dreamt of them one last time, telling them both: *You can't be here anymore.*

Because it was fresh on my mind, I'd been telling Nisha, my friend, that story, too, at the pub, catching up on the last decade-plus of each other's lives. She'd never known David; she was a friend from before he came into my life. And now we'd both wound up in the same city, and somehow had made friends with circles that overlapped enough for us to realise, 'Hey! We went to school together!' The whole evening was the definition of serendipity.

'I found out about a year ago that they'd moved here,' I'd told her, over two-for-one cocktails in a basement bar with loud music and cute barmen. 'Occasionally I look out of the bus window and think somebody walks like him, or I'll turn around without knowing why, understanding that somebody sounded like him only after I'd realised that's what I was searching for. I forget those things as they happen, really, because the chances of running into each other are so small . . .'

Nisha had held my eye as I said that, as we both silently acknowledged that we, ourselves, had beaten the odds to find common friends in a city of millions, but she didn't say as much out loud.

It was the damnedest thing. Nisha and I had gotten tipsy enough that it seemed like a hilarious idea to bow out of the bar without settling our tab – something I had never done before, or since. We'd held on to each other's arm as we stumbled up the steps into the night air, confronted by ghosts and witches of a Halloween night that caused us to inexplicably laugh even more.

'Just one more drink,' one of us said to the other. 'Over there, look. That casino.'

We were heading towards the purple flickering lights of the gambling hall when I noticed a smaller, quieter place across the street. 'There,' I said. 'It's better in there.' It was a pub I'd never set foot in, in my life.

It happened in slow motion. Nisha went first, pulling open the door, and I felt him before I saw him. I waited for the rationalisation to kick in. *Of course it's not him*, I waited to think. But it was. I'd known for twelve months, in one way or another, that London wasn't big enough for the both of us. I'd known in the four years since we'd broken up that the *world* wasn't big enough for the both of us. I'd see him again, somewhere along the way.

'Nisha,' I said. 'Nisha!' I was backtracking my steps, hissing her name over and over. 'Nisha, no. Come here. Nisha!' I pulled the strap of her bag, guiding her back outside, around the corner, dizzy and shocked, heart pounding.

His gold band flashed in the light, held up against his pint. I knew who he was with almost before I knew it was him. It was the older version of him, the one with grey hair and a slightly slimmer frame. His dad.

For years I'd imagined what I'd say to him. David. What words would tumble out when our life paths crossed, in whatever way, at whatever time. I imagined I'd be stony-faced and serious, I'd look him dead in the eye to say simply and hurtfully: 'You broke me, and you never even said sorry.'

But, that's not what I said.

Nisha shook my arm. 'Laura? Let's go. Come on. You don't have to talk to him.'

'No,' I explained to her. 'I have to do this. I have to say something.' She followed me back inside.

'Is it you?' I croaked, re-entering the pub. He stopped talking mid-sentence. His grin slipped like mud off a shovel. Colour drained. His mouth fell open.

'Hello.'

My performance began. The Laura Show. Light arm touches, silly jokes, funny voices. Total enthusiasm. My defence mechanism was to be as fabulous as possible. To demonstrate, after all this time, that I was fine. Look how fine I am!

I asked about his brother and sister, about his mother and his work. His dad stood and watched the exchange, my friend laughing extra loud and long at my jokes as proof of how much I didn't need him. She was the best unsuspecting supporting actress I could've hoped for.

I said, 'And how's . . .?' But her name stuck in my throat. '. . . everything else?' I told him about writing a book, about meeting with publishers and thinking about getting my PhD and how my parents were getting blessed after thirty years together. He said he liked my hat. I thanked him. Silence hung, then, with nothing left to say.

I remembered the email I'd sent him, after I'd banned him from my dreams and moved to Detroit and had been to Italy and Paris without him. I'd forgotten I'd sent it. Our story was always being rewritten with new details. I forgot until I didn't that I had said: *For six years, I've felt that you were too good for me, and that in some unspoken way I was holding you back. But, I was only holding myself back. The day you left me was the day you cut my wings free, and now I'm flying. Thank you.*

As we danced around our history in that pub, wide-eyed and perplexed to stand before each other again, all this time later, my wings on full show-off display, I thought to myself how four years is a long time to build up an image of a monster in your mind. Betrayal can do that. Seeing him – talking with him – he was just a person. A person with bigger jowls than I recalled, and a broader North Yorkshire accent than I remembered. He was just a person, and not even my person. He was a memory. A fading one. A yesterday. I didn't miss him anymore.

'See you, then,' I said, leaning in to kiss his cheek, and his father's, too. Nisha shook their hands and, as we walked away, David said, 'Good luck, Laura.'

*

Nisha insisted on a drink to debrief, and I spent a full half an hour saying, 'I can't believe that just happened.' I didn't know her well enough to dissect it like I wanted to, and so we bid goodnight and I began a walk towards the river. Halloween ghosts danced around me drunkenly as I made my way out of the centre of town and towards somewhere a little quieter. I kept walking, letting the cold air pull at the hair escaping from my hat, taking a route I'd never taken before. *I wonder if he'll tell her,* I mused, passing a homeless man bundled up outside Greggs, and pulling change from my purse to slip into his cardboard cup. *I wonder if what happened means as much to him as it does to me.*

'Bless you, love,' the man on the ground said, and we smiled.

I realised it didn't matter. It didn't matter if he told her, it didn't matter what he thought, it only mattered how I felt. And I felt fine. Relieved it was over, and that she hadn't been there, and that he was, in the absolute, just a person.

*I'm okay,* I thought, crossing the road, making up my directions. *I'm really, truly, okay.*

My phone beeped and Calum's named appeared on my screen. *'Hey bb! Wanna come over and make me dinner tomorrow night? We*

*can Google naked celebs and eat krispies in melted chocolate. It's
been a while!'*

I sent back a *Yes please!* and put my phone on silent. I wanted to
be with my own thoughts. I wanted to enjoy the sublime aloneness,
now that I no longer felt lonely. I wanted to carry on walking, carry on,
carry on, carry on. The unnecessary history I'd gripped on to like life
support slipped away with each step I took. I was closer to home
every time I placed another foot in front of the other – not entirely
sure of the way, but knowing that I'd get there.

# ACKNOWLEDGEMENTS

*Becoming* is a product of the knowledge, expertise and passion of a publishing house with vision, balls and a staff who is human before they are a job title. From my very first meeting at Hodder & Stoughton I knew the story of how I came to be myself had found its home.

To the woman who commissioned me, Liz Caraffi: what fortune I've been bestowed to have you be so bloody smart, so detail-oriented, so in tune with what I'd ever hoped this manuscript could be. Thank you seems such a small word for being the 'yes' that made this happen. There's not a single element – from editorial notes, to design, to font choice, to everything else I hadn't even realised was 'a thing' – that you did not consult me on, and the generosity of that is staggering. It's because of you that I see myself in this pink tome so vividly. The hardest work was yours. Vero and Caitriona: every interaction has been a dream. Thank you for the enthusiasm, and always making sure there's biscuits. Jo, your copy-edits saw things nobody else saw. Anna – this cover! It's worth me telling you that when I first saw it I sobbed with my all. It is perfect.

Ella. Oh, fuck – I'm crying now I have typed your name. Ella, agent extraordinaire: do you realise the strength, the belief, the confidence you have imbibed me with on this wild ride to publication? You're so good at what you do! It makes me rise to the challenge of being my best, too. You have class, and also bollocks of brass: two things I both envy and admire. To have you as my teammate for this book is one thing, but to know you're my teammate for this career, well. I'm the luckiest author in the world.

Thanks to my first readers, Alice Judge-Talbot, Dan Draper, Jamie Varon and Eric Sun: you were so gentle with me, and so straight with me, too. Your notes made me lean all the harder into staring out my truth, damned square in the eye, and refusing to look away. Alex Cameron, thank you for daring to suggest I could dedicate my own book to myself. Damned right I can! Daisy Buchanan, The Guyliner, Jen Grieves, Cate Sevilla, Victoria Saddler and Jamie Klingler: thank you for the testimony you gave me for the initial book proposal. Your words carry weight, and that weight got me noticed.

Emma Gannon: I would never have leapt before I felt ready had you not so doggedly tugged on my sleeve to say, 'If I can get an agent, you can too. Jump, Laura.' That's friendship. I'm honoured to have shared this book-writing road with you. Fiona Barrows – to think a single re-tweet could have started all of this . . . I owe you a Balinese coconut. To everyone who gave me a place to stay as I travelled the world and reworked the thing: Maria and Eugene for the Rome apartment, Candy and Neil for the Swiss penthouse, Kristy and Maggie for Istanbul, and Lauren for Modena.

And then, there's the house that made me. My girls. Jo, Fern, Amy: *Becoming* is my love letter to you. I don't know how else to tell you that all I am is because of your unwavering affection. You broke down all of my walls, with the strength of your love. You're my sisters.

Calum: I fell for you on that very first day at university, and from that very first day you were the only one who understood the size of the dream, and the dedication it takes to make it a goal. Nobody else comes to close to 'Competency Club' status. Nanny Anna, my oldest school friend: you continue to hold my hand through life's most important bits, and the power of that humbles me. I'm so thankful for you. Megan Gilbride – nobody tells me how awesome I am with such frequency as you. I appreciate you, you nob head. Meg Fee: there's not enough space to do your role in my life justice. How funny that on writing this we still have not met, and yet you know me oft-time better than I know myself. I live for your words, for your friendship, for your kindness.

Auntie Shirley, Auntie Rose, Mandy Frost: you out of everyone never doubted me, and I promise I will never forget that. Mum, Dad, Jack: I love you so much.

Finally: in the past eight years there has been a small, committed and incredibly vocal group of cheerleaders who have read my blog, followed me online and graced my inbox with words of encouragement and shared stories. I haven't met most of you, but this book only exists because of you. You've made me feel less alone, and more like myself. You told me I could. I wish I could name every last one of you, but since I can't I trust you to know who you are. I see you. I value you. You are remarkable. Thank you.

**Follow Laura Jane Williams' blog Superlatively Rude
and read one of her favourite posts here...**

'Do you do stand-up, then?' she said, testing lighting and angles and other things I won't pretend to understand. It's about the best compliment she could've given, really, since I've harboured longings on giving it a go since about 2007. It made me warm to her immediately. I thought, thank goodness SOMEBODY has spotted my immense and undeniable talent for being spontaneously hilarious.*

She asked me to smile, and tilt my chin, and contort my shoulder, and I knew then she'd been overly complimentary so that I was putty in her hands, and as such would do whatever she told me to. Move my back like this? Swerve my hip like that? WHATEVER YOU NEED, PHOTOGRAPHER LADY WHO HAS COMPLIMENTED ME SO! Whatever. You. Want.

The Tweet had fluttered towards me only the week before. 'Laura,' the features director of the national magazine had crammed into 140 characters. 'Can you follow me so I can DM you? V. important!'

It transpired she'd seen *The Book of Brave*, and wanted me to help launch a campaign for Marie Claire UK on – and I quote – saying no to the crap stuff women have to put up with, complete with fancy-pants photoshoot.

Me.

Part of a national movement.

(*My immense and undeniable talent for *The Laura Show* when confronted with more than one set of eyeballs.)

Because of a PDF file I'd charged folks money for through a website I made on Blogger.

That's the thing about opportunity. They tell you to make your own but nobody ever really breaks that down. Pinterest quotes allude to "the hustle" and "owning it", and I didn't realise until I was in the make-up chair, dressed by a stylist and my hair being pulled at by a professional, talking about bravery and fearlessness and fearfulness, that I made that opportunity by being unabashedly myself. I doggedly got on with the business of what thrills me, what makes my heart sing, and then somebody vibing on the same level noticed. And that person just happened to work at Time Inc. I don't think it's about "fake it 'til you make it" so much as "geek out on whatever ever makes you the most you, you can be, and trust the process of it." Admittedly, my slogan is less catchy, but my point remains: this is certainly never something I could've pitched for.

I was invited the other side of the computer screen after she snapped me, after they got me on video, to see, to know, and I declined. 'I have a chin thing,' I said. 'It's not my job to be beautiful, it's somebody else's. And if I look at those I will forget that. So. Just pick the non-troll-like one, please.' I'm not here to be hot, or sexy, or photogenic, you see. I'm here to laugh like a drunk sailor and get cold sweats over story ideas. I'm here to get so engrossed in what I love – words – that I forget to wash my hair or have children.

Anyway, not that you'll be surprised but – I digress.

The Marie Claire #BREAKFREE campaign is designed to challenge society, and ourselves, in breaking free from shame, ageism, mother guilt, body hate, gender, labels, likes, Islamophobia and fear. I got photographed alongside eight other businesswomen, bloggers and campaigners all shouting about how life is scary, that being a woman is hard, that it's okay to want what we want, how we want it.

New Year-life – isn't, for me, about becoming a new person. New Year-life – is about becoming the person you already are, but hide away, because it can take an alarming amount of courage to be yourself in a world that tells you to be anything but. I was bullied in high school for my passion. For my hyperbole. For *The Laura Show*. I've been bullied by so-called friends in the years since. It took me ten years to stop apologizing for having a voice, and to understand I am entitled to the space I take up, along with the next person.

I don't do New Year resolutions anymore, because I set monthly ones – it suits my short-sightedness better. But I do set an annual theme. 2013 was The Joy of Missing Out to combat my FOMO. 2014 was #StrongandSexy, as I prioritised my health. Last year I said, sit at the grown-up's table. This year, my theme is circling somewhere around Let It Scare You.

I do my best – rise to the challenge of myself – when I'm shitting bricks. When I'm not sure if I can. When what I'm chasing is as terrifying as the notion of not going for it at all. I might be the poster child for breaking free from fear, but what I actually mean is being fearful and knowing we're not alone in that. Trying anyway. Knowing that fucking up isn't the end – not trying is.

And so, as I write this, here as a national magazine's bravery ambassador, I'm not shy in saying: screw up. Make mistakes. Give yourself permission to see what feels good. Decide for yourself. Dare to be who you are. That – most of all. In 2016, be more you. You're a marvel. Own that. That's how to #BREAKFREE.

Perfectly flawed women talk about \*their\*

# BECOMING

on The Becoming Podcast.

Because we all have one.
We all have a story.
Share them using...
#thisismybecoming

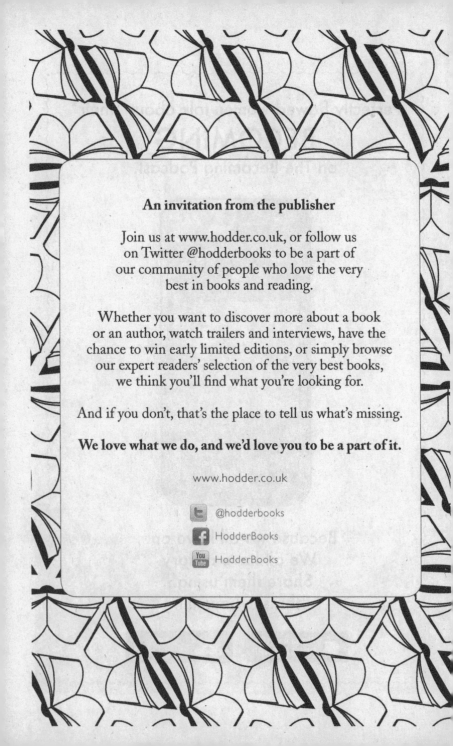

**An invitation from the publisher**

Join us at www.hodder.co.uk, or follow us
on Twitter @hodderbooks to be a part of
our community of people who love the very
best in books and reading.

Whether you want to discover more about a book
or an author, watch trailers and interviews, have the
chance to win early limited editions, or simply browse
our expert readers' selection of the very best books,
we think you'll find what you're looking for.

And if you don't, that's the place to tell us what's missing.

**We love what we do, and we'd love you to be a part of it.**

www.hodder.co.uk

@hodderbooks

HodderBooks

HodderBooks